STATE, LAND AND DEMOCRACY IN SOUTHERN AFRICA

State, Land and Democracy in Southern Africa

Edited by

ARRIGO PALLOTTI and CORRADO TORNIMBENI

University of Bologna, Italy

ASHGATE

© Arrigo Pallotti and Corrado Tornimbeni 2015

All rights reserved. No part of this publication may be reproduced, stored in a retrieval system or transmitted in any form or by any means, electronic, mechanical, photocopying, recording or otherwise without the prior permission of the publisher.

Arrigo Pallotti and Corrado Tornimbeni have asserted their right under the Copyright, Designs and Patents Act, 1988, to be identified as the editors of this work.

Published by
Ashgate Publishing Limited
Wey Court East
Union Road
Farnham
Surrey, GU9 7PT
England

Ashgate Publishing Company
110 Cherry Street
Suite 3-1
Burlington, VT 05401-3818
USA

www.ashgate.com

British Library Cataloguing in Publication Data
A catalogue record for this book is available from the British Library

Library of Congress Cataloging-in-Publication Data has been applied for

ISBN 9781472452405 (hbk)
ISBN 9781472452412 (ebk – PDF)
ISBN 9781472452429 (ebk – ePUB)

Printed in the United Kingdom by Henry Ling Limited,
at the Dorset Press, Dorchester, DT1 1HD

Contents

List of Figures	*vii*
List of Tables	*ix*
List of Abbreviations	*xi*
List of Contributors	*xiii*
Series Editor's Preface	*xv*

1   State, Land and Democracy: Reflecting on Agrarian Change
in Southern Africa   1
Mario Zamponi

PART I   LAND AND RURAL DEVELOPMENT IN SOUTHERN AFRICA: HISTORICAL AND POLITICAL PERSPECTIVES

2   An Unfinished Agenda in a Neoliberal Context:
State, Land and Democracy in Malawi   23
Blessings Chinsinga

3   Rural Development and the Fight against Poverty in Tanzania:
A Fifty-Year Perspective   39
Arrigo Pallotti

4   State, Poverty and Agriculture in Zambia: The Impact of State
Policies after Democratization   61
Federico Battera

5   Land and Labour Contestation in Manica, Mozambique:
Historical Issues in Contemporary Dynamics   83
Corrado Tornimbeni

PART II   LAND REFORM IN ZIMBABWE: NATIONAL AND INTERNATIONAL DIMENSIONS

6   Proposed Large-Scale Compensation for White Farmers as an
Anglo-American Negotiating Strategy for Zimbabwe, 1976–1979   105
Timothy Scarnecchia

7	Land Reform, Livelihoods and the Politics of Agrarian Change in Zimbabwe *Ian Scoones*	127
8	Women and Land in Zimbabwe: State, Democracy and Gender Issues in Evolving Livelihoods and Land Regimes *Rudo B. Gaidzanwa*	149
9	Ecolonization and the Creation of Insecurity Regimes: The Meaning of Zimbabwe's Land Reform Programme in Regional Context *Pádraig Carmody*	169

Index of Names 183

List of Figures

7.1	Map of Masvingo province, showing study areas	128
7.2	Annual rainfall totals (mm) across three stations in Masvingo province	132
7.3	Percentage of farmers growing cotton in Uswaushava, 2001–2013	142

List of Tables

2.1	Targets versus achievements	27
4.1	Province level poverty estimates (percentage)	63
4.2	Parliamentary majorities since 1991	66
7.1	Changes in the national distribution of land, 1980–2013	130
7.2	A socio-economic profile of the study sites (average amounts across survey households)	133
7.3	Livelihood strategies in Masvingo province	134
7.4	Settler profiles across schemes	135
7.5	Land owned and cleared	137
7.6	The value of investments in the new resettlements: from settlement to 2008, and from 2008 to 2012	139
7.7	Percentage of farmers harvesting greater than a tonne of maize	141
7.8	Mean cattle holdings: changes by scheme type and success group	142
7.9	Farm labour: temporary (temp) and permanent (perm)	144
8.1	Provincial land allocations by gender	158

List of Abbreviations

ASDP	Agriculture Sector Development Programme
ASDS	Agricultural Sector Development Strategy
AU	African Union
AZ	Agenda for Zambia
CAADP	Comprehensive Africa Agriculture Development Programme
CBNRM	Community-Based Natural Resources Management
CBRLDP	Community-Based Rural Land Development Programme
CCB	Companhia Colonial do Búzi
CCM	Chama Cha Mapinduzi
CoCs	Community Oversight Committees
CSOs	civil society organizations
CTR	Código do Trabalho Rural
DFID	Department for International Development
FAO	Food and Agriculture Organization of the United Nations
FCO	Foreign and Commonwealth Office
FCP	Fertilizer Credit Programme
FDI	Foreign Direct Investment
FISP	Farm Input Subsidy Programme
FISP	Farmer Input Support Program
FRA	Food Reserve Agency
FRELIMO	Frente de Libertação de Moçambique
FTLR	Fast Track Land Reform
GBI	Green Belt Initiative
GDP	Gross Domestic Product
IFI	International Financial Institutions
IMF	International Monetary Fund
INDECO	Industrial Development Corporation
LAA	Land Apportionment Act
MDC	Movement for Democratic Change
MGDS	Malawi Growth and Development Strategy
MoL	Ministry of Land
MMD	Movement for Multiparty Democracy
MPRS	Malawi Poverty Reduction Strategy
MUZ	Mineworkers Union of Zambia
NAIP	National Agriculture Investment Plan
NAIVS	National Agricultural Inputs Voucher Scheme
NAMBOARD	National Agriculture Marketing Board

NAP	National Agriculture Policy
NASSPFU	National Association of Small-Scale and Peasant Farmers Union
NEPAD	New Partnership for Africa's Development
NLHA	Native Land Husbandry Act
NLP	National Lima Party
NP	National Party
NSGRP	National Strategy for Growth and Reduction of Poverty
OAU	Organization of African Unity
PCILR	Presidential Commission of Inquiry on Land Reform
PEDSA	Plano Estratégico Para o Desenvolvimento do Sector Agrário
PF	Patriotic Front
PFUZ	Peasant Farmers' Union of Zambia
PRPs	Poverty Reduction Programmes
PRSP	Poverty Reduction Strategy Paper
RDS	Rural Development Strategy
REDD	Reduce Emissions from Deforestation and Forest Degradation
RENAMO	Resistência Nacional Moçambicana
RTI	Regulamento de Trabalho Indígena
SADC	Southern African Development Community
SAP	Structural Adjustment Programme
SSE	Sena Sugar Estates
TANU	Tanganyika African National Union
TNCs	trans-national capitals
UNIP	United National Independence Party
UPND	United Party for National Development
USAID	United States Agency for International Development
VPCs	Village Productivity Committees
WB	World Bank
WDCs	Ward Development Committees
ZANLA	Zimbabwe African National Liberation Army
ZANU-PF	Zimbabwe African National Union – Patriotic Front
ZAPU	Zimbabwe African People's Union
ZCCM	Zambia Consolidated Copper Mines
ZCF	Zambia Cooperative Federation
ZCTU	Zambia Congress of Trade Unions
ZIPA	Zimbabwe People's Army
ZLA	Zambia Land Alliance
ZNFU	Zambia National Farmers' Union

List of Contributors

Federico Battera is Senior Lecturer of African Political Systems at the Department of Political and Social Sciences – University of Trieste, Italy. He is the author of a series of articles and chapters on Somali, Kenyan and Zambian politics and history, including "Ethnicity and the Degree of Partisan Attachment in Kenyan Politics." *Journal of Asian and African Studies*, 48(1) (2013).

Pádraig Carmody is Associate Professor in Geography at Trinity College Dublin, where he co-directs the TCD-UCD Masters in Development Practice. His research centres on the political economy of globalization and economic restructuring in Southern and Eastern Africa. He is an editor-in-chief of *Geoforum* and his most recent books are *The Rise of the BRICS in Africa: The Geopolitics of South-South Relations* (Zed Books, 2013) and (with James T. Murphy) *Africa's Information Revolution* (Wiley-Blackwell, 2015).

Blessings Chinsinga is Associate Professor at the Department of Political and Administrative Studies (PAS) and Deputy Director of the Centre for Social Research (CSR), Chancellor College, University of Malawi. His main research interests include political economy of development, poverty reduction and rural livelihoods, and local level politics. Some of his recent publications include: (with C. Poulton) "Beyond Technocratic Debates: The Significance of Political Incentives in the Malawi Farm Input Programme (FISP)." *Development Policy Review* 32(2), (2014), and (with E. Chirwa) "The Political Economy of Food Price Policy in Malawi," in *Food Price Policy in an Era of Market Instability: A Political Economy Analysis* (ed. P. Pinstrup-Anderson, Oxford University Press, 2014).

Rudo B. Gaidzanwa is Professor of Sociology at the University of Zimbabwe and is the current Dean of the College of Social Sciences, Zimbabwe Academy of Sciences. She is author of *Images of Women in Zimbabwean Literature* (College Press, 1985), *Policy Making Issues in Southern Africa* (ed., SAPES Books, 2001) and *Speaking for Ourselves: Masculinities and Femininities at the University of Zimbabwe* (ed., AAP/GSA/Ford Foundation, 2001). She has published extensively on women and land in Zimbabwe, and is currently writing on the music of Oliver Mtukudzi, a Zimbabwean musician.

Arrigo Pallotti is Associate Professor of History of Africa at the Department of Political and Social Sciences of the University of Bologna (Forlì Campus), Italy, and Research Fellow in the Centre for Africa Studies at the University of the Free State, South Africa. He is the author of two monographs, co-author of two books and has edited two books and three special issues of the peer-reviewed journal on African and Middle East studies *afriche e orienti*. He is also author of more than 20 chapters or articles in edited books and journals in both Italian and English. His research interests focus primarily on democratization in sub-Saharan Africa, the decolonization of Southern Africa, and relations between Africa and the European Union.

Timothy Scarnecchia is Assistant Professor of African history at Kent State University. He is the author of *The Urban Roots of Democracy and political violence in Zimbabwe: Harare and Highfield, 1940–1964* (University of Rochester Press, 2008) and a series of articles and chapters in Zimbabwean history, including "Rationalizing Gukurahundi: Cold War and South African Foreign Relations with Zimbabwe, 1981–1983." *Kronos* 37(1) (2011).

Ian Scoones is Professorial Fellow at the Institute of Development Studies, and Director of the ESRC STEPS Centre, University of Sussex, Brighton. He is an agricultural ecologist by original training and works on the intersections of science, politics and policy in rural development and environmental change in Africa. He has worked for nearly 30 years in Zimbabwe on land and agrarian change, and is a co-author of *Zimbabwe's Land Reform: Myths and Realities* (James Currey, 2010).

Corrado Tornimbeni is Lecturer of History of Africa at the Department of Political and Social Sciences of the University of Bologna, Italy. He is co-editor of the peer-reviewed journal on African and Middle East studies *afriche e orienti*. He has worked and researched on Portuguese colonialism, labour migration in Mozambique and Southern Africa, land and natural resources management in Mozambique and on citizenship in sub-Saharan Africa. Currently, he is working on nationalism and international relations in Mozambique, Southern Africa and the Portuguese-speaking Africa countries. Among his publications: *Working the System in Sub-Saharan Africa: Global Values, National Citizenship and Local Politics in Historical Perspective* (ed., Cambridge Scholars Publishing, 2013).

Mario Zamponi is Associate Professor of African and Development Studies at the Department of Political and Social Sciences of the University of Bologna, Italy, where he is the Director of the Master programme "Local and Global Development." He is the editor of the peer-reviewed journal on African and Middle East studies *afriche e orienti*. He has published extensively in journals and edited books. His main research interests are: democratization in sub-Saharan Africa, history of Southern Africa, land and rural development.

Series Editor's Preface

Once seen only as a continent of poverty, violence and corruption, the Africa of today is a vibrant place where social forces demand representative governance, in the process generating fresh forms of complexities in the political, social and economic life of ordinary Africans. Whether what we are witnessing is a third liberation of the continent: the first from colonialism, the second from autocratic indigenous rule and now something far more different, is a work in progress.

This series seeks original approaches to furthering our understanding of the ensuing changes on the continent. The series includes work that progresses comparative analysis of African politics. It looks at the full range and variety of African politics in the twenty-first century covering the changing nature of African society, gender issues, economic prosperity and poverty to the development of relations between African states, external organisations and between leaders and the people they would govern. The series aims to publish work by senior scholars as well as the best new researchers and features original research monographs, thematically strong edited collections and specialised texts.

Nana K. Poku,
Health Economics and AIDS Research Division (HEARD),
South Africa

Chapter 1

State, Land and Democracy: Reflecting on Agrarian Change in Southern Africa

Mario Zamponi

Agrarian Question(s)

In the last two decades there has been a stimulating debate on the role that the practices of development may have in the South of the world, with particular attention to rural development and the role of the peasantry in today's global economy (van der Ploeg 2010). There have also been extensive debates within development studies, with a particular interest in developing countries, which have significant implications for our understanding of the agrarian question(s) and agrarian transition (see e.g. Akram-Lodhi and Kay 2010a, 2010b).

This is linked to the discussion within development studies about the role that primitive accumulation can play in development (Moore 2004): it is a complex debate, since in most developing countries – and in particular sub-Saharan Africa – no overall economic transformation through processes of primitive accumulation has ever been completed (Helliker and Murisa 2011). Indeed, the periphery has remained locked within disarticulated models of accumulation (Moyo and Yeros 2005), which have impacted on the characteristics of agrarian transformation.

Moreover, we have to consider the role played by agriculture in sub-Saharan Africa. NEPAD declared 2014 the 'Year of Agriculture': 'The Year of Agriculture intends to: consolidate active commitments towards new priorities, strategies and targets for achieving results and impacts, with special focus on sustained, all Africa agriculture-led growth, propelled by stronger, private sector investment and public–private partnerships' (NEPAD 2014). In addition, according to some recent data produced by NEPAD itself,[1] the role of agriculture is still important in most sub-Saharan African countries: the same document states that the agricultural sector remains a major sector in most African economies – though it accounts for less than 15 per cent of GDP in South Africa and Namibia; it is the main creator of jobs, while industry is very weak and extractive industries have little impact on employment and revenue (NEPAD 2013: 15). Despite rapid urbanization, the rural population is growing and land pressure is mounting (ibid.: 17). As mentioned by Borras (2009), although the rural population is diminishing, the percentage of poor

---

1 See for general information: http://www.nepad.org/foodsecurity/knowledge/doc/3232/agriculture-africa; for detailed data see NEPAD (2013).

people in rural areas continues to be higher than in urban areas: world poverty still represents a largely rural phenomenon. Borras reminds us how important the relationship is between agriculture and access to livelihoods, poverty and inequality in the rural areas of developing countries (and Africa in particular).

Thus, to debate and reflect on the agrarian question in Africa – and in Southern Africa more specifically – is of primary importance because the agrarian question is strictly intertwined with the anti-colonial struggle, state formation and the 'unsolved national question' (Moyo and Yeros 2005). In this regard, land reform needs economic and agrarian transformations in order to achieve the goal of sustainable rural development (Helliker and Murisa 2011).

The creation of new capitalist classes, the transformation of property rights, and patterns of primitive accumulation are in progress in the global economy. This is also the case with most of rural Africa (see e.g. Peters 2004; Cotula 2007). As recently mentioned by Lund and Boone (2013: 1), 'land issues are often not about land only. Rather, they invoke issues of property more broadly, implicating social and political relationships in the widest sense'.

As Bernstein (2012: 16) suggests: 'It is useful to begin with a familiar "founding" moment: Marx's enclosure model of primitive accumulation in the original transition to agrarian capitalism.' This starting point is pertinent because – he continues – it is useful to remember that

> (i) the English transition, as the first, had features unlikely to be repeated subsequently and (ii) Marx's historical materialism provides some of the essential means for investigating transformations of land and labour in different times and places of the diverse histories of capitalism. Central to these processes is the dynamic of 'the commodification of subsistence' that is, commodification of the conditions of reproduction of labour. (Bernstein 2012: 16–17)[2]

The classical agrarian question, that is the evolution from the feudal to the industrial capitalist model, has not been completed in many third world regions – a fact which happened in Europe, as we have already mentioned. As Byres (2012: 13) reminds us: 'The agrarian question may be defined as the continuing existence in the countryside of a poor country of substantive obstacles to an unleashing of the forces capable of generating economic development, both inside and outside agriculture.' Following the discussion raised by Byres' wide-ranging research,[3] Lerche (2012) raises the issue of the failure of accumulation in the countryside and the failure of the state to mediate the agrarian transition successfully.

Bernstein (2003) suggests that it would be useful, in describing Byres' agrarian transition, to consider the role of agrarian classes, the transformation of the social relations of production in the transition to capitalism, and how such transformations

---

2 The chapter has been published in Italian. The quotation is taken from the original English version.

3 For a review of Byres's work see Bernstein and Brass (1996).

may, or may not, contribute to the accumulation process. He also suggests that the processes of transformation include: intensified exploitation of land incorporated within colonial rule, and commoditization of peasant agriculture, frequently linked to export-orientated forms of agriculture. This is certainly the case in Southern Africa, as we will see, where the role of settler agriculture transformed the agrarian landscape. In addition 'what is specific about the forms of domination in Southern Africa is not just the importance of its legacies of settler colonialism, but also the enduring legacy of politically organized regional systems of migrant labour' (O'Laughlin et al. 2013: 3).

In this regard, Bernstein (2004; 2010) maintains that there is an agrarian question of capital and an agrarian question of labour. The agrarian question of capital is related to the processes of transition to capitalism, which is the question at the core of Byres' analysis. However, due to the processes of globalization, the classical agrarian question seems no longer to be central to the processes of capitalist development. Thus, in his opinion there does exist an agrarian question of labour, that is the relationship between access to employment and social policy, the definition of the working classes and the dynamics of transformation related to access to land.

This theme is developed by other authors. Lerche (2012) points out that Bernstein's analysis represents one of the challenges to the classical agrarian question and to agricultural transformation, while a second challenge finds its main reference in movements such as Via Campesina, GRAIN and the Movement for Food Sovereignty. These last believe that because of the dominant neoliberal globalization, it is today necessary to revise the agrarian question (and land reform proposals) to give more power to the producers in the South. Nor, indeed, can we ignore the present-day agrarian question of food, linked to tensions between the interests of large transnational companies and claims to food sovereignty by many social sectors in the South (McMichael 2008). Other authors (Akram-Lodhi and Kay 2009; Lipton 2009) argue that traditional agrarian and land reforms, in particular, express the potential for contemporary transformation of agriculture, especially in relation to issues such as property and land redistribution.

In Africa the agrarian question is related to many other issues. Some authors have tried to grasp the complexity of agrarian problems in Africa by examining issues such as: insecurity of tenure, the role of the market in agricultural transformation, patterns of land alienation and concentration, undemocratic structures of local government, the construction of customary tenure, and conflicts and competition over the land (see among others: Toulmin and Quan 2000; Wily 2011; Lund and Boone 2013; Peters 2013a and 2013b). According to Manji (2006: 41 ff.), the land question in Africa also depends on the diverse regional contexts, and in the case of the former colonies of Southern Africa the main problems are concentration and inequality (with ownership of land being concentrated in the white minorities), and the role of the regional labour systems, thus emphasizing the issue of land redistribution.

The release of rural dwellers from pre-capitalist social relations has meant that a modern, fragmented reserve of labour forces has formed. Bernstein refers to the so-called 'classes of labour': a highly differentiated social group including proletarian or semi-proletarian rural groups, small farmers, and also highly market-orientated entrepreneurial farmers (Bernstein 2010: 110 and ff.). They all have to attain their reproduction in conditions of growing income insecurity (and in many cases pauperization) as well as employment insecurity.

Nowadays, neoliberal globalization and land deals in Africa, based on a vision of the world as a globally organized 'free trade' economy managed by a largely unaccountable political and economic elite, only intensify the issues of access to the land and of the economic role of the peasantry (White et al. 2012). In this regard, Wily (2012) argues that land rushes are based on and legitimized by legal manipulation which usually fails to recognize customary rights to the land; land grabbing is being legalized, to the detriment of the poor and marginalized. Woodhouse (2012), specifically focuses on the supply side of land deals in Africa, placing the current 'enclosures' in a longer historical context. He outlines the ways in which the two dominant institutional models – large-scale mechanized farms and contract farming – are seen capable to respond to productivity challenges.

On this issue Oya (2013) has recently suggested that the return of capital to agriculture and the renewal of the agrarian question of capital do not bring any resolution to the agrarian question of labour, since displacement is experienced as more significant than the creation of new livelihood opportunities. We should hence pay more attention to the twin agrarian questions of capital and labour, to use Bernstein's terms.

Agrarian Change, Land and the State

'The historical puzzles' (Byres 1996: 15) and the lack of any clear explanation of the agrarian question(s) have led to a broad re-examination of the characteristics of both the agrarian question and the agrarian transition since the 1990s, in the light of a changing global context (Akram-Lodhi and Kay 2010b). Since the 1980s, structural adjustment programmes have reinforced processes of economic integration at a global level, and reduced the role of the state, while increasing commoditization of agriculture, and – in many cases – worsening the crisis of the agriculture sector (Helliker and Murisa 2011).

In many African countries during the last 30 years, emphasis on promotion of an agricultural export-led strategy as the principal means of enhancing rural accumulation has brought renewed interest by both the state and investors in closer agricultural integration with the global economy and agro-food commodity chains:

> The policy conditionalities of the international development institutions did this as a means of boosting access to foreign exchange, facilitating debt repayments, increasing funds for investment, promoting technological change and boosting rural productivity and profits. In other words, increasing and intensifying integration into the global economy – globalization – has been argued by

State, Land and Democracy

> neoliberals to be the most effective means of enhancing rates of accumulation, in the rural economy and more generally. (Akram-Lodhi and Kay 2010b: 263)

In the face of this, Patnaik (2011) argues that stronger integration into export markets through free trade has contributed to the present agrarian crisis. In Africa, more specifically, Moyo (2012) explains the 'failed agrarian transition' in the light of colonial and neoliberal accumulation by dispossession and exploitation of labour. He argues that neoliberal policies have accelerated the process of undermining and dispossessing small peasants and encouraging large-scale investments, thus creating the basis for contemporary land grabbing, a 'new scramble over African lands' which expresses 'the escalation of capital's speculative tendency to accumulate by dispossession ... ' (Moyo 2011: 73 and 78).

Meanwhile, we should not forget that, since the 1990s, the debate has been strongly orientated towards marked-led agrarian reforms, and rural development aiming to support smallholder agriculture. The main sponsors of this approach have been international institutions such as the World Bank (WB) and bilateral donors as well, with the emphasis on the central role of agriculture for development, particularly in order to alleviate poverty (WB 2003 and 2008. For a critical analysis and the debate, see Akram-Lodhi 2008, Oya 2009). One recent WB document states that: 'The dominant focus of support is on smallholder agriculture' (WB 2013: xvi). In particular the WB programme in 93 countries has supported longer-term investments such as agricultural research and extension, improved water management, agricultural management practices, adoption of new technologies, and gender mainstreaming.

More recently international thinking on development has connected the issue of security of tenure and land reform with development, and more specifically, with poverty reduction. Some authors have argued that the solution to rural poverty is redistribution of land to small farmers. The argument in favour of redistribution hinges on the idea of the inverse relationship. Thus, land should be redistributed to small producers who are able to use it in a more efficient and productive way (Griffin, Khan and Ickowitz 2002). On this point, a recent study by Otsuka and Place finds that inverse relationship had historically seldom been reported in sub-Saharan Africa, 'at least because the farming system was relatively extensive, requiring little hired labour. If an extensive farming system, such as slash and burn farming, is practiced, we can hardly expect to observe any correlation between *cultivated* farm size and productivity' (Otsuka and Place 2014: 4). However, they have accepted that the inverse relationship has been recently found by numerous studies about sub-Saharan Africa.

Byres (2004) disputed the view supporting contemporary redistributive land reform since it calls for major investments that states are not able to sustain. He also criticized the position for encouraging a populist utopia, given that contemporary neoliberal discourse dismisses the historical path of capitalist relations in the countryside – which include peasant agriculture.

However, nowadays this issue is still part of the thinking of international development agencies which claim the economic and political importance of rural development and land reform: according to Lipton (2009) land reform is an unresolved and hence topical issue, keenly debated throughout the world.

Understanding the political economy that underpins smallholder agriculture is of critical importance, as more than 90 per cent of the world's 1.1 billion poor live on small family farms (Lipton 2005). While the future of smallholders hangs in the balance, there is substantial evidence that the contribution of agriculture to growth and poverty reduction will continue to depend on broad participation by smallholder farmers. Birner and Resnik took their cue from Karl Kautsky's 'The Agrarian Question': 'peasant producers persisted due to self-exploitation and under consumption, which were not deemed to be socially desirable situations. He was convinced of the technical superiority of large farms and saw no justification for agricultural policies designed to support small farmers' (Birner and Resnik 2010: 1442). By contrast, Birner and Resnik claim that 'the experience of the 20th century seems to tell a different story; implementing policies to support the economic development of small farmers has proven to be a particularly successful strategy to reduce rural poverty and to use agriculture as an engine of growth on the road to industrialization' (ibid.).

However, for all the rhetoric of market-led land reforms and support for small-scale commodity producers, there is a growing crisis among the smallest and poorest producers in developing countries (Bernstein 2010: 82 ff.), accompanied by an increase in claims for the right to food and to food sovereignty (McMichael 2012). Despite growing evidence of smallholder productivity (Lipton 2009), small and medium farmers are often pushed into the ranks of the extremely poor because of their vulnerability to shocks such as drought or flooding, and deteriorating terms of exchange.

Within the idea of supporting small farmers, programmes aiming to confer registered title deeds on land to local farmers and communities could be a way to offer security of tenure to wider groups of rural dwellers (in Africa in particular); it might generate a new class of small peasants, even within the global capitalist system (for discussion of this point, see Zamponi 2007). However, within the framework of contemporary neoliberal policies there is the risk that the sole beneficiary would be small groups of rural (and sometimes urban) elites, while conflicts over land increase.

As mentioned by Hall, further testing through new research is needed, bearing in mind that: pre-existing customary institutions could mean that tenure insecurity may not be the primary productivity constraint in Africa; African farmers are less able to transform investment into production due to constraints in access to inputs; there is a lack of public investments in infrastructure and services. Therefore 'Titling alone is likely insufficient to unleash greater productivity' (Hall 2014a). Indeed, as Susan Minae of FAO observed 'while there is a need for technical expertise and governance solutions: "Securing land rights is not just about governance, it's about politics!"' (Hall 2014b).

On the other hand one is witnessing initiatives based on 'alternative views' which are trying to strengthen the peasants' role by empowering them politically and supporting their social struggle (Desmarais 2007; Edelman and James 2011). Against this, others believe that in the current context radical reform and transformation is simply not feasible. Lerche (2012) notes that land reform is no longer an achievable goal as a way of generating growth based on the role of the peasantry and on accumulation from below. On this point, Bernstein (2002) notes that land reform has re-emerged within the 'rhetoric' of development policies related to poverty reduction, the emphasis being on reform models entrenched on the classical bourgeois system, that is clarifying and defining patterns of private ownership of land.

Privatization and commoditization of land may end by turning subsistence producers into either proletarians or petty commodity producers, as well as creating new groups of capitalist producers from village leaders, traditional chiefs, local elites and government officials. Today, we find an anomalous situation in which, despite large-scale commoditization of the land, systems still follow customary rules (Chimhowu and Woodhouse 2006). In this framework a sort of partial primitive accumulation occurs. Lund and Boone (2013: 10) describe how 'The fusion of customary, state-leveraging, and market strategies of land access promote accumulation on the part of well-positioned actors, but appear to reproduce fluidity in the norms and terms of land access, rather than institutional closure'.

Broadly speaking, during the twentieth century a capitalist system developed which subordinated agriculture, though without implementing sustainable industrial processes. Hence, in developing countries the agrarian question remains still unsolved and closely tied to the national question (Moyo and Yeros 2005). Meanwhile, the 'traditional' pre-capitalist agrarian systems, characterized by a close social relationship between agrarian property and labour, have not been completely replaced by a transition to capitalism via primitive accumulation (Bernstein 2004; Moyo 2012; Oya 2013).

We may thus say that the agrarian question and land reform are still relevant in international development policies and debates. In particular, in Southern Africa (see *infra*) the land question is closely related to state-building and citizenship, as a key factor in the formation of political consensus, in defining citizenship rights, and in the implementation of development policies – including the management of natural resources through legitimate systems of land access. Thus, independent states have sought to set up institutions of land governance designed to control, discipline and deliver development to the people (Alexander 2006).

The Land Question in Southern Africa

In taking a closer look at the agrarian question in Southern Africa, we should start by considering that large-scale commercial farms remain a model of viability in the region (with the exception of Zimbabwe after its Fast Track Land Reform (FTLR) programme – see *infra*). The contemporary agrarian and land question in the region is still deeply marked by its distinctive history of colonial conquest, alienation and dispossession, and uneven patterns of capitalist accumulation, including a high degree of land concentration (particularly in former settler economies) (O'Laughlin et al. 2013; Helliker and Murisa 2011; Kleinbooi 2010). Colonial systems were based on expropriation of the land, spatial segregation of indigenous peoples in native reserves, systematic regulation of migrant labour, taxation of the peasants, and massive state support for the development of a white settler farming class (Cousins and Scoones 2010; Moyo 2012). A highly dualistic and racially divided agrarian structure emerged. The system was composed of a large-scale white capitalist farming sector, on the one hand, which dominated production on both the domestic and international markets, and a struggling peasant sector, on the other. Although a few smallholder peasants became successful producers of agricultural commodities, the general pattern was one of rural poverty. Thus, the establishment of colonial rule through state action in direct support of the settlers forged a specific link between land, race and inequality, which resulted in a deep legacy for post-colonial state-building. O'Laughlin (2008: 199) argues that 'Southern Africa's agrarian crisis is rooted not in what it does not have – liberal economic and political institutions – but in what it does have: a history of integration into global markets and the class relations of capitalism through violence and colonial domination'.

Land reform in Southern Africa is thus still a hot issue. The former settler colonies in the region inherited racially skewed patterns of land distribution, and each country has had to cope with its own history in which peasant production was dispossessed and undermined (Bernstein 2003). However as Cousins and Scoones (2010: 33) phrase it, ' ... should land reform involve the break-up of large-scale farms into smaller production units allocated to large numbers of the rural poor, as happened in Zimbabwe ... or, alternatively, should a productive large-scale commercial farming sector be retained but de-racialized, as a contribution to national reconciliation?'. We may also say that the specific history of the region has impacted, albeit in different ways, on the current national policies of the states in the region: 'when we think about land issues, what is immediately apparent is how overwhelmingly important is *the national level*. Debates over land law and policy and realities on the ground are hugely influenced by the national political landscape' (Palmer 2008: 6; italics in the original).

These historical legacies in post-settler societies (Namibia, South Africa[4] and Zimbabwe) have left unsolved a number of issues, such as the national question, the definition of citizenship, human rights, democratic governance, and the redistribution of resources. The legacy of colonial dispossession remains evident in the land issue, and in the ongoing struggle for land in the region as a whole, as it is well described by Timothy Scarnecchia's chapter about Zimbabwe; he deals

---

4   The South African case is not discussed in this book. For a detailed review of the land question in South Africa see Zamponi (2015 forthcoming).

with the relevance of history in understanding the land question in Zimbabwe and how international politics was involved in finding a negotiated solution. A key issue for the newly elected democratic governments in Zimbabwe, Namibia, and South Africa was whether or not to fundamentally alter the agrarian structure through a large-scale and rapid redistribution of productive land. For many reasons, including doubts as to the productive capacity of small-scale producers, the idea of promoting an economically viable agriculture through removing barriers to racial ownership of commercial agriculture through market-based land reforms, as well as by preserving the productive role of commercial agriculture, is still a central feature of rural policies (Cousins and Scoones 2010) (with the partial exception of Zimbabwe since 2000).

Having said that, if we now turn our attention to Zimbabwe, we see a new path which has the aim of redressing historical injustice, solving the national question and tackling the political struggle for land. Since 2000, the debate on land issue and the FTLR programme has been controversial (for further references, see Zamponi 2013). The discussion over state and land has become more and more dichotomous: on the one hand, the rhetoric of human rights, on the other hand, the rhetoric of social justice and the anti-colonial struggle. All commentators have highlighted the political significance of the land question in relation to state, democracy, and citizenship rights. The land question was presented by the government of Zimbabwe as a way to solve the historical legacy and colonial injustices which still influenced the process of state formation, thus affording a 'convenient legitimization of the ruling party's twenty-year political hegemony' (Compagnon 2011: 167). For some scholars, land reform is a process of social transformation: 'the revolutionary situation in Zimbabwe has given rise *not* to a revolutionary state but a *radicalized* state; this is a peripheral state which has rebelled against neocolonialism' (Moyo and Yeros 2007: 105, italics in the original). For others land reform is just a 'charade' that led to famine; land reform is just an 'inappropriate name for a political strategy that has little to do with rural development' (Compagnon 2011: 166). The research carried out by Scoones et al. (2010: 236–40) critically reviews the characteristics of the land reform programme, highlighting the complexity and variety of the phenomena, for what is concerning with output decline and the lack of investment by small producers. About investments the study points out that the problems related to investment are connected to the country's economic crisis, and the weak agricultural and extension support.

In addition to his previous works, Ian Scoones' chapter discusses the characteristics of and debate surrounding the FTLR programme, drawing on particularly rich research data, and in particular its consequences for rural people's livelihoods and its effects on the political economy of the country.

The need to broaden the land debate in Zimbabwe beyond its current confines and focus on aspects previously underestimated by both policy prescriptions and academic research is particularly emphasized: Rudo Gaidzanwa in her chapter invites us to consider gendered industrial and commercial land use as equally deserving of policy attention, and demonstrates the gendered impact of agrarian policies in the country through a number of case studies. Gaidzanwa's chapter illustrates the relation between land, state and democracy and demonstrates that, from this perspective, the land policies and practices of successive governments have simply stayed static.

Equally important is the extent to which Zimbabwe's experience can be considered unique or whether it may represent broader political dynamics at play in the Southern African region with respect to the classical agrarian question and capitalist social relations of production affecting African agriculture (or not). Pádraig Carmody examines this issue by addressing large-scale land acquisitions and land reform in Zimbabwe from a 'biopolitics' perspective.

Whereas in Zimbabwe the land question is inevitably influenced by its historical roots in colonial dispossession policies and post-colonial contradictions, outside Zimbabwe it is largely seen in relation to legitimacy and democratization, and so the land question becomes a key priority for each country's development policies and political stabilization.

In the other cases discussed in this book, since the 1990s all countries, each in its own way, have tried to address the rural situation through National Land Policies or Laws (Zambia 1995, Mozambique 1997, Tanzania 1999, Malawi 2002).

In the case of Malawi, the rural question has always been, and still is, a crucial element of development practices (Zamponi 2009). With the transition to multiparty democracy in 1994 the theme of land reform became central to the country's political agenda and was considered as the most important way to reduce poverty and promote sustained economic development. Land reform is advocated as a means to bolster the process of democratization and national unity. Particularly important was the 1998 Commission of inquiry on land reform, which stressed the need for a National Land Policy, paving the way for a new land law approved by Parliament in 2002. Nonetheless, to date there is still no coherent framework for implementing the new land law, while rural policies are still unable both to meet the needs of the population and settle rural disputes (Chinsinga 2011; Peters and Kambewa 2007).

As a result of these issues, in recent years three main programmes have driven the Malawian land policy. First, the WB sponsored the Community-Based Rural Land Development Programme (CBRLDP), a pilot programme which draws on a market-led land reform model. Second, starting from the 2005/06 growing season, the Malawian government implemented the Farm Input Subsidy Programme (FISP), with the intent of subsidizing maize production as a way to improving food security. In this regard there are many similarities with the programme launched in Zambia in 2002 (Fertilizer Support Programme): both are concerned with supporting smallholders and attracting the rural vote. Third, as a response to some of the questions raised by international donors, in 2009 the Malawian government introduced the Green Belt Initiative. This programme aims to support the commercialization of agricultural produce by supporting the development of small and large-scale irrigation and maximization of rain-fed agricultural practices.

However, in his chapter Blessings Chinsinga argues that in Malawi, although political liberalization touted the land question as one of the priority policy issues, both vested internal interests and the private agenda of influential external actors have successfully obstructed any real or fast progress, as witnessed by former president Joyce Banda's veto against the 2013 Land Act Bill.

In the cases of Mozambique, Zambia and Tanzania too, governments drew up documents defining rural development policies; more specifically they launched programmes promoting land registration of title deeds, though by differing approaches and regulations.

Wily (2011: 752) states that, broadly speaking, in African countries 'fairer legal terms affecting customary land rights would make it less easy for governments to wilfully remove lands from communities.' Land laws are the only way to protect communities from having their land usurped by foreigners working in conjunction with their own government. However, while in some African countries land laws serve to legitimize the grabbing of customary lands, in others they act as an obstacle to peasant dispossession. As mentioned by Tygesen with reference to Zambia (2014: 31), 'a crucial argument for land titling and thus for the transformation of customary land to state/titled land is based upon the presumption that increased security for land users will increase their willingness to invest in it'.

Coming to Mozambique, the 1997 Lei de Terra (Land Law) is often lauded as one of the most progressive in Africa (Fairbairn 2013). In Mozambique land has never been an issue as it has in neighbouring former settler colonies, but has increasingly attracted policy attention and scientific debate as foreign investments in land have increased in the country since the 1990s.

Many documents about land and rural development have been drawn up by the government since the 1990s (for a wider analysis, see Mosca 2011). Among them, the Plano Estratégico Para o Desenvolvimento do Sector Agrário (PEDSA) which 'is based on the 2025 Vision for Mozambique: an integrated, prosperous, competitive and sustainable agrarian sector.' In pursuing this goal the document defines a general aim: 'to contribute towards the food security and income of agricultural producers in a competitive and sustainable way, guaranteeing social and gender equity' (Republic of Mozambique, Minister of Agriculture 2010: vi).

We should note, however, that most traditional land rights are not formally recognized and above all are not recorded in a national land register. The issue of delimitation and registration has highlighted several problems including that of conflicts among peasants, traditional authorities and the state, very often in a context of persisting lack of procedural transparency and the absence of clear rules. Moreover, there is evidence that the registration of titles has actually produced instances of land concentration, demonstrating the fact that often the more powerful are able to obtain registration of the land (Fairbairn 2013), while rural development policies seem unable to support smallholders, in what Mosca has called 'the politics of not having policies' (Mosca 2014).

There can be little doubt that this also has to do with the fact that the country (and the region as a whole, with the exception of Zimbabwe) is going ahead with a model of liberalization and privatization supported by the WB, seen as the key to increasing production and reducing poverty: securing title deeds, in this model, is held to be a prerequisite for improving production, reducing inefficiency and, ultimately, drawing up a legal framework for more effective usage of the land (Saul 2011).

As Carmody does for Zimbabwe, Corrado Tornimbeni addresses a number of current issues linked to land reform and rural development in contemporary Mozambique. He discusses their implications for the land issue and its role in the country's political economy. Arguing from a historical perspective in which great emphasis is given to the main characteristics of rural development as consolidated during the colonial period, Tornimbeni questions how the developments of the last two decades can be said to fit the history of a country in which labour has always been considered more important than land in shaping local politics and power relations. His chapter takes the Mozambican province of Manica as a case study: bordering with Zimbabwe, this province has land and natural resources endowments in common with Zimbabwe; furthermore, it has always been considered as one of the main food-producing areas of the country in both colonial and post-colonial times.

In the case of Tanzania current land tenure is still guided by the 1999 Land Act and the 1999 Village Land Act (and amendments thereto). All land in Tanzania is public land vested in the president as trustee on behalf of all citizens. Many initiatives involving land registration and definition of access to the land are based on the Property and Business Formalization Programme, also known as Mkururabita, a programme which aims to promote the formalization of citizens' land rights and the procedure of land titling and registration (United Republic of Tanzania, President's Office – State House 2007).

However, as mentioned by Maghimbi, Lokina and Senga (2011: 50) 'It is not clear why the country has two land laws, but the logic appears to derive from colonial dualism … . Traditional land tenure has sat well with the philosophy of the country's rulers since the days of colonialism.' The authors also state in their study that

> conflicts over land and other natural resources offer the best reflection of the agrarian question in Tanzania. The 1999 land laws give too much power to the government in allocating land. … The people should have full control of their own land (for example, through freehold). The government has its own land which is more abundant than the peasants' and pastoralists' land. (Maghimbi, Lokina and Senga 2011: 59)

Arrigo Pallotti scrutinizes the relationship between land reform (within wider processes of agricultural transformation in the country) and the policy of decentralization in Tanzania in marshalling his argument as to the shaping of post-Ujamaa citizenship rights and the political limits of neoliberal development in this country, with particular reference to agricultural and land policies. As in previous works (see for example Pallotti 2008), his chapter focuses on conflict and inequality over land: the registration of new title deeds is exacerbating tensions, since there is often confusion over access to the land while national land and agricultural policy do not offer adequate support to small-scale agriculture.

The difficulties concerning land titling are also confirmed by a recent study which identifies a number of problems linked to inequality (in particular for women) and to the fact that titled land remains de facto controlled by wealthy households and, within households, men (Ali et al. 2014). The issues of inequality, dispossession, and inefficiency are again shown to be relevant in this country (Myenzi 2006), confirming and supporting Pallotti's analysis.

Finally, in focusing on the land issue and land policies in Zambia since independence, Federico Battera analyses the impact of State policies on poverty reduction after democratization: against a background of weak links between economic interests and the party system, and fragmentation of farmers' interests, he demonstrates that the uneven economic achievements have penalized the poorest rural households.

In the case of Zambia, one should note that since enactment of the 1995 Land Act which allows for conversion of customary land to state land with private leasehold interests, only 10 per cent of land held under customary tenure has been privatized through conversion to leasehold (USAID 2010: 1). A recent study (Tygesen 2014) advances two major conclusions on this matter:

> First of all, foreign private investors are few, but acquire large tracts of land. When foreign investors buy land, there are often no or very few consultations with local communities whose land they buy … . Secondly, local elites have shown a rapidly growing interest in taking ownership of Customary Land. (Tygesen 2014: 6)

Moreover:

> Although the 1995 Land Act opened for holders of traditional tenure rights on Customary Land to title this, few have opted for this. Reasons vary, but the most commonly cited are lack of awareness of the option, unsurmountable economical costs or formalities, or resistance to such transfers from chiefs or headmen fearing loss of control over their area and subjects. (ibid.)

In addition, a study by Sitko and Jayne suggests that 'much of the growth of the emergent farming sector can be explained by a legislative and public spending framework that favours both the alienation of large tracts of agricultural land by non-smallholder farmers, coupled with the disproportionate capture of agricultural public spending by a rural minority' (Sitko and Jayne 2014: 201).

These points are clearly related to Battera's analysis of land, state and the political system, a theme that is also part of Gould's work, which again links the land question to democracy and the political system. More specifically, he criticizes the results attained in the country in terms of land and rural development: 'despite two decades of deregulated development in Zambia, agrarian transformation is still stalled at square one for much of the country. The fundamental problems of low productivity and ineffective demand persist ... ' (Gould 2010, part 7. Epilogue).

Gould conclusions on Zambia are particularly meaningful for the region and for the present collection, notably when he points to persistent agrarian stagnation related to various factors such as social exclusion and broad marginalization of small farmers who encounter many difficulties in accessing input, facilities and services (Gould 2010).

Conclusions

The whole issue of contemporary development hinges on the possibility of a profitable relationship between rural development policies, redistributive land reform, and support of small-scale producers.

However, tensions and conflict over land involving a wide range of social actors are marked by acutely local features and are widespread in third world countries. They appear to be intensifying in many African contexts. Peasants are having to cope with the ongoing processes of transformation if they wish to avoid being destroyed as a class, in complex and diverse situations, varying from region to region.

We may say that because of globalization, the classical agrarian question is no longer central to the global economy. However, we must recognize that the question of national accumulation in most African countries has not yet been resolved. What does exist is an agrarian question of labour (or classes of labour), namely, what relationships exist between classes of labour and rural transformation (Bernstein 2010).

In most African rural societies, which are less and less cohesive, and at the same time, more globalized, an acute struggle is taking place against inequalities. The global process of accumulation of natural resources (including land) has perpetuated the agrarian crisis. More attention is needed to the interactions between process and structure, between the role of the state – both colonial and contemporary – in defining land tenure and the alliances (both national and international) the state forms with capital, social classes and groups over the land question (Maghimbi, Lokina and Senga 2011).

The twentieth century has generated a rich and diverse experience regarding the role of small farms in reducing poverty and generating economic development (Birner and Resnik 2010). For many analysts, smallholder development is still one of the main ways to reduce poverty in low-income countries. As Hazell et al. (2010: 1358) point out,

State, Land and Democracy   15

new thinking on the role of the state in agricultural development, wider changes in democratization, decentralization, the introduction of participatory policy processes, and a renewed interest in agriculture among major international donors presents opportunities and gives ground for hope that greater and more effective support to small farm development can be delivered.

More research on the political economy of smallholder-orientated politics is urgently needed now that, after years of neglect, agriculture has re-appeared on the international development agenda.

In conclusion, as Peters suggests (2013a: 562)

> any attempt to understand 'the question of land' in contemporary Africa has to grapple even more than in the past with the dynamics of social transformation at multiple levels – global, regional, national, subnational – that are reshaping not merely access to land itself but the very bases of authority, livelihood, ownership and citizenship. And in reverse, any attempt to understand the multiple transformations taking place on the continent has to include 'the question of land' as a central element.

In the Southern African region, the historical legacy of land and the socio-economic inequalities in contexts of high poverty is weakening governments' legitimacy and represents a challenge to the models of economic development promoted by governments for years with the support of the international community. In this context, given the peculiar history of colonial domination experienced by the region, the land question still appears to be a central issue. It can jeopardize citizenship and democracy: no government seems able to fully cope with this challenge and to find a viable and sustainable solution.

References

Akram-Lodhi, A. Haroon. 2008. "(Re)imagining Agrarian Relations? The World Development Report 2008: Agriculture for Development." *Development and Change* 39(6): 1145–62.

Akram-Lodhi, A. Haaron and Cristóbal Kay. eds. 2009. *Peasants and Globalisation, Political Economy, Rural Transformation and the Agrarian Question*. London: Routledge.

——. 2010a. "Surveying the Agrarian Question (Part 1): Unearthing Foundations, Exploring Diversity." *Journal of Peasant Studies* 37(1): 177–202.

——. 2010b. "Surveying the Agrarian Question (Part 2): Current Debates and Beyond." *Journal of Peasant Studies* 37(2): 255–84.

Alexander, Jocelyn. 2006. *The Unsettled Land: State-making and the Politics of Land in Zimbabwe 1893–2003*. Oxford: James Currey.

Ali, Daniel Ayalew, Matthew Collin, Klaus Deininger, Stefan Dercon, Justin Sandefur, and Andrew Zeitlin. 2014. "The Price of Empowerment: Experimental Evidence on Land Titling in Tanzania." June, World Bank Policy Research Working Paper No. 6908. Accessed 16 December 2014. http://elibrary.worldbank.org/doi/pdf/10.1596/1813-9450-6908.

Bernstein, Henry. 2002. "Land reform: Taking a Long(er) View." *Journal of Agrarian Change* 2(4): 433–63.

——. 2003. "Land Reform in Southern Africa in World-Historical Perspective." *Review of African Political Economy* 30(96): 203–26.

——. 2004. "'Changing Before Our Very Eyes': Agrarian Questions and the Politics of Land in Capitalism Today." *Journal of Agrarian Change* 4(1–2): 190–225.

——. 2010. *Class Dynamics of Agrarian Change*. Halifax: Fernwood.

——. 2012. "Alcune dinamiche di classe del lavoro rurale nel Sud del mondo." *Sociologia del lavoro* 128(4): 16–31.

Bernstein, Henry and Tom Brass. 1996. *Agrarian Questions Essays in Appreciation of T.J. Byres*. London: Frank Cass.

Birner, Regina and Danielle Resnik. 2010. "The Political Economy of Policies for Smallholder Agriculture." *World Development* 38(10): 1442–52.

Borras, Saturnino M. Jr. 2009. "Agrarian Change and Peasant Studies: Changes, Continuities and Challenges – An Introduction." *Journal of Peasant Studies* 36(1): 5–31.

Byres, Terence J. 1996. *Capitalism from Above and Capitalism from Below: An Essay in Comparative Political Economy*. London: Macmillan.

——. 2004. "Introduction: Contextualising and Interrogating the GKI Case for Redistributive Land Reform." *Journal of Agrarian Change* 4(1–2): 1–16.

——. 2012. "The Agrarian Question and the Peasantry," in *The Elgar Companion to Marxist Economics*, edited by Ben Fine and Alfredo Saad-Filho, 10–15. Cheltenham: Edward Elgar Publishing.

Chimhowu, Admos and Philip Woodhouse. 2006. "Customary vs Private Property Rights? Dynamics and Trajectories of Vernacular Land Markets in Sub-Saharan Africa." *Journal of Agrarian Change* 6(3): 346–71.

Chinsinga, Blessings. 2011. "The Politics of Land Reforms in Malawi: A Case Study of the Community-Based Rural Land Development Programme." *Journal of International Development* 23(3): 380–93.

Compagnon, Daniel. 2011. *A Predictable Tragedy: Robert Mugabe and the Collapse of Zimbabwe*. Philadelphia, PA: University of Pennsylvania Press.

Cotula, Lorenzo. Ed. 2007. *Changes in "Customary" Land Tenure Systems in Africa*. London: IIED.

Cousins, Ben and Ian Scoones. 2010. "Contested Paradigms of 'Viability' in Redistributive Land Reform: Perspectives from Southern Africa." *Journal of Peasant Studies* 37(1): 31–66.

Desmarais, Annette. 2007. *La via campesina*. London: Pluto Press.

Edelman, Marc and Carwil James. 2011. "Peasants' Rights and the UN System: Quixotic Struggle? Or Emancipatory Idea Whose Time Has Come?" *Journal of Peasant Studies* 38(1): 81–108.

Fairbairn, Madeleine. 2013. "Indirect Dispossession: Domestic Power Imbalances and Foreign Access to Land in Mozambique." *Development and Change* 44(2): 335–56.

Gould, Jeremy. 2010. *Left Behind: Rural Zambia in the Third Republic*. Lusaka: Lembani Trust.

Griffin, Keith, Azizur Rahman Khan, and Amy Ickowitz. 2002. "Poverty and the Distribution of Land." *Journal of Agrarian Change* 2(3): 279–330.

Hall, Ruth. 2014a. "Does Land Titling Work?" *Future Agricultures blog*, 14 November. Accessed 15 December 2014. http://www.future-agricultures.org/blog/entry/does-land-titling-work.

——. 2014b. "Land Policy for the Next Decade: Taking Stock and Moving Forward." *Future Agricultures blog*, 12 November. Accessed 15 December 2014. http://www.future-agricultures.org/blog/entry/conference-on-land-policy-ruth-hall.

Hazeel, Peter, Colin Poulton, Steve Wiggins, and Andrew Dorward. 2010. "The Future of Small Farms: Trajectories and Policy Priorities." *World Development* 38(10): 1349–61.

Helliker, Kirk and Tendai Murisa. 2011. *Land Struggles and Civil Society in Southern Africa*. Trenton: Africa World Press.

Kleinbooi, Karin. Ed. 2010. *Review of Land Reforms in Southern Africa 2010*. Bellville: Institute for Poverty, Land and Agrarian Studies (PLAAS), School of Government, University of the Western Cape.

Lerche, Jens. 2012. "Questioni agrarie o questioni del lavoro? La questione agraria e la sua irrilevanza per il lavoro rurale nell'India neo-liberista." *Sociologia del lavoro* 128(4): 76–105.

Lipton, Michael. 2005. "The Family Farm in a Globalizing World." 2020 Vision. Discussion Papers 40. Washington DC: International Food Policy Research Institute. Accessed 30 November 2014. http://www.ifpri.org/sites/default/files/publications/vp40.pdf.

——. 2009. *Land Reform in Developing Countries: Property Rights and Property Wrongs*. New York: Routledge.

Lund, Christian and Catherine Boone. 2013. "Introduction: Land Politics in Africa – Constituting Authority over Territory, Property and Persons." *Africa* 83(1): 1–13.

Maghimbi, Sam, Razack B. Lokina, and Mathew A. Senga. 2011. "The Agrarian Question in Tanzania? A State of the Art Paper." *Current African Issues* no. 45. Uppsala: Nordiska African Institute.

Manji, Ambreena. 2006. *The Politics of Land Reform in Africa: From Communal Tenure to Free Markets*. London: Zed Books.

McMichael, Philip. 2008. "Peasants Make Their Own History, But Not Just as They Please … " *Journal of Agrarian Change* 8(2–3): 205–28.

——. 2012. "The Land Grab and Corporate Food Regime Restructuring." *Journal of Peasant Studies* 39(3–4): 681–701.

Moore, David. 2004. "The Second Age of the Third World: From Primitive Accumulation to Global Public Goods?" *Third World Quarterly* 25(1): 87–109.

Mosca, João. 2011. *Políticas agrária de (em) Moçambique*. Maputo: Escolar Editora.

——. 2014. "Agricoltura familiare in Mozambico: la politica di non avere politica?" *afriche e orienti* Numero Speciale: 24–43.

Moyo, Sam. 2011. "Primitive Accumulation and the Destruction of African Peasantries," in *The Agrarian Question in the Neoliberal Era: Primitive Accumulation and the Peasantry*, edited by Utsa Patnaik and Sam Moyo, 61–85. Cape Town: Fahamu Books and Pambazuka Press.

——. 2012. "Transizione agraria mancata e sotto-consumo in Africa." *Sociologia del lavoro* 128(4): 106–21.

Moyo, Sam and Paris Yeros, eds. 2005. *Reclaiming the Land: The Resurgence of Rural Movements in Africa, Asia and Latin America*. London: Zed Books.

——. 2007. "The Radicalised State: Zimbabwe's Interrupted Revolution." *Review of African Political Economy* 34(111): 103–21.

Myenzi, Yefred. 2006. "Land Privatization in Tanzania: The State of Art, Implications and Lessons for Policy and Practice." Hakiardhi working paper. Accessed 10 December 2014. http://www.hakiardhi.org/index. php?option=com_docman&task=cat_view&gid=67&Itemid=81&limitstart=1 5.

NEPAD. 2013. *African Agriculture, Transformation and Outlook*. November. Johannesburg: NEPAD. Accessed 12 December 2014. http://www.nepad.org/ system/files/Agriculture%20in%20Africa.pdf.

——. 2014. "2014 Year of Agriculture, Transforming Africa's Agriculture: harnessing opportunities for inclusive growth and sustainable development." Visited 15 December 2014. http://pages.au.int/caadpyoa.

O'Laughlin, Bridget. 2008. "Gender Justice, Land and the Agrarian Question in Southern Africa," in *Peasants and Globalisation: Political Economy, Rural Transformation and the Agrarian Question*, edited by A. Haaron Akram-Lodhi and Cristóbal Kay, 190–213. London: Routledge.

O'Laughlin, Bridget, Henry Bernstein, Ben Cousins, and Pauline E. Peters. 2013. "Introduction: Agrarian Change, Rural Poverty and Land Reform in South Africa since 1994." *Journal of Agrarian Change* 13(1): 1–15.

Otsuka, Keijiro and Frank Place. 2014. "Changes in Land Tenure and Agricultural Intensification in sub-Saharan Africa." WIDER Working Paper, No. 2014/051. UNU-WIDER. http://www.econstor.eu/bitstream/10419/96348/1/779696611. pdf.

Oya, Carlos. 2009. "Introduction to a Symposium on the World Development Report 2008: Agriculture for Development?" *Journal of Agrarian Change* 9(2): 231–4.

——. 2013. "The Land Rush and Classic Agrarian Questions of Capital and Labour: A Systematic Scoping Review of the Socioeconomic Impact of Land Grabs in Africa." *Third World Quarterly* 34(9): 1532–57.

Pallotti, Arrigo. 2008. *"*Tanzania: Decentralising Power or Spreading Poverty?" *Review of African Political Economy* 35(2): 221–35.

Palmer, Robin. 2008. "Land Reform in the Broader Context of Southern Africa." Paper presented at the Conference "Land Reform from Below: Decentralised Land Reform in Southern Africa," Kopanong Hotel, Johannesburg, 22–23 April 2008. Accessed 10 December 2014. http://www.mokoro.co.uk/files/13/file/lria/land_reform_in_broader_context_southern_africa_dlrsa.pdf.

Patnaik, Utsa. 2011. "The Agrarian Question in the Neoliberal Era," in *The Agrarian Question in the Neoliberal Era: Primitive Accumulation and the Peasantry*, edited by Utsa Patnaik and Sam Moyo, 7–60. Cape Town: Fahamu Books and Pambazuka Press.

Peters, Pauline E. 2004. "Social Conflict over Land in Africa: Time to Reorient Research." *Journal of Agrarian Change* 4(3): 269–314.

——. 2013a. "Conflicts over Land and Threats to Customary Tenure in Africa." *African Affairs* 112(449): 543–62.

——. 2013b. "Land Appropriation, Surplus People and a Battle over Visions of Agrarian Futures in Africa." *Journal of Peasant Studies* 40(3): 537–62.

Peters, Pauline E., and Daimon Kambewa. 2007. "Whose Security? Deepening Social Conflict over Customary Land in the Shadow if Land Tenure Reform in Malawi." *Journal of Modern African Studies* 45(3): 447–72.

Republic of Mozambique, Ministry of Agriculture. 2010. Strategic Plan for Agricultural Development PEDSA 2010–2019, draft, October.

Saul, John. 2011. "Mozambique: Not Then but Now." *Review of African Political Economy* 38(127): 93–101.

Scoones Ian, Nelson Marongwe, Blasio Mavedzenge, Jacob Mahenehene, Felix Murimbarimba, and Chrispen Sukume. 2010. *Zimbabwe's Land Reform. Myths and Realities*. Harare: Weaver Press.

Sitko, Nicholas J., and Thomas S. Jayne. 2014. "Structural Transformation or Elite Land Capture? The growth of 'Emergent' Farmers in Zambia." *Food Policy* 48: 194–202.

Toulmin, Camilla, and Julian Quan. Eds. 2000. E*volving Land Rights, Policy and Tenure in Africa*. London: DFID/IIED/NRI.

Tygesen, Peter. 2014. "No Clear Grounds. The Impact of Land Privatisation on Smallhold Farmers' Food Security in Zambia." A desk study on behalf of DanChurchAid. Accessed 29 November 2014. http://www.mokoro.co.uk/files/13/file/NoClearGrounds.pdf.

United Republic of Tanzania, President's Office – State House. 2007. *Property and Business Formalization Programme*, Mkururabita. Dar es Salaam.

USAID. 2010. "Zambia Country Profile. Property Rights and Resource Governance." Accessed 12 December 2014. http://usaidlandtenure.net/sites/

default/files/country-profiles/full-reports/USAID_Land_Tenure_Zambia_Profile.pdf.

Van der Ploeg, Jan D. 2010. "The Peasantries of the Twenty-first Century: The Commoditisation Debate Revised." *Journal of Peasant Studies* 37(1): 1–30.

White, Ben, Saturnino M. Borras Jr., Ruth Hall, Ian Scoones, and Wendy Wolford. 2012. "The New Enclosures: Critical Perspectives on Corporate Land Deals." *Journal of Peasant Studies* 39(3–4): 619–47.

Wily, Liz Alden. 2011. "'The Law is to Blame': The Vulnerable Status of Common Property Rights in Sub-Saharan Africa." *Development and Change* 42(3): 733–57.

——. 2012. "Looking Back to See Forward: The Legal Niceties of Land Theft in Land Rushes." *Journal of Peasant Studies* 39(3–4): 751–75.

Woodhouse, Philip. 2012. "New Investment, Old Challenges: Land Deals and the Water Constraint in African Agriculture." *Journal of Peasant Studies* 39(3–4): 777–94.

World Bank (WB). 2003. *Land Policies for Growth and Poverty Reduction.* Oxford: Oxford University Press.

——. 2008. *World Development Report: Agriculture for Development.* Washington DC: World Bank.

——. 2013. *Implementing Agriculture for Development: World Bank Group Agriculture Action Plan (2013–2015).* Washington DC; The World Bank Group. Accessed 20 November 2015. http://www-wds.worldbank.org/external/default/WDSContentServer/WDSP/IB/2013/05/23/000333037_20130523100445/Rendered/PDF/779110WP0Ag0Ac0than0the0Board0paper.pdf.

Zamponi, Mario. 2007. "Governance della terra, diritti di cittadinanza e sviluppo rurale in Africa australe." *Africa (Roma)* 52(1): 54–77.

——. 2009. "'Promoting Sustainable pro-Poor Growth.' The Policy of Poverty Reduction in Malawi." *afriche e orienti* Special Issue II: 177–87.

——. 2013. "Land, State and National Citizenship in Zimbabwe." In *Working the System in Sub-Saharan Africa. Global Values, National Citizenship and Local Politics in Historical Perspective*, edited by Corrado Tornimbeni, 65–82. Newcastle upon Tyne: Cambridge Scholars Publishing.

——. 2015 forthcoming. "The South African Land Reform Since 1994: Policies, Debate, Achievements." In *Unfinished Transition. South Africa Twenty Years after the End of Apartheid*, edited by Ulf Engel and Arrigo Pallotti.

PART I
Land and Rural Development in Southern Africa: Historical and Political Perspectives

Chapter 2

An Unfinished Agenda in a Neoliberal Context: State, Land and Democracy in Malawi

Blessings Chinsinga

Introduction

The land question is increasingly becoming important since Malawi remains predominantly agrarian five decades after independence (Chinsinga and Wren-Lewis 2014). The land question lies at the heart of Malawi's political economy because up to 85 per cent of Malawians earn their livelihood out of agriculture. In fact, agriculture contributes about 90 per cent of the country's export earnings; adds 39 per cent to Gross Domestic Product (GDP); accounts for 85 per cent of total employment; and 65 per cent of total rural income. It is therefore not surprising that there is a direct correlation between the magnitude of a household's poverty and its overall access to land as the single most important productive asset in the country (Chirwa 2008; GoM 2013a).

The main concern, however, is that the land question remains unsettled five decades later (Kanyongolo 2005; Chinsinga, Chasukwa and Zuka 2013). The ownership of land is highly unequal with some recent estimates projecting that land ownership per capita has dwindled to as low as 0.4 hectares (GoM 2013a). This has potentially catastrophic consequences for Malawi's development since land still remains the most productive asset for the majority of the people. The paradox is that the land question has always been on the country's policy and development agenda since independence although, relatively speaking, it was not as pronounced as in other countries such as Mozambique, Namibia, South Africa and Zimbabwe which experienced deeply entrenched white settler colonialism (Breytenbach 2003). Of course, radical land reforms were an integral part of the independence struggle rhetoric but were not implemented as envisaged and championed. The reforms that were introduced under the auspices of the 1967 Land Act essentially perpetuated the colonial land tenure system which distinguished three categories of land, namely: public, freehold/leasehold and customary (N'gong'ola 1982; Chinsinga 2002; Kanyongolo 2005). These reforms maintained the colonial dualistic agrarian structure that distinguished between estate and smallholder sectors whereby land could be transferred from the latter to the former but not the other way round. Moreover, smallholder farmers were not allowed to cultivate high value crops such as burley tobacco, tea, coffee and sugar (Chinsinga 2002; Chirwa 2004).

The major beneficiaries of the land reforms under the auspices of the 1967 Land Act included mainly politicians, traditional chiefs, senior civil servants, parastatal and private sector employees. It is actually estimated that by 1993, over a million hectares of land had been transferred from the smallholder to the estate sector with most of the land estimated at 28 per cent lying idle following the enormous decline of the agricultural sector (Chirwa 1998; GoM 2002). These massive tracts of land were appropriated from the smallholder sector usually with little or no compensation at all. Signs of mounting land pressure among rural Malawians became apparent in the lead up to the 1992–1994 democratic transition as small-scale land invasions were reported especially in the tea and coffee growing districts of Thyolo and Mulanje as well as in some protected forest reserves around the country (Kanyongolo 2005; Chinsinga 2008). These developments were seized by the proponents of democratization to advocate for radical land reforms should they be brought into power as a springboard for rapid, sustainable and equitable socio-economic development.

It is against this backdrop that this chapter undertakes a critical review of the progress that Malawi has made in addressing the land question since the transition to democracy in May 1994. The main argument of this chapter is that while the advent of democratization pushed the land question onto the agenda, and advocates for political liberalization touted it as one of the priority policy issues, vested and deeply entrenched interests have successfully obstructed swift progress. The land reform agenda has further been compromised by external actors who have been providing technical assistance to the government in its attempt to address the land question. The majority of these external actors have their own interests rooted in their ideological beliefs that they would like to achieve most of which run counter to the ideals of a broad based land reform agenda informed by, and rooted in the specificities and particularities of the historical context. The rest of the chapter is organized as follows. Following this introduction, the second section provides an overview of the land reforms in the democratic context. The third section examines two initiatives that have been implemented in the context of the apparent stagnation of the land reform efforts since May 1994. These initiatives are the Community-Based Rural Land Development Programme (CBRLDP) and the Green Belt Initiative (GBI). The main purpose is to examine the extent to which these initiatives have enabled or constrained progress in the country's land reform efforts. The fourth section considers some of the key challenges in the country's land reform efforts while the fifth and final section offers some concluding remarks.

Land Reforms in Democratic Malawi

Malawi reinstated a multiparty political dispensation in May 1994 after 30 years of authoritarian one party rule but it was not until 1996 that some notable action began in relation to addressing the land question (Kishindo 2004; Chinsinga 2011).

The first major initiative was the constitution of the Presidential Commission of Inquiry on Land Reform (PCILR). Its overall mandate was 'to promote scholarly discourse, gather the opinion of the private sector, ordinary citizens and non-governmental organizations and to organize their findings in such a manner as to aid the land policy efforts' (GoM 1999: 13).

The PCILR produced its report in 1999 which formed the basis for producing a draft land policy which was endorsed by Cabinet in July 2002. This was followed by the empanelment of a Special Law Commission in 2003 whose main task was 'to review existing land legislation and develop new legislation for effective land administration by consulting as widely as possible with relevant stakeholders' (Chinsinga 2011: 381). The Special Law Commission completed its work in 2005. Further developments in as far as the land reform question is concerned have included the development of the Malawi Land Reform Implementation Strategy 2003–2007, the implementation of the CBRLDP in 2004 and the GBI in 2010.

All these efforts have not culminated in the adoption of a new legislative framework. This means that initiatives such as the GBI are being implemented in the context of a virtual legislative impasse (Chinsinga and Chasukwa 2012). The draft Land Act Bill was tabled in Parliament in June 2013 and endorsed for enactment into law but former President Joyce Banda declined to assent to it. The President declined to sanction the draft Land Act Bill into law due to strong resistance against it particularly from traditional leaders and civil society organizations largely due to its predominant neoliberal orientation (Chinsinga and Chasukwa 2013). The draft Land Act Bill was purportedly informed by the apparent success of the CBRLDP, which piloted the neoliberal orientated land reforms anchored in the willing seller willing buyer philosophy.

The chiefs are opposed to the draft Land Act Bill because it dispossesses them of their authority over customary land, which is construed as 'unallocated land' (GoM 2013b) while the civil society organizations are wary about the unrestrained land markets that shall result following the enactment of the Bill into law. They fear that this new land law will result in large-scale dispossession of rural poor of their land, which is their only meaningful productive asset. The major reason the President declined to assent to the draft Land Act Bill is that she did not want to risk her election chances. The elections were scheduled for May 2014 and antagonizing the chiefs around this period can be costly since they are generally considered as critical power brokers in view of the enormous power and influence they wield over their subjects (Chinsinga 2006; Chiweza 2007).

In addition to the PCILR's report, the development of the 2002 land policy was further informed by several land utilization studies commissioned by donors such as the European Union (EU), the Department for International Development (DFID) and the World Bank (Chinsinga, Chasukwa, and Zuka 2013). These studies collectively established that Malawi has farmable land to the tune of 9.4 million hectares and out of this 7.7 hectares are available for estate and smallholder agriculture. It is estimated that estate agriculture takes up to 1.2 million hectares leaving the rest for smallholder farmers. However, out of the remaining 6.4 million hectares smallholder farmers only effectively cultivate 2.4 million hectares, which implies that 4.1 million hectares lie idle. These studies also concluded that much of the land devoted to estate agriculture lies idle bringing the total of unutilized land to about 28 per cent of the total farmable land in the country.

The 2002 land policy was developed with technical support from the World Bank. In fact, the policy drafting exercise was led by a consultant hired on behalf of the Malawi government by the World Bank. The drafting of the land policy was informed, to a very great extent, by the findings of the land utilization studies which, overall, painted an imagery of the existence of vast tracts of empty and idle land in the country. The picture about the existence of abundant land in Malawi is further reinforced by claims of the apparent unproductivity of smallholder farmers. According to Kaarhaus and Nyirenda (2006), smallholder agriculture productivity is particularly undermined by exorbitant prices of agricultural inputs, poor infrastructure, weak and collapsing extension services, fluctuating markets and dismal returns.

The main concern about the land reform efforts in the democratic context is that they have not been guided by the recommendations made by the PCILR. It, *inter alia*, recommended that it should principally be the idle estate land that should be targeted for redistribution to the landless or near landless (Kishindo 2004; Chinsinga 2011). This was, however, effectively resisted until the introduction of the CBLRDP which, on a pilot basis, propagated land reform efforts guided by the willing seller willing buyer philosophy. The PCILR's recommendation was resisted because the majority of the owners of the idle estates happen to be political, bureaucratic and business elites who, ironically, were in the forefront pushing for the democratization agenda and flagging a comprehensive land reform programme as key to achieving rapid, sustainable and equitable socio-economic development.

CBRLDP and GBI: Necessary Detours?

This section examines the extent to which the implementation of the CBRLDP and GBI have either facilitated or obstructed the land reform efforts. While the CBRLDP was conceived as an integral part of the efforts to spearhead the implementation of land reforms, GBI has totally different origins but has had significant implications on the land reform efforts. The GBI was initiated in 2010 as a strategic attempt to expand the volume of land under irrigated agriculture from 78,000 to about 1 million hectares. It was further justified as a mechanism for consolidating the gains of the Farm Input Subsidy Programme (FISP) by guaranteeing the expansion of land under irrigated agriculture especially in the context of unfavourable climatic patterns (GoM 2010; Chinsinga and Chasukwa 2012).

The CBRLDP

The CBRLDP was launched in 2004 as a three year pilot programme targeting four districts (two sending districts and two receiving districts). The sending districts were Thyolo and Mulanje while the receiving districts were Mangochi and Machinga. The districts designated as sending were deemed to be land constrained while the receiving districts were considered fairly land rich (Chirwa 2008; Chinsinga 2008). The CBRLDP was thus conceived as a pilot initiative that involves purchasing and redistributing land to farmers on a willing buyer, willing seller basis with the view of building on its lessons to scale it up as a framework for land redistribution in the country.

The CBRLDP was funded to the tune of US$28.75 million under a tripartite funding arrangement. The World Bank contributed US$24 million; the Malawi Government provided US$2.4 million; and the beneficiary communities contributed US$2.30 million mostly in kind and labour (World Bank 2004). The main objective of the CBRLDP was to facilitate access by the poor to underutilized land through redistribution and resettlement. This would, in turn, reduce rural poverty, promote growth, and increase consultation and participation of key stakeholders in the implementation of land reforms (GoM 2005; Chirwa 2008; Chinsinga 2011).

The goal of the CBRLDP was to resettle 15,000 poor rural families thereby enhancing their income through provision of land for viable agricultural production. The programme targeted Malawians that were landless or near landless, facing food insecurity and willing to give up the land they owned in the sending districts as a means of easing the mounting pressure on land (GoM 2005; Chirwa 2008). The beneficiaries self-selected themselves into groups of 10–35 households designated as trusts to seek relocation from sending to receiving districts. These groups were screened to certify their eligibility according to the programme guidelines by Community Oversight Committees (CoCs). In the host communities, the CoCs facilitated the integration of the new settlers into their respective new communities. Each beneficiary received a grant of US$1050 to buy land, cover resettlement costs, and other start up costs in the new location.

Table 2.1 below presents a summary of progress in the implementation of the CBRLDP as of 2009 when it was winding down.

Table 2.1   Targets versus achievements

Objective	Target	Achievement
Groups resettled	450	358
Households resettled	15,000	8,222
Land acquired (hectares)	33,750	18,254
Group titles transferred	450	153
Trust deeds registered	450	299
Maize yield	962 kg/ha prior to settlement	2,269 kg/ha after resettlement

Source: Ministry of Lands and Natural Resources, 2009.

The main issue of concern is that the CBRLDP has been declared a success despite the numerous shortfalls that characterized its implementation. It was actually the principal basis for the draft legislative framework that former President Joyce Banda declined to endorse for it to become law. Several evaluations and scholarly studies including Chirwa (2008) and Chinsinga (2008) have raised a wide range of challenges that cast doubt on whether CBRLDP can be projected as an absolute success so as to inform, almost exclusively, the development of the land legislative framework. Some of the challenges included the following:

i. The yield levels of the CBRLDP beneficiaries were not sustained beyond the first year of settlement. This was due to the fact that the settlers were not able to afford improved farm inputs in the subsequent years due to severe cash constraints since most of these areas lack viable markets for farmers to dispose of their produce at a profit.

ii. A good number of the settlers have ended up abandoning their land and returned to their original homes in the sending districts. For most of them, life in the new settlements became unbearable since most of them were not properly served with basic social amenities such as health, education and water. The situation was further exacerbated by lack of lucrative markets that made farming on the newly acquired land hardly sustainable.

iii. There were considerable overt and covert protests against the programme especially by the host communities. An example of overt protests entailed members of the host communities encroaching onto the land of the new settlers. They justified the encroachment on the basis that the land on which the new settlers had been given originally belonged to them and had been alienated from them under the auspices of the 1967 Land Act. The major act of covert protest involved the chiefs abdicating their role in mediating land conflicts of this nature. Most settler communities have therefore lost their land through encroachment. This was further exacerbated by the proposal both in the policy and legislative framework to relieve chiefs of their direct involvement in land matters and transactions.

iv. The programme also suffered from elite capture especially by the chiefs which, in a way, undermined the success of the CBRLDP. The chiefs through CoCs extracted rents through imposing some kind of a fee estimated at about US$20 in the sending districts for households to qualify for selection. This meant that it was not exactly the landless or the near landless who benefitted from the programme. In addition, the chiefs encouraged the beneficiaries not to give up their land in the sending districts. Most of the beneficiaries therefore commute between the sending and receiving districts which greatly undermined the overarching objective of the CBRLDP pilot initiative.

v. The implementation of the CBRLDP precipitated cultural clashes between incoming and original communities. This created conditions of perpetual instability and tension between the new settlers and host communities. This is inevitable because the settler communities are predominantly Christian whereas the host communities are predominantly Moslem.

The GBI

The GBI was conceived in 2010 as an integral part of concerted efforts to achieve sustainable economic growth and development through the Malawi Growth and Development Strategy (MGDS), which is flagged as the country's overarching development planning framework (GoM 2010). The overriding aim of the GBI is to reduce poverty, improve livelihoods and sustainable food security at both household and national levels through increased production and productivity of agricultural crops, livestock and fisheries.

The GBI is thus seen as a mechanism to protect the gains in food security, reduce vulnerability to drought, and diversify crop production by irrigating a million of hectares of land lying within the 20 km radius of the country's three lakes and 13 perennial rivers (Chinsinga and Chasukwa 2013). At the time the GBI was conceived, the amount of land under irrigated agriculture was estimated at 78,000 hectares. The specific objectives of the GBI include the following: 1) increasing production and productivity of crops, livestock and fisheries; 2) increasing agricultural exports and foreign exchange earnings; 3) promoting diversification of crops and livestock enterprises; 4) increasing household incomes; 5) improving value chain linkages and operations; 6) increasing private sector participation in agricultural production; 7) adding value through processing of raw materials; 8) reducing rural-urban migration; and 9) improving availability of quality water for domestic and industrial use.

The desirability of the GBI is not questionable at all given the country's troubled history in relation to the question of food insecurity especially since the turn of the 1990s. Nonetheless, the main concern is that the GBI essentially promotes supply driven orientated land grabs in a country where land ownership per capita has dramatically declined. It is estimated that about 25 per cent of smallholder farmers cultivate less than 0.5 hectares; 55 per cent cultivate less than 1.0 hectares; 31 per cent cultivate between 1.0 and 2.0 hectares and only 14 per cent cultivate more than 2.0 hectares. However, despit The drafting of the land policy was informed, to a very great extent, by the findings e being resource constrained, the smallholder farmers in Malawi produce about 80 per cent of Malawi's food and 20 per cent of the total agricultural exports (Anderson 2011; IFAD 2011; Chinsinga, Chasukwa, and Zuka 2013).

The supply driven land grabs orientation of the GBI is self evident in the concept paper that outlined its implementation mechanisms. It clearly states that government will facilitate the acquisition of land (lease or sublease) for both local and international investors, and wherever appropriate, it will promote out-grower schemes. The following sentiments aptly capture the position of the government:

> The large growers need vast acres for large-scale production … land has to
> be identified for them along the [GBI] and these have to be linked to banking

30   *State, Land and Democracy in Southern Africa*

> institutions for inputs such as machinery, fertilizers, seeds, pesticides, labour, and cash. Large growers will have to engage in discussions with local assemblies to relocate villages for intensified farming by use of heavy machinery. Irrigation schemes [will] be owned by large-scale commercial farmers and cooperate companies [who] ... will be responsible for developing and operating them. (GoM 2009: iii-iv)

The supply driven land grabs orientation of the GBI is, to a very great extent, inspired by the conclusions of studies that informed the development of the 2002 land policy (Breytenbach 2003). To reiterate, these studies paint an imagery of the existence of plentiful land that is both idle and underutilized. The main concern is that the GBI does not target the idle land owned by political bureaucratic elite but that held by smallholder farmers, which in the absence of a definitive legislative framework, is defined as state land (Chinsinga and Chasukwa 2012). This is the case because the draft land policy designates a new category of land, private customary land, which cannot be achieved in the absence of an enabling legislative framework. Thus until a new legislative framework is enacted, customary land will be treated as state-owned as stipulated in the 1967 Land Act, and which the 2002 land policy and the 2013 draft Land Act Bill construe as 'idle, empty and unallocated land'.

Key Challenges in Land Reform Efforts

The land reform efforts have encountered several challenges since the transition to democracy in May 1994. There is no doubt that the transition to democracy gave land reform a new lease of life but the progress has been painfully slow. The country does not have a definitive legislative framework for land matters and transactions two decades later. Meanwhile several developments such as the implementation of the GBI, which essentially touts some kind of supply driven land grabs, have added some measure of complexity to the land reform efforts. The rest of this section therefore explores some of the major challenges that have slowed down the land reform efforts in a democratic context.

Elite Capture

The land reform efforts have fallen prey to elite capture driven largely by their selfish interests (Chinsinga 2008). This is quite striking because the debate about land reform was initially instigated internally by the elites that led the pro-democracy movement against the one party authoritarian rule who argued that the implementation of land reforms portended the dawn of a new socio-economic order for the country. However, the elites did not act on the land question, or have not acted on it decisively because most of the pro-democracy elites had benefitted from the 1967 land reforms. They had simply fallen out of favour with the regime. It is therefore not surprising that their success at the polls did not necessarily translate into swift implementation of land reforms even though this was one of the flagships of the pro-democracy movement.

With the benefit of hindsight, it is fair to say that land reform was opportunistically flagged by the advocates of democratization to gain support for their cause. Once in office, the elites developed cold feet to the idea of a swift overhaul of land tenure and ownership patterns underlined by the lack of momentum to push on with the reforms. A critical review of the land reform efforts since May 1994 shows that a coalition of elites spanning the political divide strategically decelerated the pace of the land reform efforts. It can actually be argued that the PCILR was set up in May 1996 to kick-start the land reform effort merely as a lip service to their pre-election pledge and not as a commitment to see through a comprehensive land reform programme as the springboard for rapid, sustainable and equitable socio-economic development (Kishindo 2004; Chinsinga 2008).

The CBRLDP stands out as the major land reform initiative to date, and the enabling land legislative framework is yet to be concluded. The major development planning frameworks that have been implemented in the post democratic era such as the Malawi Poverty Reduction Strategy (MPRS) and the MGDS (I and II) have strikingly shied away from explicitly addressing the land question (Chinsinga 2007). Although the CBRLDP was projected as a home grown initiative, it would not be an overstatement that it had been pushed, and funded, by the World Bank following the ugly turn of events in the Zimbabwe's land reform programme. The elites perhaps accepted the CBRLDP because the owners of the land targeted for redistribution were handsomely compensated at competitive market rates. Thus the apparent commitment of the pro-democracy advocates to the question of land reform was essentially a strategic ploy to woo voters into ushering them into power.

Dominance of Informality

The land reform efforts have to contend with deeply entrenched informality in the conduct of formal transactions in Malawi. The dominance of informality on the continent is widely recognized (Bratton 2007). In fact, the argument is that Africa is the best starting point for exploring the role of informal institutions, which derive from a social logic of the economy of affection. According to Adam and Dercon (2009), a systematic understanding of the interface between formal and informal institutions permits to get beneath the formal structures to reveal the underlying interests, incentives and institutions that enable or frustrate change.

The role of traditional leaders has been particularly important as an embodiment of informality in the land reform efforts. As noted earlier, traditional leaders are vested with the guardian role of customary land as defined by the 1967 Land Act. This implies that in the absence of a definitive legislative framework that supersedes the 1967 Land Act, traditional leaders own customary land on behalf of their subjects. Although in terms of the 1967 Land Act this was meant as a nominal role, it has evolved over time and has empowered chiefs to distribute this land, facilitate transactions and preside over disputes over this land. These roles and responsibilities have accorded traditional leaders streams of benefits and rents that make it almost impossible for them to support any reform efforts that would divest them of their dominance in land matters and transactions.

The traditional leaders have resisted the proposed land reforms because both the land policy and the draft Land Act Bill propose to divest traditional leaders of the roles and responsibilities in land matters and transactions. Both the policy and draft Land Act Bill abolish the customary land category. It proposes that there should be only two categories of land, namely: public and private. This implies that customary land can be owned under private arrangements with title deeds. The roles and responsibilities played by traditional leaders will be taken over by a committee constituting an equal number of men and women representatives to ensure transparency, accountability and responsiveness in land matters and transactions (GoM 2002). The constitution of the committees in a gender balanced manner would ensure that the women are not unfairly disadvantaged in land matters, ownership and inheritance.

The traditional leaders have fiercely resisted against the adoption of the new land legislative framework because it would mean losing the stream of rents and benefits the current setting provides. They have also argued that divesting them of these roles and responsibilities that they currently play in land matters and transactions would undermine their position as traditional leaders (Chinsinga 2006). Their strongly held position is that one can only be called chief if he or she has people to look after and land to call his or her own. They argue that it is not possible to stake one's claim to chieftaincy if they do not have a piece of land over which they can exercise authority. It is against this backdrop that traditional leaders mobilized themselves to lobby former President Joyce Banda not to assent to the draft Land Act Bill, which, if had been endorsed into law, would have divested traditional leaders of the roles and responsibilities that they currently exercise over land.

Irrelevant Legislative Framework

The legislative impasse makes it very complicated for the momentum towards comprehensive land reforms to be sustained. The main challenge is that although the underlying spirit of the reforms advocated by the ongoing efforts proposes some radical changes, the 1967 Land Act remains the principal legislative framework. The land policy was endorsed by Cabinet as early as July 2002 but it does not yet have an enabling legislative framework more than a decade later.

As noted earlier, the legislative impasse presents serious challenges to the land reform efforts because several developments have taken place, for example, the implementation of the GBI and the development of informal land markets especially in the peri-urban areas. This legislative impasse has created space for legal pluralism particularly on the part of government. When it suits them, they invoke the provisions of the 1967 Land Act or refer to the provisions of the 2002 land policy to justify their actions. This has been particularly manifested in the government's quest to expand the sugar industry in the context of a virtual legislative impasse to create an enabling framework for land matters and transactions.

The sugar industry has become quite important in Malawi following the fierce global anti-smoking lobby that threatens to decimate the tobacco industry which is the country's principal foreign exchange earner (Chinsinga, Chasukwa and Zuka 2014). The expansion of the land devoted to sugar is therefore seen as a significant potential alternative cash crop to tobacco to keep the country's economy afloat. The legislative impasse makes the land efforts to essentially mount to putting new wine in old bottles. This has simply multiplied the challenges that stand in the way of the land reform efforts.

Ill-Conceived Metaphor

The land reform efforts have been beset by the usage of an ill-conceived metaphor about the existence of idle land in the country. Both the policy and the draft Land Act Bill project customary land as unallocated, empty and idle land when in reality it is not. If this were the case, then reports about constant running battles between communities and investors would have been hardly existent. Communities would not have been petitioning the President, Ministers, Members of Parliament and District Commissioners almost on a daily basis (Chinsinga and Chasukwa 2013).

The claim by the land policy that about 28 per cent of the country's land lies idle is difficult to sustain empirically. The actual land that might be available is far less than the projections made by the land policy on which most of decisions and choices including the GBI are based for two reasons. Firstly, the data on the amount of idle land usually takes a long time to be updated. In Malawi, for example, the documentation of available idle land is based on 1994 estimations (GoM 2002). With population growth pegged at 2.8 per cent (GoM 2008), demographic changes over the decade have likely reduced the magnitude of idle land, if any. Secondly, most of the arguments about available land are based on total available land in the country and not really on agro-ecological analysis. Bearing in mind that most large-scale agricultural investments go for fertile arable land (Stephens 2011; Kachika 2010; Borras, McMichael and Scoones 2010), use of agro-ecological data may provide better estimations of available idle in the country. In the case of Malawi, it is doubtful that the 28 per cent figure presents the accurate estimate of available idle land for investment in Malawi. Only 34 per cent of the country's land is arable land. The country has also the highest population density in Africa pegged at 126 people per km^2, which rises to as high as 466 people per km^2 if only arable land is considered (Chinsinga, Chasukwa, and Zuka 2014).

The perception of the existence of plentiful land in Malawi reflects the global competing narratives over the definition of idle and empty namely: physical availability of empty idle lands versus availability of unproductively utilized land (Borras et al. 2012; Matondi, Havnevik, and Beyeme 2011). The first classification of available land for large-scale agricultural investment in Malawi is based on the existence of empty unoccupied and uncultivated land. In the existing legal framework, ownership rights of this land belong to the state, which grants land lease to investors. For instance, in line with this understanding, government identified 1 million hectares of idle irrigable land to be offered to investors under the auspices of the GBI who have the potential to utilize land that smallholders cannot utilize because of capital and technology constraints (GoM 2010). The drive to expand the sugar industry is based on the argument that the investors shall utilize marshy empty and unoccupied lands.

There are, however, serious theoretical flaws with the definition of empty lands as it confuses emptiness with usefulness. In particular, most of the land that is declared empty is, or may be physically unoccupied but is very useful to local communities. Besides playing a critical role in biodiversity conservation, tracts of land defined as empty are critical livelihood assets for the local communities. For instance, local communities whose land has been grabbed for the expansion of the sugar industry have consistently argued that they have been using the land for grazing livestock, sourcing grass for thatching their houses, collecting wild products such as mushrooms, vegetables and traditional medicine. This clearly shows that it is erroneous to equate existence of unoccupied land to existence of idle land (Cotula et al. 2009; Borras et al. 2012; Nunow 2012).

The metaphor of vast, empty and idle land is further predicated on the existence of 'unproductively' utilized land. As noted earlier, this perception is based on the idea that smallholder farming is ineffective and cannot adequately achieve increased crop productivity due to a number of constraints it faces (GoM 2002; Kaarhus and Nyirenda 2006). However, there are actually several studies that have found that smallholder farmers are efficient, or could considerably increase their productivity levels through relevant and viable support systems (Byerlee and de Javnry 2009). Moreover, the evidence across countries where land deals have been sealed reflects rational calculations on the part of local communities to maximize livelihood options. In most cases, communities leave one part of the land uncultivated for collection of grass thatch, livestock pasture, traditional medicine and other wild products. The argument that vacant land exists in the country based on farming inefficiencies therefore reflects lack of knowledge of relevant support mechanisms to smallholder agriculture as well as local peoples' livelihood practices. To avoid this fatal error, identification of vacant land needs adequate community consultation and accurate prediction of future needs of host communities.

Limited Capacity for Land Matters

The limited capacity to facilitate land reform efforts has contributed to slowing down progress. The capacity to facilitate the implementation of neoliberal orientated land reforms, at least, successfully does not exist. This is further exacerbated by lack of political will (Chinsinga 2011).

Granted that the CBRLDP was a viable initiative to facilitate and speed up the land reform efforts, it was not fully exploited to build the requisite capacity. It provided an opportunity to test the capacity of district and sub-district participatory structures outlined in the land policy to mediate land transactions (Chirwa 2008; Chinsinga 2008). This would have been tremendously useful because it would have generated contentious and unending debates during the subsequent phases including the enactment of the draft Land Act Bill into law. Overall, the main concern is that there is inadequate technical staff at national, district and local levels that would provide the administrative infrastructure to the efficient and effective functioning of the neoliberal land markets. According to Woodhouse (2006), when capacity is deficient to provide the requisite administrative support infrastructure, central land registers quickly become out of date as land transfers are often not notified to the central registry.

Concluding Remarks

There is no doubt that the advent of democratization in Malawi promised quite a lot in as far as settling the land question once and for all was concerned. Yet two decades later not much has been achieved that guarantees the resolution of the land question in the near future. While a land policy was endorsed by Cabinet in July 2002, an enabling legislative framework is yet to be concluded. Parliament endorsed the draft Land Act Bill in June 2013 but former President Joyce Banda vetoed it. She deferred to the fierce lobby of chiefs who are against the neoliberal orientation of the draft land law particularly because it divests them of their roles and responsibilities over land matters and transactions. The new land law would circumvent the stream of benefits and rents that the 1967 Land Act, which still remains the principal legislative framework for land matters and transactions in Malawi, affords traditional leaders.

This chapter demonstrates that while the advent of democratization pushed the land question onto the agenda, and advocates of democratization touted it as one of their priority interventions to bring about a new socio-economic order in the country, it has been captured by vested elite interests. This has invariably held back progress on the land reform efforts. The protracted delays in the implementation of the land reforms inevitably created a favourable milieu for legal pluralism to thrive. The elites tend to switch around between the 1967 Land Act and the 2002 land policy as a strategy to promote and safeguard their interests as they wish. The situation is further complicated because external agents that are providing technical support to the government have their own interests heavily coloured by their ideological beliefs, which they seek to promote. It is very clear, for example, that the World Bank seeks to promote an entirely neoliberal land legislative framework without taking into account at all some peculiarities of the local context. The history of the land question in Malawi poses some unique challenges that cannot be dealt with the neoliberal land reform took kit.

The intervening experiments in the context of the land reform efforts, namely, the CBRLDP and the GBI, have further complicated the land reform landscape in the country. This is inevitable because while these initiatives have posed some new challenges that cannot be dealt with by the existing legislative framework, or have advanced certain positions taking advantage of the existing legislative impasse, the long drawn battle to shape up the enabling legislative framework has meant that the land question in Malawi remain in a state of flux. The most unfortunate part is that the loser in this long drawn out legislative impasse is the ordinary Malawian whose land is insecure and often the primary target for appropriation either for public use or private investment. The main conclusion of this chapter is that a detailed political economy analysis of the land question is quite imperative in order to successfully break the legislative jinx in the land reform efforts.

References

Adam, Christopher and Stefan Dercon. 2009. "The Political Economy of Development: An Assessment." *Oxford Review of Economic Policy* 25(2): 173–87.

Anderson, Agnes. 2011. "Maize Remittances, Smallholder Livelihoods and Maize Consumption in Malawi." *Journal of Modern African Studies* 49(1): 1–15.

Borras, Saturnino M., Philip McMichael, and Ian Scoones. 2010. "The Politics of Bio-Fuel, Land and Agrarian Change: Introduction." *Journal of Peasant Studies* 17(4): 575–92.

Borras, Saturnino M., Jennifer C. Franco, Sergio Gómez, Cristóbal Kay, and Max Spoor. 2012. "Land Grabbing in Latin America and Caribbean." *Journal of Peasant Studies* 39(3–4): 845–72.

Bratton, Michael. 2007. "Formal Versus Informal Institutions in Africa." *Journal of Democracy* 18(3): 97–110.

Breytenbach, Willie. 2003. "Land Reform in Southern Africa," in *Monitoring Regional Integration in Southern Africa*, edited by Dirk Hansihon, Willie Breytenback, and Trudi Hartenberg, 51–65. Windhoek: Gramsberg Macmillan.

Byerlee, Derek, and Allain de Javvry. 2009. "Smallholders Unite," in *Foreign Affairs Case Studies on Agricultural and Bio-fuel Investment*. New York: NYU School of Law.

Chinsinga, Blessings. 2002. "The Politics of Poverty Alleviation in Malawi: A Critical Review," in *A Democracy of Chameleon: Politics and Culture in New Malawi*, edited by Harri Englund, 25–42. Uppsala: Nordiska Afrika Institutet.

——. 2006. "The Interface between Tradition and Modernity: The Struggle for Political Space at the Local Level in Malawi." *Civilizations* LIV(1&2): 255–74.

——. 2007. *Democracy, Decentralization and Poverty Reduction in Malawi*. Cologne: Rudiger Kuppe Verlag.

——. 2008. "Exploring the Politics of Land Reforms in Malawi: A Case Study of the Community Based Rural Land Development Programme (CBRLDP)." *IPPG Discussion Paper No. 20.* Manchester: University of Manchester.

——. 2011. "The Politics of Land Reforms in Malawi: The Case of the Community Based Rural Land Development Programme (CBRLDP)." *Journal of International Development* 23: 380–93.

Chinsinga, Blessings and Michael Chasukwa. 2012. "Youth, Agriculture and Land Grabs in Malawi." *IDS Bulletin* 43(6): 67–77.

——. 2013. "Trapped between the Farm Input Subsidy Programme (FISP) and the Green Belt Initiative (GBI): An Audit of Malawi's Contemporary Agrarian Political Economy." Paper presented at the Political Economy of Agricultural Policy in Africa, Pretoria, South Africa, 19–21 March.

Chinsinga, Blessings, Michael Chasukwa, and Sane Zuka. 2013. "The Political Economy of Land Grabs in Malawi: Investigating the Contribution of Limphasa Sugar Corporation to Rural Development." *Journal of Agricultural and Environmental Ethics* 26(2): 1065–84.

——. 2014. "Large-Scale Land Deals in the Sugar Industry and Rural Development in Malawi: A Political Economy Inquiry," in *International Land Deals in Eastern and Southern Africa,* edited by Paul Miyo, 63–94. Addis Ababa: OSSREA.

Chinsinga, Blessings and Liam Wren-Lewis. 2014. "Grabbing Land in Malawi," in *Corruption, Grabbing and Development: Real World Challenges*, edited by Tina Soreide and Aled Williams, 93–102. Massachusetts and Northampton: Edward Elgar Publishing.

Chirwa, Ephraim. 2004. *Access to Land, Growth and Poverty Reduction.* Zomba: Chancellor College, University of Malawi.

——. 2008. "Land Tenure, Farm Investments and Food Production in Malawi." *IPPG Discussion Paper Series No. 18.* Manchester: University of Manchester.

Chirwa, Wiseman. 1998. "Democracy, Ethnicity and Regionalism: The Malawi Experiment, 1992–1996." In *Democratization in Malawi: A Stocktaking*, edited by Kingd Phiri and Martin Ott, 52–69. Blantyre: Christian Literature Association of Malawi (CLAIM)

Chiweza, Asiyati. 2007. "The Ambivalent Role of Chiefs in Malawi's Rural Decentralization Initiative." In *A New Dawn for Traditional Authorities: State Recognition and Democratization in Sub-Saharan Africa*, edited by Lars Buur and Helene Kyed, 53–78. London: Palgrave Macmillan.

Cotula, Lorenzo, Sonja Vermeululen, Rebeca Leonard, and James Keeley. 2009. *Land Grab or Development Opportunity? Agricultural Investment and International Land Deals in Africa.* London and Rome: IIED/FAO/IFAD.

Government of Malawi (GoM). 1999. *Final Report of the Presidential Commission of Inquiry on Land Policy Reform.* Lilongwe: Ministry of Lands, Housing and Surveys.

——. 2002. *Malawi National Land Policy.* Lilongwe: Ministry of Lands, Housing and Surveys.

——. 2005. *Malawi Land Reform Programme Implementation Strategy (2003–2007)*. Lilongwe: Ministry of Lands, Housing, Physical Planning and Surveys.

——. 2008. *Malawi Population and Housing Census*. Zomba: National Statistical Office (NSO).

——. 2009. *The Green Belt Initiative (GBI). Concept Paper*. Lilongwe: Ministry of Agriculture and Food Security.

——. 2010. *The Green Belt Initiative: Concept Paper*. Lilongwe: Ministry of Agriculture and Food Security.

——. 2013. *Draft Land Act Bill*. Lilongwe, Malawi: Ministry of Justice and Constitutional Affairs.

——. 2013. *Integrated Household Survey III*. Zomba: National Statistics Office (NSO).

International Fund for Agricultural Development (IFAD). 2011. *Enabling Poor Rural People to Overcome Poverty in Malawi*. Rome: IFAD.

Kaarhus, Randi, and Ramji Nyirenda. 2006. "Decentralization in the Agricultural Sector in Malawi: Policies, Processes and Community Linkages." *Noragric Report No. 32*. Norway: University of Oslo.

Kachika, Tinyade. 2010. *Land Grabbing in Africa: A Review of the Impacts and the Possible Policy Responses*. London: Pan Africa Programme of Oxfam International.

Kanyongolo, Edge. 2005. "Land Occupations in Malawi: Challenging the Neoliberal Order." In *Reclaiming the Land: The Resurgence of Rural Movements in Africa, Asia and Latin America*, edited by Sam Moyo and Paul Yeros, 118–41. London and New York: Zed Books.

Kishindo, Paul. 2004. "Customary Land Tenure and the New Land Policy in Malawi." *Journal of Contemporary African Studies* 22(2): 213–25.

Matondi, Prosper, Kjell Havnevik, and Atakilte Beyeme. 2011. *Biofuels, Land Grabbing and Food Security in Africa*. London: Zed Books.

Ng'ong'ola, Clement. 1982. "The Design and Implementation of Customary Land Reforms in Central Malawi." *Journal of African Law* 26(2): 115–82.

Nunow, Abdirizak. 2012. "The Dynamics of Land Deals in Tana Delta." Paper presented at the International Conference on Global Land Grabbing, Institute of Development Studies, University of Sussex, 6–8 April.

Stephens, Phoebe. 2011. "The Global Land Grab: An Analysis of Extant Governance Institutions." *International Affairs Review* XX(1): 1–21.

Woodhouse, Philip. 2006. "Legitimizing Markets or Legalizing Custom? Land Commoditization and Land Tenure Reform in Africa." In *"Competing Rights: Land and Natural Resources in Africa."*, edited by Corrado Tornimbeni and Mario Zamponi, *afriche e orienti*, Special Issue 2007: 20–31.

World Bank. 2004. *The Community Based Rural Land Development Programme (CBRLDP). Project Document*. Lilongwe: The World Bank.

Chapter 3

Rural Development and the Fight against Poverty in Tanzania: A Fifty-Year Perspective

Arrigo Pallotti

Since independence in 1961, fighting poverty has constantly been a major goal of the Tanzanian government's development strategies.[1] In spite of this, not only does Tanzania remain one of the poorest countries in the world today, but there is also a growing consensus among scholars, donors and policy makers that the high rates of economic growth recorded during the last decade in the country have not translated into a significant reduction of poverty, because of the disappointing performance of the agricultural sector (Mashindano et al. 2011: 5; World Bank 2012a: 11–12). This is all the more striking if we consider that around 80 per cent of the Tanzanian population live in the rural areas and depend primarily (but seldom exclusively) on agriculture, which is mostly practised by small farmers.

This chapter analyses the rural development policies implemented by the Tanzanian government during both the socialist and the post-socialist period, and investigates the reasons why, in spite of the centrality of rural development within Tanzania's post-colonial state-building process, the agricultural sector has generally recorded a disappointing performance after independence. In so doing, the chapter highlights some points of historical and political continuity and discontinuity between the socialist and the post-socialist development strategies, and investigates their effects on citizenship rights in the rural areas of Tanzania.

The analysis presented in this chapter aims to overcome some of the limitations of the contemporary literature on rural development in Africa, with its almost exclusive attention to the positive and negative effects of the multiple processes commonly referred to as 'land grabbing' (Zoomers 2011; Matondi and Mutopo 2011), or the technicalities of the land titling programmes implemented in a number of African countries (Ubink, Hoekema, Assies 2009). This chapter argues that these processes, which today are hotly debated in Tanzania itself, can only be fully understood within an analytical framework that investigates both the changing role of agriculture within African countries' political economy, and the intrinsically political nature of the rural development policies pursued

---

1 The analysis presented in this chapter refers to mainland Tanzania only and excludes the Zanzibar archipelago.

by their national governments. As Du Toit has recently remarked, although the latter are often 'framed as elements of a seamless narrative of enlightened humanist modernization' (Du Toit 2013: 17), they are a product of prevalent power configurations, and have important implications for the democratization processes in Africa.

The chapter is organized so that the next section analyses the socialist rural development policy implemented by the Tanzanian government from the mid-1960s to the early 1980s. It highlights the many contradictions that plagued the implementation of the policy of *ujamaa vijijini* and the vibrant academic debate during the 1970s and the early 1980s that tried to explain the main weaknesses of the socialist development strategy in the country. The second section examines the impact of structural adjustment reforms on agriculture, and critically analyses the provisions of the new land laws adopted by the Tanzanian parliament in 1999. The third section scrutinizes the government's policies aimed at promoting rural development after the adoption of the first Tanzanian Poverty Reduction Strategy Paper in 2000, and their contradictory outcomes. The chapter concludes that rural development is today a marginal priority for the Tanzanian government and that the subsidy programme which the latter has recently implemented has been guided, as in the past, by a paternalistic approach to smallholder farmers.

Ujamaa and Rural Development

According to the Arusha Declaration, adopted by the National Executive Committee of the Tanganyika African National Union (TANU) in February 1967, rural development was to play a crucial role in the 'fight against poverty' (Arusha Declaration 1967: 235). The Arusha Declaration on the one hand presented a very negative assessment of the development plans implemented in the first years after independence, and on the other hand put forward a development vision which conferred priority to the agricultural sector. In the words of the Declaration:

> We have made [a] big mistake [thinking] that development begins with industries. It is a mistake because we do not have the means to establish many modern industries in our country. ... Because the main aim of development is to get more food, and more money for our other needs, our purpose must be to increase production of ... agricultural crops. This is in fact the only road through which we can develop our country – in other words, only by increasing our production of these things can we get more food and more money for every Tanzanian. (Nyerere 1968a[1967]: 241–4)

After the adoption of the Arusha Declaration the government nationalized industries and banks, established a number of parastatal organizations, heavily regulated import and export trade, imposed price controls on most commodities, and kick-started a new rural development policy.

The Tanzanian president Julius Nyerere outlined the priorities of the latter in an essay published in September 1967 and entitled: *Socialism and Rural Development*. According to Nyerere, the agrarian structure of Tanzania would be transformed by the creation of ujamaa villages, where production would be based on the 'traditional' African principles of equality, solidarity, and communal work. As the Tanzanian president explained:

> the principles upon which the traditional extended family was based must be reactivated. ... The basis of rural life in Tanzania must be the practice of cooperation in its widest sense – in living, in working, and in distribution, and all with the acceptance of the absolute equality of all men and women. (Nyerere 1968b[1967], 348)

According to Nyerere, *ujamaa vijijini* would also facilitate state provision of social and extension services for the rural population, and modernization of smallholder agriculture. Nyerere also insisted on the voluntary nature of the villagization policy, arguing that 'socialist communities cannot be established by compulsion. [They] can only be established with willing members; the task of leadership and of Government is not to try and force this kind of development, but to explain, encourage, and participate' (ibid.: 356).

The implementation of the policy of *ujamaa vijijini* took place at different times and in different stages in the various regions of the country. Political considerations and local power configurations heavily influenced the outcomes of the villagization policy (von Freyholf 1979). Initially, the government limited its role to the provision of some inputs to the (few) new ujamaa villages. Then, in order to speed up the villagization process, in November 1973 it decreed that by the end of 1976 all the rural population of Tanzania had to live in villages. The regional resettlement operations carried out under the supervision of the local bureaucracy were tarnished by coercion (Schneider 2004). In spite of Nyerere's emphasis on communal work as the basis of the Tanzania's Rural Development Strategy, this aim was abandoned, and the increase in agricultural production became the government's priority. The government's paternalistic attitude towards the small peasants and the use of coercion in the resettlement operations reflected the ascendency of a technocratic and top-down approach to the promotion of rural development that stifled popular participation and fuelled multiple forms of resistance in the rural areas of the country (Feierman 1991). The latter ranged from political apathy to a decline in the share of agricultural output sold through the official marketing channels, and a few outbreaks of violence against local government representatives (such as the killing of the Commissioner of the Iringa Region at Ismani in 1971) (Awiti 1973).

As James Scott remarked, the bureaucratization of the policy of *ujamaa vijijini* and recourse to coercion revealed the ambiguous nature of a rural development policy which aimed at 'reconfigur[ing] the rural population into a form that would allow the state to impose its development agenda and, in the process, to control the work and production of cultivators' (Scott 1998: 241). In spite of Nyerere's emphasis on the need to promote the modernization of Tanzanian agriculture on the basis of the pre-colonial values of equality and solidarity, the policy of *ujamaa vijijini* shared the colonial assumption that 'the practices of African cultivators and pastoralists were backward, unscientific, inefficient, and ecologically irresponsible [and that] only close supervision, training, and, if need be, coercion ... could bring them and their practices in line with a modern Tanzania' (ibid.).

TANU's and central government's control over local politics and development activities was reinforced by the new decentralization policy adopted in 1972. District councils were abolished and replaced by local development bodies whose members were not popularly elected but nominated by the central government. In 1976 the government also abolished the local producers' cooperatives and their federations, officially because of their inefficiency and corruption. In this way, the cooperative movement, which was perceived by the TANU leadership as an autonomous power base, ceased to represent a potential threat to the party's hegemony in the rural areas. The producers' cooperatives and their federations were replaced by village cooperatives and parastatal organizations, respectively. The latter were tasked with providing the peasants with input and credit as well as purchasing and commercializing their crops.

Extensive state intervention in the agricultural sector and the villagization policy did not bring about the expected results (Raikes 1986). Between the late 1960s and the early 1980s Tanzania's agriculture recorded a disappointing performance. The food crisis of the early 1970s led the government to raise the official prices of food crops. As a consequence, exports of cash crops diminished, while food crop production increased until the end of the decade (Wuits 1994: 171, 176–7, 184).

The bureaucratization of *ujamaa vijijini* and the disappointing growth performance of the agricultural sector sparked a vibrant scholarly debate on the nature and limitations of the Tanzanian socialist experiment (Barker 1979).

Some scholars argued that Tanzania lacked the material bases for implementation of the socialist modernization project envisaged by Nyerere. French agronomist René Dumont wrote that the difficulties the implementation of ujamaa encountered in Tanzania 'result[ed] more from underdevelopment than from socialism' (Dumont 1983: 173). Nyerere's vision of rural development 'overestimated the technical capabilities of the administrative staff at all levels, from the regional officials down to the villagers' (ibid.: 153), and so a top-down, bureaucratic and at times coercive approach to development prevailed. Andrew Coulson questioned the economic rationale of the villagization policy, arguing that the pre-ujamaa growth rates of agricultural output had already shown that 'if new technology was clearly profitable [the Tanzanian farmers] could take it up even if they were living dispersed on their farms' (Coulson 1982: 256). According to Coulson, the policy of *ujamaa vijijini* improved social indicators in the rural areas, but had such negative repercussions on agricultural output that social improvement proved unsustainable (ibid.: 260–62).

While not questioning the political vision at the basis of the policy of *ujamaa vijijini*, a number of left-wing scholars brought to light a fundamental contradiction in the implementation of the latter. Contrary to Nyerere's egalitarian rural development vision, a political alliance had formed between the better-off peasants (*kulaks*) and the bureaucracy in rural areas. This alliance not only benefitted the better-off economically at the expense of the majority of smallholders, but brought about political marginalization of the latter (van Velzen 1973; Cliffe 1973; von Freyholf 1979).

Other scholars argued that ujamaa had never been a truly revolutionary development policy. According to Issa Shivji, the de-politicized version of socialism outlined in the Arusha Declaration clearly reflected the class project of the 'bureaucratic bourgeoisie' that had taken hold of the Tanzanian state (Shivji 1975: 107). Boesen argued that ujamaa never translated into a coherent strategy of transformation of the economic and social relations in the rural areas of Tanzania. It was within this context that the bureaucratization of *ujamaa vijijini* strengthened the political hegemony of the state bourgeoisie and its control over the national economy (Boesen 1979).

Some economists pointed to the internal contradictions of the Tanzanian economic development strategy. As in many other African countries (Bates 1981), so in Tanzania the government drained resources from the agricultural sector in order to finance a strategy of import substitution industrialization (Ellis 1983). However, the large state investments in the industry and service sectors and the rapid expansion of the public service were followed by stagnation in industrial production and a huge increase of the public debt. So, when in the late 1970s war against Idi Amin's Uganda, adverse weather conditions and international oil shocks hit the Tanzanian economy, state support for food crop production rapidly contracted (Wuyts 1994). More generally, the decay of state extension services and the financial difficulties of the agricultural marketing boards and parastatal organizations dealt a serious blow to the rural economy, and led to the emergence of a thriving informal market (Bryceson 1982).

In spite of the economic difficulties it encountered, the policy of ujamaa brought about a marked improvement in social indicators in the country. Universal primary education was almost achieved in 1981 (World Bank 1999: 47). The number of dispensaries and health facilities in the rural areas increased as a result of the new preventive approach to health care which the government had adopted in the early 1970s (Kopoka 2002). Life expectancy at birth rose from 30 years in 1960 to 51 years in 1980 (Kaijage and Tibaijuka 1996: 36).

These data highlight the contradictions of a top-down socialist development policy which on the one hand consolidated the Tanzanian national identity and strengthened social peace in the country, and on the other promoted a practice of passive citizenship. As Gaspar Munishi has remarked, the welfare policies implemented during ujamaa improved social indicators in the country, but also contributed to stifling local political activism, since:

the development of welfarist inclinations on Tanzania has not only made the state an interventionist one but one that actually takes away responsibility from beneficiaries and local organizations in pursuit of its own national integration, political mobilization and the maintenance of legitimacy. ... In this political messiahnist approach, enabling the poor to fend for themselves is not a primary concern of the state, the major concern is to centralize and administer the available services more equitably than before and to score political credits through redistributive policies. (Munishi 1998: 57)

The Structural Adjustment Era

After a prolonged arm-wrestling with the international financial institutions, in 1986 the Tanzanian government adopted an Economic Recovery Programme sponsored by the International Monetary Fund (IMF). During the presidency of Ali Hassan Mwinyi the government devalued the Tanzanian shilling, raised interest rates, liberalized foreign trade, abolished price controls, privatized or liquidated most state-owned industries and parastatal organizations, cut the size of the public service, abolished farmer subsidies and introduced fees and 'tickets' in the social services (van der Geest and Köttering 1994; Gibbon 1995).

The economic outcomes of the structural adjustment reforms were contradictory at best. Growth remained stagnant until the late 1990s, and in the period 1986–1997 per capita income growth averaged 0.6 per cent (Bigsten and Danielson 2001: 21). During the 1990s production of the main food crops recorded modest and fluctuating growth rates, which were constantly below the rate of population growth (World Bank 1998: 18; World Bank 2000: 63). The weak performance of the agricultural sector led to the share of agriculture declining in the Gross Domestic Product (GDP) (World Bank 2002: 17; URT 2004a: 18). While during the 1990s the contribution of 'traditional' export crops (coffee, cotton, sisal, etc.) to Tanzania's export earnings increased, it later declined. By contrast, since the late 1990s the contribution of 'non-traditional' export sectors such as mining and manufacturing has been constantly increasing (URT 2000a: 45; URT 2007: 57; URT 2013a: 55). As a consequence, the share of 'traditional' cash crops in the total exports of Tanzania decreased from 56.8 per cent in 1996 to 15 per cent in 2010 (Wuyts and Kilama 2014b: 25).

Based on the assumption that market liberalization would bring about the speedy recovery of the agricultural sector, the structural adjustment reforms contributed to further derangement of production and reproduction strategies in the rural areas of the country. In spite of the improved availability of consumer goods, smallholders faced several obstacles in adapting to the new economic dispensation, such as lack of credit, higher prices of inputs, absence of information on market prices, difficulties in accessing markets, and the declining state of the extension services (Pallotti 2008).

The structural adjustment reforms set in motion new patterns of capital accumulation that left the majority of the rural dwellers out on a limb. As Chachage remarked: 'the main beneficiaries of the SAPs [Structural Adjustment Programmes] have thus been the traditional private bourgeoisie and party, government and parastatal officials, rather than the general rural population – the manifest focus of SAPs' (Chachage 1993: 216).

It was within the context of market liberalization reforms that land once again became a hotly contested issue in Tanzania. While growing urbanization and financial speculation heightened land pressures in the urban and peri-urban areas, in the countryside land ownership was made more precarious by the courts' apparent inclination to legally enforce pre-ujamaa land rights (Shivji 1998: 26–40; Kiondo 1999: 48).

The Land Laws

The urgent need for a land tenure reform led to the appointment of a Presidential Commission of Inquiry into Land Matters, chaired by Issa Shivji. In its final report, presented in November 1992, the Commission put forward a number of proposals designed to overcome the rigid (colonial) distinction between 'granted rights of occupancy' and 'deemed rights of occupancy' (Coldham 1995), as well as strengthening the security of tenure of smallholder farmers. The Commission recommended that access to village land be disciplined by customary law and that a maximum limit of 200 acres be imposed on the individual ownership of village land (URT 1994: 153–8). The Commission's report attracted some criticism, in particular for the insufficient attention it paid to gender discrimination in access to land (Tibaijuka and Kaijage 1995: 41–4). However, Shivji defended the Commission's proposals, arguing that 'such an evolution of Tanzanian "common law" [as proposed by the Commission] would be more organic and would have greater legitimacy than statutory law imposed from above' (Shivji 1998: 54).

In 1995 the government published the National Land Policy. The document included the Shivji Commission's proposal to provide smallholder peasants with individual title deeds, but espoused a political vision of land tenure reform radically different from the Commission's one. The National Land Policy not only placed emphasis on the need to stimulate a land market and to facilitate private investments in land, but also suggested that the 'radical title' be vested in the President, and not in the village assembly (URT, MLHSD 1995).

In January 1999 the Parliament passed Land Act No. 4 and the Village Land Act No. 5. These two very complex and lengthy pieces of legislation were inextricably interlinked from both a legal and a political point of view. Given that 'All land in Tanzania is public land vested in the President as trustee on behalf of all citizens' (URT 1999: §3.1.b), the President was given the power to transfer 'any area of village land to general and reserved land for public interest' (ibid.: §4.1). This and other provisions on land transfer reflected the investor-friendly nature of the land laws (Maoulidi 2004: 5–6), showed the central government's determination to maintain tight control over land allocation to private investors (Shivji 1998: 82), and added further pressure on village authorities to directly grant land to non-resident investors in the form of a customary right of occupancy (URT 1999: §24), or a derivative right (ibid.: §34).

The crucial innovation introduced by the Village Land Law was the possibility for an individual (or a family or an association) to get a certificate of 'customary right of occupancy' (*Hakimiliki ya kimila*) on village land. The introduction of this new title deed and the complex procedures laid down in the Village Land Law for obtaining it sparked off a heated debate among scholars and activists. While Alden Wily argued that Tanzania had adopted 'a community-based land tenure management system' (Alden Wily 2003: 1), other commentators highlighted the risk that, instead of strengthening tenure security, the new bureaucratic and costly titling system would set in motion a process of land grabbing by the wealthier villagers, and would further undermine the political legitimacy of the local government authorities (Pallotti 2008).

Activists' fears that the Village Land Act might undermine land tenure security for the majority of rural dwellers were confirmed by the Land (Amendment) Act passed by the Tanzanian parliament in February 2004. The amendment made it easier for mortgagees to enter into possession of and sell mortgaged land (URT 2004b). The amendment was the government's response to intense lobbying by banking and financial institutions, which lamented the fact that the 1999 land laws 'tended to inhibit bankable projects especially mortgages from accessing finance' (Tanzania Bankers Association 2005: 4). So, in spite of the official emphasis on the need to provide security of tenure for the mass of smallholders, the new land laws largely subscribed to a neoliberal vision of rural development, and aimed at stimulating a land market in the country and promoting large-scale commercial farming.

From Structural Adjustment to Poverty Reduction?

In the late 1990s the Tanzanian government revised the country's rural development priorities in line with the new international agenda of poverty reduction (van Waeyenberge 2006). The government's official documents on the one hand emphasized the need both to sustain the smallholders and to promote large-scale commercial farming, and on the other hand called for an active role by the private sector in providing economic and social services in rural areas.

Rural Development and Poverty Reduction

The Poverty Reduction Strategy Paper (PRSP) adopted by the government in October 2000 committed it to maintaining macroeconomic rigour, furthering liberalization of the economy and increasing social spending within the limits of tight budgetary constraints (URT 2000b: 18).

The PRSP devoted only scant attention to rural development. It confirmed the policy shift from state-based to market-based agriculture (ibid.: 20), and stated that 'the Government will confine its own interventions mainly to the elaboration of sound policies', the promotion of research, the development of infrastructures, and to 'putting into effect the new Land Act' (ibid.: 21).

The aims and priorities of the government's rural development policy were set out at length in the Agricultural Sector Development Strategy (ASDS) of October 2001. The document stressed the need to stimulate agricultural production in order to foster food security in the country (URT 2001: 2), and committed the government to sustaining the livelihoods of smallholders, and at the same time to promoting large-scale commercial agriculture. The ASDS stated that: 'The overarching Government objective is poverty reduction. The preponderance of poverty in the rural areas and the importance of agriculture as the mainstay of rural livelihoods calls [*sic*] for strategies that are capable of raising the incomes and living standards of a large portion of the rural population', and then added that: 'This does not preclude the simultaneous creation of the enabling environment to encourage larger scale activities and investments in agriculture by the private sector' (ibid.: 16). According to the ASDS, the 'potential opportunities for strategic partnerships between these enterprises and smallholder farmers' would help overcome the apparent contradiction between the two policy objectives (ibid.: 10).

The ASDS stressed the fact that state intervention in the agricultural sector would be undertaken within the limits of the government's broader macroeconomic policy, which 'rule[s] out the possibility of profligate government expenditure or subsidies to "enhance" rural incomes [and] limit[s] the role of government to policy formulation, the establishment of a regulatory framework to reduce transaction costs ... and the provision of safety nets for the most vulnerable in society' (ibid.: 16).

The ASDS also placed strong emphasis on the private sector's role in the provision of services in the rural areas, as it argued that: 'The success of the ASDS will depend on the private sector playing a key role in commercial activities and the provision of many services, especially after the withdrawal of Government from these activities' (ibid.: 25). Finally, the local government authorities, together with the Ministry of Lands and Human Settlements, were called to play a more active role in the implementation of the new land laws. In particular, their task was 'to sensitize the public to the provisions of the new Land Acts regarding legal and physical access to land, and use of land titles as collateral for loans' (ibid.: 30).

As the ASDS, so the Rural Development Strategy (RDS) adopted in December 2001 mapped out a rural development vision whose priorities were to strengthen food security, to improve rural livelihoods, and 'to encourage and facilitate private sector investment and the establishment of large-scale commercial farmers in agricultural and livestock activities' (URT, PMO 2001: 36).

Contrary to the ASDS, the development of off-farm activities in the rural areas was a central priority of the RDS. In the light of both the increase in rural-urban migration (ibid.: 51–67), and the lack of job opportunities in the formal sector of the economy, the RDS stated that: 'Poverty in Tanzania will not decline without growth in rural incomes, and rural incomes will not grow without improving productivity of the agriculture sector, and growth of rural non-farm businesses' (ibid.: 27). As a result, according to the RDS, 'economic diversification and the promotion of non-farm economic activities is [*sic*] a key aspect of rural development' (ibid.: 39). In order to promote the latter, and in line with the government's neoliberal development vision, the RDS emphasized both 'the informal sector [as] a major source of income generation, particularly for youth and women, [and] the promotion of small and medium-sized enterprises [through] policies and institutions that encourage private investment in rural enterprises and complementary businesses' (ibid.: 39).

As both the ASDS and the RDS considered private sector investments as the key to promoting economic and social transformation of the rural areas, later government documents insisted on the need to accelerate reform of the land tenure system, so as to overcome the fragmentation of land ownership, promote large-scale commercial farming and facilitate the growth of off-farm activities. According to the National Strategy for Growth and Reduction of Poverty (NSGRP), adopted by the government in 2005 as a follow-up to the PRSP, implementation of the new land laws would spark off new patterns of capital accumulation in the rural areas, since the 'regularization and titling of land is [*sic*] expected to facilitate residents' use of their land and property thereon (dead capital) as collateral with which they may obtain credit from banks and building societies for socio-economic investment' (URT, VPO 2005: 7). In this way, as envisaged in the NSGRP II of 2010, the land laws would not only bring about the modernization of the agricultural sector through 'a shift away from small scale farming' and the consolidation of large-scale commercial farming (URT, MFEA 2010: 43), but would also foster the productivity of the agricultural sector, accelerate the growth of the national economy, and reduce poverty in the country (ibid.: 31).

From Policies to Politics: What Rural Development?

In spite of the emphasis which the government and donors have placed on the need to promote the growth of agriculture in order to reduce poverty, achieving these two objectives has proved elusive in Tanzania.

The annual growth rate of the agricultural sector has averaged 4.4 per cent in the period 1999–2011, much below the average growth rate of the economy as a whole (7 per cent in the period 2002–2012) (World Bank 2014: 11). However, these high rates of economic growth have not translated into a significant reduction of poverty rates in the country. According to the 2011/12 Household Budget Survey, currently 28.2 per cent of the Tanzanian population lives below the basic needs poverty line. The figure rises to 33.3 per cent in the rural areas, where 84.1 per cent of the poor population lives (National Bureau of Statistics, Ministry of Finance 2014: 98). The slow pace of poverty reduction in the rural areas of Tanzania clearly emerges when we consider that in 2000/01 it was estimated that

Rural Development and the Fight against Poverty in Tanzania   49

38.6 per cent of the rural population of the country lived below the basic needs poverty line (National Bureau of Statistics 2002: 81).

During the last decade the sluggish growth of agriculture (URT 2013: 15) has led to a decrease in its agricultural share of the GDP (ibid.: 18).[2] However, agriculture still provides the greatest contribution to GDP in absolute terms (URT 2013b: 8). While cash crop production has recorded modest and highly fluctuating growth rates (URT, MAFSC 2008: 16), food crop production has kept pace with population growth, thanks to a large increase in the extension of cultivated land (ibid.: 13–15). Recently the contribution of 'traditional' export crops to Tanzania's export earnings has increased (from US$507.3 million in 2008 to US$956.7 million in 2012). However, their share in Tanzania's total export earnings remains limited (16 per cent in 2012). Not only do export earnings from manufacturing goods (US$1,047.3 million in 2012) exceed those of traditional cash crops, but export earnings from the mining sector are more than twice those of traditional cash crops (US$2,187.8 million in 2012) (URT 2013a: 54–5). Tanzania's agriculture also remains heavily dependent on rainfall and is mostly practised by smallholders using low-tech equipment (MAFAP 2013: 49).

Several explanations for the disappointing performance of Tanzania's agriculture during the last decade and its poor impact on poverty reduction have been advanced. Some scholars have pointed to the lack of productivity growth in the agricultural sector (Skarstein 2005; Lokina, Nerman and Sandefur 2011). According to Skarstein, the stagnation of agricultural productivity has been a perverse outcome of economic liberalization, which has driven smallholders to diversify their income sources, and 'to produce agricultural crops only for their own consumption' (Skarstein 2005: 359–60). The difficulty in accessing credit (URT, MAFSC 2008: 46), the crisis of extension services (ibid.: 39), the high cost of inputs and fertilizers and the ruinous condition of roads in rural areas (Cooksey 2012: 8) have further added to the difficulties of smallholder agriculture.

According to Wyuts and Kilama, the contraction of the agricultural contribution to the GDP has not been followed by a significant reduction in the number of people employed in the agricultural sector. On the contrary, since the 1990s 'the share of agriculture in total employment has remained constant or declined only slightly' (Wuyts and Kilama 2014b: 35). As a result, at present 'agriculture acts as a refuge sector of excess labour' which cannot find employment in other sectors of the economy (Wuyts and Kilama 2014a: 27).

Thus, the neoliberal development strategy pursued by the Tanzanian government during the last two decades has brought about neither a significant expansion of employment in the service and industry sectors (in spite of the impressive growth rates which these economic sectors have recorded), nor a

---

2   The interpretation of these data requires some caution, not least for the different reference year of various time data series. Wuyts and Kilama have estimated that during the last two decades agricultural contribution to GDP has decreased by 10.7 per cent, but they also argue that their own estimate is probably low (Wuyts and Kilama 2014b: 23).

modernization of smallholder agriculture that could translate into a significant reduction of poverty rates in the rural areas.

A number of factors have contributed to this outcome. In the first place, the array of rural development projects financed by international donors and the various initiatives launched by different branches of the executive (the presidency, the Ministry of Agriculture and Human Settlements, the Prime Minister's Office – Regional Administration and Local Government, etc.) have lacked any effective coordination mechanism and so fed bureaucratic fragmentation.

In the second place, investments in the rural sector have not matched expectations. Private sector activities have remained mainly concentrated in the marketing of agricultural inputs and crops. The development of agro-processing industries is still in its infancy (URT, MAFSC 2011: 20, 31, 35). Brian Cooksey has recently argued that the reason for the private sector's lukewarm response to the liberalization of the agricultural sector is to be found in the state's failure to establish conditions conducive to development of private entrepreneurship in the rural areas (Cooksey 2012: 14, 23). At a deeper level of analysis it could be argued that the ideological vision of rural sector transformation espoused by the Tanzanian government during the last decade has proved deeply contradictory. While on the one hand the emphasis on market-led agricultural growth has been instrumental in fostering new patterns of capital accumulation, on the other hand the long-term marginalization of agriculture within the Tanzanian political economy has continued almost unabated. This process has been sharpened by the reduction of state budget for agriculture, which in turn reflects the structural transformation of the Tanzanian political economy. At the same time, since the majority of the Tanzanian population live in the rural areas and still depend on agriculture, the government has manipulated public spending for agriculture in order to nurture electoral support for the ruling Chama Cha Mapinduzi (CCM).

In addition to the evidence above, the economic marginalization of agriculture within Tanzania's political economy clearly emerges from the sector distribution of foreign direct investments. In the period 2008–2011 foreign investment flows have mainly been directed at the manufacturing, mining and quarrying sectors. As a consequence, while the stock of foreign direct investments in the manufacturing sector has grown from US$870.7 million in 2008 to US$1.5 billion in 2011, in the mining and quarrying sector it has increased from US$3.7 billion in 2008 to US$4.1 billion in 2011. The agricultural sector has attracted more modest flows of foreign direct investments, whose stock has risen from US$202.3 million in 2008 to US$355.4 million in 2011 (NBS, TIC 2012: 21). These data confirm anecdotal evidence as to the relatively limited extension of large-scale foreign land acquisitions in Tanzania (Sulle and, Nelson 2009; Sulle, Nelson and Lekaita 2012).

The data presented in this chapter unequivocally point to the central relevance of the mining and manufacturing sectors in the Tanzanian economy. It is within this context that the *Tanzania Five Year Development Plan 2011/12–2015/16*, released by the government in 2011, has argued that: 'The mining industry has a crucial role to play in the country's industrialisation [because] an increased growth path in the sector will provide high levels of revenue to the Government, which can then be used in order to promote the interventions mentioned in the other sectors' (URT, PO, PC 2011: 72). Thus, while in the first three decades after independence the government's development plans envisaged that agriculture would provide the financial resources to implement an import substitution industrialization strategy, today the mining sector is supposed to boost the Tanzanian economy and provide revenues for the government. The profound transformation of the Tanzanian political economy has recently been underlined by President Kikwete, who has declared that: 'it is envisaged that by 2025 Tanzania will have transformed into a middle-income country, characterized by high quality livelihood; ... and a diversified semi-industrialized economy with a substantial industrial sector' (Kikwete 2014: 1). Unfortunately, questions such as how economic growth is going to translate into shared prosperity and poverty reduction, or what role agriculture will play in the future Tanzanian economy find no answer in Kikwete's vision.

In spite of the growing consensus as to the need for the government to stimulate agricultural growth in order to fight poverty in the country, the Food and Agriculture Organization of the United Nations (FAO) has noted that the development of agriculture has become a marginal priority for the government, given that 'budget allocations in support of the agricultural and food sector declined from almost 13% of total government spending in 2006/07 to about 9% in 2010/11 [and] actual spending in relative terms also decreased significantly in the period' (MAFAP 2013: 140). According to the World Bank, the contraction in budget allocations to agriculture is partly explained by the fact that the 'government continuously assumes that agriculture will be financed by private sector investments' (World Bank 2012b: 23).

While the rural development vision of the Tanzanian government has facilitated capital accumulation strategies by local and national elites, who have benefitted from their close relations with members of the CCM establishment (Kamata 2012: 296; Peters 2013a: 557), the multiple processes of land commodification, speculation and concentration have intensified processes of social stratification and stirred local resistance and conflicts (Odgaard 2006; Hakiardhi 2009; Lawyers' Environmental Action Team 2011; Sulle, Nelson and Lekaita 2012). As the same time, as in many other African countries, it remains to be seen if and how the new practices of contract farming introduced by multinational companies will translate into practical benefits for the smallholder farmers (Oya 2012).

It is within this context that recently the government has expressed some concern for the potentially negative effects of large-scale land investments (see the following section), and has also tried to cultivate the political consensus of the rural population by allocating a growing share of the decreasing state budget for agriculture to direct transfers to smallholders through input subsidies (MAFAP 2013: 145). While in 2003 the government reintroduced fertilizer subsidies in the Southern Highlands, since 2008 the National Agricultural Inputs Voucher Scheme (NAIVS) has extended the geographical scope of the subsidy programme, which today also covers the purchase of seeds.

The NAIVS, which has been financed by the World Bank, has been heavily criticized not only for its too evident electoral purposes (the scheme was inaugurated before the 2010 presidential and parliamentary elections) (Therkildsen 2011), but also because its benefits have mostly been reaped by the better-off farmers (Cooksey 2012). The FAO has voiced international donors' concern about the long-term effects of the NAIVS on the agricultural sector, arguing that: 'input subsidies may be an important policy instrument for stabilizing the incomes of producers in developing countries in the short run, but they should not compromise the allocation of resources to categories of spending that improve incomes over the long run' (MAFAP 2013: 152).

In a broader perspective input subsidies seem aimed not only at nurturing political support for the CCM in the rural areas, but also at exerting a form of paternalistic control over the rural 'surplus' population within the context of the deep structural transformations of the Tanzanian economy (Peters 2013b). This conclusion seems confirmed by President Kikwete's decision in 2005 to redirect implementation of the Agriculture Sector Development Programme (ASDP) and to give priority to irrigated-rice cultivation. According to Cooksey, this move aimed to strengthen central government's political control over the rural areas through its patronage networks with the local political and economic elites (Cooksey 2012: 20).

Back to the Future: the National Agriculture Policy

Despite the blatant failure of the land titling programme (Pallotti 2013), the National Agriculture Policy (NAP) adopted by the Tanzanian government in October 2013 reasserted the key role of the Land Act and the Village Land Act in promoting agricultural growth. According to the NAP:

> the existing land tenure system is not conducive to long-term investment. Insecurity of land tenure has led to decline in the productive capacity of agricultural land because of non-sustainable land use practices. ... This is aggravated by ... inadequate titling of land for agricultural investment; delays in issuance of title deeds; ... and insecurity of agricultural land especially in premium areas. (UTR, MAFSC 2013: 18)

Within the context of both increasing public concern at the negative effects of large-scale land investments and the local conflicts sparked off by the processes of land speculation and alienation in the rural and peri-urban areas, the NAP commits the government to protecting 'agricultural lands ... against encroachment', and at the same time to guaranteeing the 'availability of land for agricultural investment' (ibid.: 19).

As previously the ASDS, so now the NAP, whose main aim is 'to facilitate the transformation of the agricultural sector into a modern, commercial and competitive sector in order to ensure food security and poverty alleviation' (ibid.: 9), calls

Rural Development and the Fight against Poverty in Tanzania 53

for an active role of the private sector in the provision of better services and the development of the agro-processing industry in the rural areas (ibid.: 19). Together with large-scale commercial farming, the latter should 'provide opportunities for creating partnerships with small farmers as well as creating a more dynamic rural jobs market' (ibid.: 7). The NAP also expresses some concern at labour conditions and the practices of economic exploitation in rural areas, and pledges the government to 'regulate contract farming while ensuring that the rights of farmers, particularly women and men, are duly respected' (ibid.: 19). However, it does not specify how the government is going to achieve such broadly worded commitments.

Thus, in spite of its emphasis on the need to promote new employment opportunities in the rural areas, not least in order to forestall rural-urban migration (ibid.: 19), the NAP does not question the neoliberal vision of rural development already espoused by the ASDS. On the contrary, paying lip service to the need to improve and safeguard the livelihoods of small farmers, the NAP still considers the consolidation of large-scale commercial farms as the key to accelerated rural development.

Conclusions

The analysis of the Tanzania's government policies aimed at promoting rural development and fighting poverty has highlighted a number of important historical continuities and discontinuities between the policy of ujamaa implemented from the late 1960s to the early 1980s and the neoliberal development vision pursued since the mid-1980s.

While fighting poverty has been one of the main priorities of both the policy of *ujamaa vijijini* and the current market-based rural development policy, the instruments adopted to achieve this goal clearly differed. Whereas during the 1960s and the 1970s the government tried to stimulate the growth of the agricultural sector and to improve the social conditions in the rural areas through extensive state intervention in the economy and public provision of social services, after the mid-1980s the emphasis shifted to market mechanisms of resource allocation. The prices and marketing of agricultural crops were liberalized and access to social services was made conditional on the payment of user fees. The implementation of both policy approaches to rural development was marked by severe limitations and contradictions. On the one hand, the policy of *ujamaa vijijini* disrupted traditional production patterns, proved unable to modernize the farming techniques of small farmers and fuelled various forms of resistance. The improvement in access to social services recorded in the rural areas during the 1960s and the 1970s proved unsustainable in the long run. On the other hand, the liberalization of the agricultural sector since the mid-1980s brought about mixed results. After growing during the 1990s, traditional cash crop exports contracted during the 2000s, and have then increased during the last few years. Food crop production stagnated during the 1990s, but has then kept pace with the rate of population growth during the last

54 *State, Land and Democracy in Southern Africa*

decade. However, agriculture is still mostly rain-fed and practised by smallholders who employ technologically poor tools.

As in many other African countries, in Tanzania during the last decade the heavy social costs of the neoliberal economic reforms drove the government and the international donors to launch a number of projects and programmes designed to improve access to social services and reduce poverty, with mixed results. In spite of the renewed official attention to poverty reduction, the present chapter has shown that the government's rural development policy remains trapped in a deep contradiction between the urgent need to improve the livelihoods of the small farmers on the one hand, and an ideological vision that aims at minimizing state intervention in the economy on the other.

The chapter has also highlighted a profound discontinuity in the role played by the agricultural sector within the Tanzanian political economy. While during ujamaa the growth of agricultural production was considered instrumental in financing implementation of the import substitution industrialization strategy, today the development of the Tanzanian economy is apparently driven by the mining sector, which is attracting a large share of Foreign Direct Investment flows to Tanzania and currently provides the bulk value of Tanzania's exports. It is within this context that the development of the agricultural sector has become a lower policy priority for the Tanzanian government. During the last decade not only have state budget allocations to agriculture declined, but the government has also left to the private sector the task of promoting the economic and social development of the rural areas, *in primis* through large-scale land investments. In spite of the fact that the latter did not match expectations, rural areas have become the site of multiple processes of capital accumulation within a context of widespread poverty, and this has resulted in local episodes of (violent) protest.

The chapter has also shown that despite its market-based development vision, the government has not refrained from actively intervening in the rural economy. In an effort to foster its political support in the rural areas, the government has devoted a growing share of the agricultural budget to input subsidies. Observers have criticized the subsidy programme for its inefficiency and its bias towards the better-off and politically well-connected farmers. At a deeper level of analysis, however, it highlights a deeper historical continuity between the socialist and the post-socialist period: the government's paternalistic approach to the small farmers, whose livelihoods are stuck in a low productivity trap and who experience precarious access to social services.

References

Alden Wily, Liz. 2003. "Community-Based Land Tenure Management. Questions and Answers about Tanzania's New Village Land Act, 1999." Issue Paper no. 120. London: International Institute for Environment and Development.

Awiti, Adhu. 1973. "Economic Differentiation in Ismani, Iringa Region: A Critical Assessment of Peasants' Response to the Ujamaa Vijijini Programme." *African Review* 3: 209–39.

Barker, Jonathan. 1979. "The Debate on Rural Socialism in Tanzania," in *Towards Socialism in Tanzania*, edited by Bismarck Mwansasu and Cranford Pratt, 95–124. Toronto: University of Toronto Press.

Bates, Robert. 1981. *Markets and States in Tropical Africa: The Political Basis of Agricultural Policies*. Berkeley: University of California Press.

Bigsten, Arne and Anders Danielson. 2001. "Tanzania: Is the Ugly Duckling Finally Growing Up?" Research Report no. 120. Uppsala: Nordiska Afrikainstitutet.

Boesen, Jannik. 1979. "Tanzania: From Ujamaa to Villagization," in *Towards Socialism in Tanzania*, edited by Bismarck Mwansasu and Cranford Pratt, 125–44. Toronto: University of Toronto Press.

Bryceson, Deborah. 1982. "Peasant Commodity Production in Post-Colonial Tanzania." *African Affairs* 81: 547–67.

Chachage, Chachage. 1993. "Forms of Accumulation, Agriculture and Structural Adjustment in Tanzania," in *Social Change and Economic Reform in Africa*, edited by Peter Gibbon, 215–43. Uppsala: Nordiska Afrikainstitutet.

Cliffe, Lionel. 1973. "The Policy of Ujamaa Vijijini and the Class Struggle in Tanzania," in *Socialism in Tanzania. An Interdisciplinary Reader*, vol. 2, *Policies*, edited by Lionel Cliffe and John Saul, 195–211. Dar es Salaam: East African Publishing House.

Cooksey, Brian. 2012. "Politics, Patronage and Projects: The Political Economy of Agricultural Policy in Tanzania." Working Paper no. 40. Future Agricultures. http://www.future-agricultures.org.

Coldham, Simon. 1995. "Land Tenure Reform in Tanzania: Legal Problems and Perspectives." *Journal of Modern African Studies* 33: 227–42.

Coulson, Andrew. 1982. *Tanzania. A Political Economy*. Oxford: Clarendon Press.

Du Toit, Andries. 2013. "Real Acts, Imagined Landscapes: Reflections on the Discourses of Land Reform in South Africa after 1994." *Journal of Agrarian Change* 13: 16–22.

Dumont, René. 1983. *Stranglehold on Africa*. London: A. Deutsch.

Ellis, Frank. 1983. "Agricultural Marketing and Peasant-State Transfers in Tanzania." *Journal of Peasant Studies* 10: 214–42.

Feierman, Steven. 1991. *Peasant Intellectuals. Anthropology and History in Tanzania*. Madison: University of Wisconsin Press.

Gibbon, Peter. 1995. "Merchantisation of Production and Privatisation of Development in Post-Ujamaa Tanzania," in *Liberalised Development in Tanzania*, edited by Peter Gibbon, 9–36. Uppsala: Nordiska Afrikainstitutet.

Hakiardhi. 2009. *The State of the NAFCO, NARCO and Absentee Landlords' Farms/Ranches in Tanzania*. Dar es Salaam: Hakiardhi.

Kaijage, Frederick and Anna Tibaijuka. 1996. *Poverty and Social Exclusion in Tanzania*. Geneva: International Institute for Labour Studies.

Kamata, Ng'wanza. 2012. "The Economic Diplomacy of Tanzania: Accumulation by Dispossession in a Peripheral State." *Agrarian South* 1: 291–313.

Kikwete, Jakaya. 2014. "Tanzania's Transformation and Vision 2025: Governing Economic Growth for Social Gain." Transcript of speech delivered at Chatham House, London, 31 March. http://www.chathamhouse. org/sites/files/chathamhouse/home/chatham/public_html/sites/default/files/20140331TanzaniaKikwete.pdf.

Kiondo, Andrew. 1999. "Structural Adjustment and Land Reform Policy in Tanzania: A Political Interpretation of the 1992 National Agricultural Policy," in *Agrarian Economy, State and Society in Contemporary Tanzania*, edited by Peter Foster and Sam Maghimbi, 42–56. Aldershot: Ashgate.

Kopoka, Peter. 2002. "Health Service Delivery in Tanzania in the 21st Century," in *The Nyerere Legacy and Economic Policy in Tanzania*, edited by Ammon Mbelle, Godwin Mjema, and Ali. Kilindo, 193–213. Dar es Salaam: Dar es Salaam University Press.

Lawyers' Environmental Action Team. 2011. *Land Acquisitions for Agribusiness in Tanzania: Prospects and Challenges*. Dar es Salaam.

Lokina, Razack, Måns Nerman, and Justin Sandefur. 2011. "Poverty and Productivity: Small-Scale Farming in Tanzania, 1991–2007." Working Paper 11/896. London: International Growth Centre. http://www.theigc.org/sites/default/files/Lokina%20et%20al_Poverty%20and%20productivity.pdf.

Maoulidi, Salma. 2004. "Critical Analysis of the Land Laws in Tanzania." A study prepared for Hakiardhi. Dar es Salaam.

Mashindano, Oswald, Kim Kayunze, Lucia da Corta, and Festo Maro. 2011. "Agricultural Growth and Poverty Reduction in Tanzania 2000–2010: Where Has Agriculture Worked for the Poor and What Can We Learn from This?" Working Paper no. 208. Chronic Poverty Research Centre. http://www.chronicpoverty.org.

Matondi, Prosper and Patience Mutopo. 2011. "Attracting Foreign Direct Investment in Africa in the Context of Land Grabbing for Biofuels and Food Security," in *Biofules, Land Grabbing and Food Security in Africa*, edited by Prosper Matondi, Kjell Havnevik, and Atakilte Beyene, 68–89. London: Zed Books.

Monitoring African Food and Agricultural Policies (MAFAP). 2013. *Review of Food and Agricultural Policies in the United Republic of Tanzania*. Rome: FAO. http://www.fao.org/fileadmin/templates/mafap/documents/Tanzania/URT_Country_Report_Jul2013.pdf.

Munishi, Gaspar. 1998. "A Social Welfare State Development: The Basis, Rationale and the Challenges of Policy Reforms," in *The Social Services Crisis of the 1990s. Strategies for Sustainable Systems in Tanzania*, edited by Anna Tibaijuka, 51–70. Aldershot: Ashgate.

National Bureau of Statistics. 2002. *Household Budget Survey, Final Report*, Dar es Salaam: National Bureau of Statistics.

National Bureau of Statistics (NBS), Tanzania Investment Centre (TIC). 2012. *Tanzania Investment Report 2012*. Dar es Salaam: National Bureau of Statistics.

National Bureau of Statistics, Ministry of Finance. 2014. *2011/12 Household Budget Survey, Tanzania Mainland, Main Report*. Dar es Salaam: National Bureau of Statistics.

Nyerere, Julius K. 1968a[1967]. "The Arusha Declaration," in *Freedom and Socialism – Uhuru na ujamaa*, Julius K. Nyerere, 231–50. Dar es Salaam: Oxford University Press.

——. 1968b[1967]. "Socialism and Rural Development," in *Freedom and Socialism – Uhuru na ujamaa*, Julius K. Nyerere, 337–66. Dar es Salaam: Oxford University Press.

Odgaard, Rie. 2006, "Land Rights and Land Conflicts in Africa: The Tanzania Case." Copenhagen: Danish Institute for International Studies. http://subweb. diis.dk/graphics/Publications/Andet2007/rod_landrights_Tanzania.pdf.

Oya, Carlos. 2012. "Contract Farming in Sub-Saharan Africa: A Survey of Approaches, Debates and Issues." *Journal Agrarian Change* 12: 1–33.

Pallotti, Arrigo. 2008. "Tanzania: Decentralising Power or Spreading Poverty?" *Review of African Political Economy* 35: 221–35.

——. 2013. "The Poverty of Democracy: From Socialism to Neoliberal Citizenship in Tanzania," in *Working the System in Sub-Saharan Africa: Global Values, National Citizenship and Local Politics in Historical Perspective*, edited by Corrado Tornimbeni, 43–64. Newcastle upon Tyne: Cambridge Scholars Publishing.

Peters, Pauline. 2013a. "Conflict over Land and Threats to Customary Tenure in Africa." *African Affairs* 112: 543–62.

——. 2013b. "Land Appropriation, Surplus People and a Battle over Visions of Agrarian Futures in Africa." *Journal of Peasant Studies* 40: 537–62.

Raikes, Phil. 1986. "Eating the Carrot and Wielding the Stick: The Agricultural Sector in Tanzania," in *Tanzania: Crisis and Struggle For Survival*, edited by Jannik Boesen, Kjell Havnevik, Juhani Koponen, and Rie Odgaard, 105–41. Uppsala: Scandinavian Institute of African Studies.

Scott, James. 1998. *Seeing like a State. How Certain Schemes to Improve the Human Condition Have Failed*. New Haven, CT: Yale University Press.

Schneider, Leander. 2004. "Freedom and Unfreedom in Rural Development: Julius Nyerere, Ujamaa Vijijini, and Villagization." *Canadian Journal of African Studies* 38: 344–92.

Shivji, Issa. 1975. *Class Struggles in Tanzania*. Dar es Salaam: Tanzania Publishing House.

——. 1998. *Not yet Democracy: Reforming Land Tenure in Tanzania*. Dar es Salaam: Hakiardhi.

Skarstein, Rune. 2005. "Economic Liberalization and Smallholder Productivity in Tanzania. From Promised Success to Real Failure, 1985–1998." *Journal of Agrarian Change* 5: 334–62.

Sulle, Emmanuel and Fred Nelson. 2009. *Biofuels, Land Access and Rural Livelihoods in Tanzania*. London: International Institute for Environment and Development.

Sulle, Emmanuel, Fred Nelson, and Edward Lekaita. 2012. "Land Grabbing and Political Transformation in Tanzania." Paper presented to the Global Land Grabbing II Conference, Cornell University, Ithaca, NY, 17–19 October. http://www.cornell-landproject.org/download/landgrab2012papers/nelson.pdf.

Tanzania Bankers Association. 2005. "The Land Reform in Tanzania: Opportunities For Agriculture and Mortgage Finance." Paper presented at the Conference: "The Role of Banks in Facilitating Economic growth in Tanzania," Dar es Salaam, 8 March.

Therkildsen, Ole. 2011. "Policy Making and Implementation in Agriculture: Tanzania's Push for Irrigated Rice." DIIS Working Paper 2011: 26. Copenhagen: Danish Institute for International Studies.

Tibaijuka, Anna and Frederick Kaijage. 1995. *Land Policy in Tanzania: Issues for Policy Consideration*. Washington: Center for International Development and Environment.

Ubink, Janine, André Hoekema, and Willem Assies. 2009. *Legalising Land Rights. Local Practices, State Responses and Tenure Security in Africa, Asia and Latin America*. Leiden: Leiden University Press.

United Republic of Tanzania (URT). 1994. *Report of the Presidential Commission of Inquiry into Land Matters*, Vol. 1, *Land Policy and Land Tenure Structure*. Dar es Salaam: Ministry of Land, Housing and Urban Development; Uppsala: Scandinavian Institute of African Studies.

——. 1999. *The Village Land Act No. 5, 1999*. Dar es Salaam: Government Printer.

——. 2000a. *The Economic Survey 1999*. Dar es Salaam.

——. 2000b. *Poverty Reduction Strategy Paper (PRSP)*. October. Dar es Salaam: Government Printer.

——. 2001. *Agricultural Sector Development Strategy*. October. Dar es Salaam: Government Printer.

——. 2004a. *The Economic Survey 2003*. Dar es Salaam.

——. 2004b. *The Land (Amendment) Act, 2004*. Dar es Salaam: Government Printer.

——. 2007. *The Economic Survey 2006*. Dar es Salaam.

——. 2013a. *The Economic Survey 2012*. Dar es Salaam.

——. 2013b. *National Accounts of Tanzania Mainland 2001-2012*. October. Dar es Salaam: National Bureau of Statistics and Ministry of Finance.

United Republic of Tanzania (URT), Ministry of Agriculture, Food Security and Cooperatives (MAFSC). 2008. *Agriculture Sector Review and Public Expenditure Review 2008/09*. November. Dar es Salaam.

——. 2011. *Evaluation of the Performance and Achievements of the Agricultural Sector Development Programme (ASDP)*. June. Dar es Salaam: unpublished.

——. 2013. *National Agriculture Policy*. October. Dar es Salaam.

United Republic of Tanzania (URT), Ministry of Finance and Economic Affairs (MFEA). 2010. *National Strategy for Growth and Reduction of Poverty II*. July. Dar es Salaam.

United Republic of Tanzania (URT), Ministry of Lands and Human Settlements Development (MLHSD) (1995), *National Land Policy*. Dar es Salaam.

United Republic of Tanzania (URT), Prime Minister's Office (PMO). 2001. *Rural Development Strategy*. December. Dar es Salaam: Government Printer.

United Republic of Tanzania (URT), President's Office (PO), Planning Commission PC). 2011. *The Tanzania Five Year Development Plan 2011/12-2015/16. Unleashing Tanzania's Latent Growth Potentials*. June. Dar es Salaam: Government Printer.

United Republic of Tanzania (URT), Vice President's Office (VPO). 2005. *National Strategy for Growth and Reduction of Poverty*. April. Dar es Salaam.

van der Geest, Willem, and Andreas Köttering. 1994. "Structural Adjustment in Tanzania. Objectives and Achievements." In *Negotiating Structural Adjustment in Africa*, edited by Wilmem van der Geest, 69–83. London: James Currey.

van Velzen, Thoden. 1973. "Staff, Kulaks and Peasants: A Study of a Political Field." In *Socialism in Tanzania. An Interdisciplinary Reader*, vol. 2, *Policies*, edited by Lionel Cliffe and John. Saul, 153–79. Dar es Salaam: East African Publishing House.

van Waeyenberge, Elisa. 2006. "From Washington to Post-Washington Consensus. Illusions of Development." In *The New Development Economics. After the Washington Consensus*, edited by Jomo Kwame Sundaran, and Ben Fine, 21–45. London: Zed Books.

von Freyhold, Michaela. 1979. *Ujamaa Villages in Tanzania. Analysis of a Social Experiment*. New York: Monthly Review Press.

World Bank. 1998. *Tanzania, Agriculture, and the World Bank: An OED Review*. Washington: World Bank.

——. 1999. *Tanzania. Social Sector Review*. Washington: World Bank.

——. 2000. *Agriculture in Tanzania since 1986: Follower or Leader of Growth?* Washington: World Bank.

——. 2002. *Tanzania at the Turn of the Century. Background Papers and Statistics*. Washington: World Bank.

——. 2012a. *Tanzania Economic Update: Stairways to Heaven*. Washington: World Bank.

——. 2012b. *Rapid Budget Analysis 2012*. Dar es Salaam: World Bank. 18 November. http://www.tzdpg.or.tz/dpg-website/aid-effectiveness/public-expenditure-review.html.

——. 2014. *Tanzania Public Expenditure Review: National Agricultural Input Voucher Scheme*. Washington: World Bank. February. https://openknowledge.worldbank.org/handle/10986/18247.

Wuyts, Marc. 1994, "Accumulation, Industrialization and the Peasantry: A Reinterpretation of the Tanzanian Experience." *Journal of Peasant Studies* 21: 159–93.

Wuyts, Marc, and Blandina Kilama. 2014a. "Economic Transformation in Tanzania: Vicious or Virtous Circle?" Special THDR Issue, ESRF Discussion Paper no. 56. Dar es Salaam: Economic and Social Research Foundation.

——. 2014b. "The Changing Economy of Tanzania: Patterns of Accumulation and Structural Change." Working Paper no. 14/3. Dar es Salaam: Research on Poverty Alleviation.

Zoomers, Annelies. 2011. "Rushing for Land: Equitable and Sustainable Development in Africa, Asia and Latin America." *Development* 51: 12–20.

Chapter 4

State, Poverty and Agriculture in Zambia: The Impact of State Policies after Democratization

Federico Battera

Introduction

In Zambia, agriculture accounted for some 21 per cent of real Gross Domestic Product (GDP) in 2009, and the sector still absorbs over two-thirds of its labour force.[1] The country has undergone stable growth since the beginning of the 2000s (more than 6 per cent per year since 2004) and nationally poverty has declined, but more than 70 per cent of rural people live in poverty.[2] Agriculture therefore remains as one of the main priorities for poverty alleviation (UNDP 2013). Big potential lies in the country's rural assets: out of its landmass of approximately 752,000 square kilometres, 56 per cent is arable land (42 million hectares). In addition, about 35 per cent of fresh water resources in the Southern African Development Community (SADC) region are in Zambia which, if profitably utilized, could make agriculture a mainstay of the economy. Despite such assets, poor policies dating back to government choices after independence have left the agricultural sector as a secondary issue that democratization after 1991 has barely reversed.

This contribution aims first to describe what has been done or not in regard to rural areas since independence by the former authoritarian regime and subsequent elected governments. Secondly, how parties have managed the land/agriculture issue in order to get access to or keep power after 1991; and finally to evaluate how government measures have impacted on poverty, in particular rural poverty.

Apparently everything indicates a lack of a strategic approach to rural lands and agriculture in general. According to the author, two main mutually reinforcing factors have determined this disappointing result: the inability of farmer associations to voice common interests because the farmers' interests are fragmented, and governing parties' preferred regulation by patronage. Furthermore, while Zambia's agriculture potentialities are luring large-scale agricultural investors (Nolte 2013), such new developments are taking place within an inadequate land governance system.

---

1 National Accounts Statistics 2011, Central Statistical Office: www.zamstats.gov.zm.
2 77.9 per cent in 2010 from 80.3 per cent in 2006 (CSO-RoZ 2010).

General Overview

Zambia is one of the most urbanized countries in sub-Saharan Africa with 31.5 per cent of the population living in the largest cities (35.7 per cent in total).[3] Lusaka and Copperbelt provinces have the highest percentage of urban population at 82 and 81 per cent respectively. The Eastern Province has the lowest one at 9 per cent (RoZ 2011). Thus, the population is concentrated in a few urban areas along the major transport corridors,[4] while the rural areas are sparsely populated. About 90 per cent of its land is therefore rural land whose tenure is mainly dominated by customary land (about 80 per cent).

In 1982, Zambia was one of the five most heavily indebted countries in the world (Rotberg 2002), importing 50 per cent of its food and dependent on copper and cobalt exports for 96 per cent of its foreign exchange.[5] This was the result of strategies which had prompted mining industries at the expense of rural development at a time of declining prices for copper.[6] The economy declined and continued to decline in the beginning of the 1990s (–1.1 per cent between 1990 and 1995). This adverse condition was only reversed towards the end of the 1990s: copper prices started to rise again and foreign investments poured in. This favoured steady growth – from about 3.8 per cent GDP per year between 2001 and 2004 to 6.8 per cent in 2012 – and a better diversification of the economy. Copper dependence declined from about 75 per cent of exports in 2005 to 65 per cent in 2010 – a percentage that remains important, however. The new conditions have generally improved the ordinary life of common people but marked differences persist between urban and rural areas. The data illustrate that poverty in rural areas is worse than in urban areas. In 2010, poverty levels affected about 60 per cent of the national population with the worst results in provinces like Western, Luapula and Eastern which are overwhelmingly rural (see Table 4.1). Notwithstanding bumper maize crops in recent years which have reduced the need for imports, Zambia's economic growth has not dramatically reversed the stubbornly high poverty rates, given the burden of high birth and high HIV/AIDS rates.

---

3 See the World Bank's 'World Development Indicators': http://data.worldbank.org/data-catalog/world-development-indicators.

4 Copperbelt and Lusaka provinces are home to about 69 per cent of urban Zambians. The remaining seven provinces are overwhelmingly rural.

5 Since 2005 Zambia has qualified for debt relief under the Highly Indebted Poor Country Initiative, consisting of approximately US$6 billion in debt relief. Therefore, the debt has been seriously reduced. Zambia's domestic and external debt for the year 2013 was projected to reach 37 per cent of the country's GDP (Zambia's 2013 debt 2013).

6 For more details see the following section.

Table 4.1 Province level poverty estimates (percentage)

Provinces	1991	1998	Change 1991–1998	2006	Change 1998–2006	2010	Change 2006–2010	Change 1991–2010	Rank 2010
Central	70	77	+7	71	-5	61	-10	-9	7
Copperbelt	61	65	+4	37	-28	34	-3	-27	8
Eastern	85	79	-6	78	-1	78	=	-7	3
Luapula	84	82	-2	74	-8	80	+6	-4	1
Lusaka	31	53	+22	25	-28	24	-1	-7	9
Northern	84	81	-3	78	-3	75	-3	-9	4
North-Western	75	77	+2	71	-6	67	-4	-8	6
Southern	79	75	-4	73	-2	68	-5	-11	5
Western	84	89	+5	83	-6	80	-3	-4	1

Sources: CSO-RoZ (2006–2010) and statistics on Central Statistical Office website: www.zamstats.gov.zm.

Agricultural Policies in Historical Perspexctive: From Independence to Multipartyism (1964–1991)

In 1973, the United National Independence Party (UNIP) became the sole legal party in Zambia, but ever since independence in 1964 it had enjoyed overwhelmingly majorities. Such strong political favour enabled President Kaunda to enforce robust policies in the economic realm. Two priorities and one asset drove the economic strategy: to ensure food security and agricultural production, and copper. By 1964, the government started to implement a series of policy measures to ensure that food security and agricultural production met the required levels: price controls and subsidies were introduced and a system of rural cooperatives and parastatals was established for the purpose of buying and marketing agricultural products and to ensure the availability of enough stock for food needs.

At the same time, in order to enhance industrialization in the country, nationalization of economic assets was also pursued. In the late 1960s, foreign firms both in rural and industrial sectors were taken over in order to strengthen the presumed state capacity to deliver jobs and credit (Baylies and Szeftel 1982). In 1972, it was the turn of the copper mines to be nationalized. Zambia's industrialization was based on import substitution relying on anticipated high prices for copper. Development was primarily seen as industrial development and Zambia made no exception, like most states elsewhere in the developing world (Bates 1981: 11). Copper production and exports remained central as this satisfied the 'revenue imperative' (Bates 1981: 13).

However, all planning efforts to attain economic diversification, self-sufficiency and provision of social welfare had abruptly failed by the end of the 1970s.[7] In particular, economic centralization proved to be a failure as mismanagement and corruption followed. For example, the Industrial Development Corporation (INDECO), which had the task of establishing small industries in rural areas, was a standing case of failure and corruption (Tangri 1999: 28–31). Projects undertaken under such plans were mainly driven by political considerations and rapidly led to mismanagement and corruption (Good 1986). Furthermore, other opportunities to implement policies in the agricultural sector were also hampered by the tenure system. As elsewhere in Africa, land tenure inherited from colonial practices had barely been touched (Jackson and Rosberg 1982): crown lands had become state lands in 1964 while the remaining ones had been placed under the authority of chiefs once these were finally co-opted by the party in power.

There were plans not only to rationalize, strengthen and diversify production but to politically mobilize peasants in favour of the UNIP through the creation of grassroots structures which could link up local development needs with priorities defined at the central level (Ollawa 1978: 117–18; Bratton 1980). However, because of lack of adequate budget and because most important decisions were imposed from the centre, such structures completely lacked power. The effects were rather a decentralization of patronage opportunities for party (UNIP) officials and local elites through control of Ward Development Committees (WDCs) (Bratton 1980: 12), while Village Productivity Committees (VPCs) which were intended to run efforts at rural development mostly remained on paper. Despite a formal commitment by Kaunda in 1968 to prioritize development in rural areas, migration to urban areas continued to be the easiest solution to rampant poverty in rural areas. Behind such formal commitments by the party in power and its official policy line, there was an important reason for both the government and the party to abdicate to effectively prioritize rural development: on the one hand, rural areas remained a field for draining political support through the pivotal role of local elites; on the other, most crucial decisions rested at the central level and were centred around the strategic need to find revenue. As for the former, chiefs were now part of the local elite. The Development of Villages and Registration Act of 1971 involved chiefs in the economic development of rural areas through their active participation in activities and projects carried out by WDCs and VPCs. Hence, after having lost much of their power to the UNIP at the early stages of independence when a series of measures such as the suppression of Native Authorities had reduced their role, in 1985 the government decided to reward the '*boma* class'[8] by conferring on it the role of deciding whenever and wherever customary land should be granted for leasehold purposes.

---

7 The first national planning started in 1965 with the Transitional National Development Plan.

8 As Chipungu (1992) defined chiefs in Zambia.

The overall result of policies centred on price controls, subsidy inputs to farmers and purchasing of rural products through the National Agriculture Marketing Board (NAMBOARD) in a period of declining copper prices[9] was that the budgetary burden of agricultural subsidies alone became burdensome, reaching almost 10 per cent of all government expenditure in 1980 and averaging 7.4 per cent of all expenditure in the 1977–84 period. This coupled with a rampant rural exodus that hampered any serious effort of planning in rural areas. By the end of the 1980s, Zambia had lost any comparative advantage over neighbouring Zimbabwe and South Africa. The land remained as it was during colonial times: divided among small and less productive lands in the hands of small rural producers and potentially better and profitable lands in the form of state properties.

The Return to Multiparty Politics: Agriculture as a Political Issue Under MMD Dominance (1991–2011)

Having won the first multiparty elections in 1991 with strong support from electors, and destined to benefit from stable majorities in parliament for a decade (see Table 4.2), the governments of the Movement for Multiparty Democracy (MMD) in the 1990s undertook one of the highest privatization schemes in sub-Saharan Africa, extending to agriculture. Price control on food (with the exception of maize) was officially removed in December 1991 leading to an enormous increase in prices, while the state-owned marketing companies were privatized by 1994–95. Such increases in prices contributed at first to the growth of poverty in urban areas (see Table 4.1). However, the initial phase of liberalization also marked a reduction in productivity due to poor market policies to sustain the sector, especially for small rural producers of food crops such as maize. About 60 per cent of maize, which is the staple food, was produced by smallholder farmers mainly living far away from markets and owning less than five hectares. About 60–70 per cent of smallholder farmers therefore did not benefit from the liberalization reforms of the 1990s. As agricultural credit finance was put into private hands, the cost of production also rose. Privatization served the requirements of the International Financial Institutions (IFI) rather than meeting local interests.[10]

---

9 Copper prices fell harshly on the world market after 1974 up to 1979, then fell again in 1981 and would only recover by 2005.

10 Although the Chiluba government was seriously committed to following IFI's request to privatize the public sector, some resistance came from core supporters of the MMD with the partial exception of the business community. For instance, the mining sector was not privatized, and then only partially, until 2000 (see Note 13). For further information on privatization and its consequences, see Simutanyi (1996).

State, Land and Democracy in Southern Africa

Table 4.2   Parliamentary majorities since 1991

Year	First party per cent seats in the NA	Second party per cent seats in the NA	Third party per cent seats in the NA
1991	MMD 83	UNIP 17	–
1996	MMD 87	Indep. 7	NP 3
2001	MMD 46	UPND 33	UNIP 9
2006	MMD 48	PF 29	UDA* 18
2011	PF 40	MMD 37	UPND 19

*UDA was a coalition composed of UPND, UNIP and FDD.
Source: By the author.

To address this deficiency, subsidies such as the Fertilizer Credit Programme (FCP) were reintroduced in 1997 to the benefit of rural producers. However, this happened after the 1996 elections, at a time when the MMD enjoyed its strongest majority, increasing its MPs from 125 to 131 (out of a total of 150), with 60.1 per cent of the votes cast. Once UNIP (the Kaunda party and the most credible opposition) dropped out of the race when its candidate for the presidential election was excluded for not having Zambian parents, the remaining votes went to a constellation of other parties some of which enjoyed limited rural support, such as the National Party (NP) in North-Western and the Agenda for Zambia (AZ) in Western. However, the support for these parties mainly came from an ethnic core, as Posner (2005: 239) demonstrates. The only party contesting the parliamentarian race with an agrarian platform at that time, the National Lima Party (NLP), managed to obtain a mere 6 per cent of the total vote and no MPs. Interestingly, NLP, at that time led by the now Vice President of Zambia Guy Scott, was the only party without any explicit ethnic profile.[11] MMD was still perceived as the most powerful and credible national party and enjoyed renewed support. Thus, apart from NLP, no party really challenged the MMD economic agenda in 1996. According to Rakner (2003: 121–2), at that time the link between economic interests and the party system had not yet developed. The miners' sector, which was potentially better able to pressurize governments, was actually ineffectual and its priorities were largely disregarded by MMD.

The re-introduction of subsidies benefiting rural producers occurred when the party in power realized the importance of rural votes. Such electoral use of subsidies before or immediately after elections as a reward for votes thus started in 1996 and inaugurated a practice widely employed thereafter by MMD. By 2001, with its

---

11   Guy Scott was Minister of Agriculture during the first post-authoritarian government and was sacked in 1993.

monopolistic position in the electoral arena beginning to be seriously questioned,[12] MMD started to cultivate a burgeoning rural profile. Such had not been the case around the turning point of the 1991 elections and not in 1996 either. During the latter elections the MMD again managed to win more than 70 per cent of the votes in urban conurbations such as those of Copperbelt, although the requests of the Zambia Congress of Trade Unions (ZCTU) for re-introduction of subsidies on food and transport to alleviate the difficulties of the workers had been regularly downplayed from 1993 to 1996.[13] Chiluba, at that time the elected President of the Republic, enjoyed a stable majority in the National Assembly, and the trade unions, especially the major ones such as the Mineworkers Union of Zambia (MUZ), acquiesced in the government decision to privatize the mines as well.[14]

By 2001 subsidies policies for the benefit of rural voters were enacted and would be scaled up before or after any electoral cycle (in 2001, 2006 and 2011) as a way to reward loyalty or as a means to gain new voters. According to Mason and Ricker-Gilbert (2013), households in areas where the ruling party won elections acquired significantly more subsidized inputs than other households. This policy of reward was reinforced by the resilience of the ethnic factor which mainly remained a rural issue.[15] At that time MMD was perceived as having its strongholds in certain ethnic constituencies (initially Bemba, though by 2001 it extended to ethnic constituencies hitherto weakly covered). Thus, self-interest drove MMD to a policy of reward more than pursuit of a policy of penetrating rural areas which were more loyal to other parties (such as the United Party for National Development – UPND).[16] Its rural

---

12   Before 2001, Chiluba attempted to amend the constitution in order to seek a third term in office. That attempt was defeated by his own party. However, quarrels over the succession led some senior MMD cadres to defect (Rakner and Svåsand 2004: 53–4).

13   Only in 1997 was a new agency – the Food Reserve Agency (FRA) – instructed to sell imported food (Rakner 2003: 76). Unlike the former agency – NAMBOARD – which was abolished in 1989 under IFI pressure as being the sole buyer and seller of grain in the country and sole fertilizer supplier, the FRA was originally conceived to stock staple food so as to dampen price variability (Chapoto 2012: 3).

14   Chiluba himself had been Chairman-General of ZCTU from 1974 to 1991. Unlike ZCTU, of which MUZ was part, MUZ endorsed privatization. As a result MUZ quitted ZCTU in 1994, only to rejoin it in 1999. ZCCM (Zambia Consolidated Copper Mines) was partially privatized in 2000. There is much debate in the literature as to the effects of mine privatization in Zambia. There is a certain general agreement that the fiscal effect was limited as well as adverse effects on work conditions (Fraser and Lungu 2006). In general, privatization stoked local protest and strengthened the relations between opposition to MMD and MUZ Copperbelt cadres by the end of the 2000s (Simutanyi 2008). The PF campaign against foreign (especially Chinese) companies helped to build Copperbelt as a powerful stronghold for the PF (Negi 2011: 87).

15   On the importance of the ethnic factor in Zambia for electoral calculation, see Posner (2005) and, more recently, Erdmann (2007) and Cheeseman and Hinfelaar (2010).

16   This was so in the Southern province, which by 2001 was strictly controlled by UPND. Since all its leaders came from Southern and were of Tonga ethnicity, the UPND

State, Land and Democracy in Southern Africa

profile was consequently more driven by electoral calculation based on the ethnic profile of the constituents. However, the 2001 elections also marked the emergence of an urban-rural divide which had been a silent factor under Kaunda. On the other hand, growing privatization of the rural landscape had changed the relation with local actors, a trend that actually already started during the last decade of the Kaunda regime when relations between the state and rural areas were resolved to the advantage of the '*boma* class.' By 1995, privatization had enhanced the role of the 'gatekeepers' of land administration (Brown 2005: 97) such as chiefs, district-level officers, and bureaucrats at the Ministry of Lands who were in a position to exploit their strategic position within a system designed to create opportunities for these officials by using their position to their own advantage.

Enjoying no more than an ancillary role under the one party system, rural organizations were now further weakened by patronage. The Zambia Cooperative Federation (ZCF) had always been of little interest to MMD since it was associated with UNIP machinery.[17] Hence, MMD tried to establish closer ties with the Zambia National Farmers' Union (ZNFU). However, at the end of the first electoral cycle ZNFU expressed scepticism about the effects of liberalization. Under pressure from the ZNFU, the ZCF and the Peasant Farmers' Union of Zambia (PFUZ), the government was forced to resume farmers' subsidies, as we have said, and this has remained the only social welfare state mechanism until the present.[18]

Today, of these entities, which are for the most part very weak, only the ZNFU still stands as a stable organization[19] notwithstanding its initial support for the NLP. Remnants of ZCF continue to try and rebuild an independent cooperative movement today and are calling for a return of subsidized government marketing and the provision of inputs for smallholders.[20] The same has happened with the PFUZ.[21]

---

has so far been perceived as a Tonga party.

17   Policies in favour of privatizing agriculture were also intended to weaken UNIP grassroots in rural society (Rakner 2003: 84). By the beginning of the 1980s, the ZCF had been affiliated with UNIP. Through this measure, ZCF representation was included in the highest decision-making body of UNIP.

18   As well as from rural organizations, pressure came from MMD MPs representing rural constituencies; this perhaps had more influence on the government's decision to resume subsidies (Rakner 2003: 177).

19   ZNFU is the only organization that represents both small- and large-scale farmers.

20   In 1973 the long-standing cooperative movement in Zambia established ZCF as its national coordinating body. Over the 1980s UNIP succeeded in drawing ZCF under party control (see Note 17). ZCF was used to pursue government agricultural policies despite the fact that these were not economically viable. In the early 1990s, ZCF was still one of the principal marketing agents. This misguided effort drove the federation to bankruptcy. On the cooperative movement today, see Lolojih (2009)

21   The Peasant Farmers' Union of Zambia (PFUZ) was a loosely organized group that called for subsidies and public inputs for small-scale farmers. Though it claimed to have a large membership, its organizational capacity was weak and it was not taken seriously by MMD. Before the 1996 election it formed a loose affiliation with UNIP, which

Thus everything indicates a weak ability by rural actors to express any stable interest apart from subsidization. Agriculture interests are voiced through several farmer associations (ZNFU, PFUZ, National Association of Small-Scale and Peasant Farmers Union – NASSPFU, ZCF, etc.) with little effect on the government commitment to endorse rural reform. As in the 1990s, Zambia's agricultural policies revolve around the question of government involvement in the marketing of fertilizer and maize (Rakner 2003: 75–6). Furthermore, the government is expected to intervene to keep retail prices down especially during election time (Taylor and Aarnes 2002). Having mainly opted for the first solution, MMD definitively lost any serious urban support by 2006. However, courting rural areas with subsidies had no substantive effect on MMD's share of votes beyond the core ethnic strongholds (Mason and Ricker-Gilbert 2013) which have constantly shifted from Bembas to other areas. The 2011 elections demonstrate MMD's inability to hold on to large majorities. Born as an urban-orientated party, the PF started during the 2008 Presidential election to campaign effectively in ethnic constituencies which now perceived they had been duped by the government (Bemba, in particular), though without losing its urban profile. When disaffection with MMD came to a head in 2011, MMD was overthrown.

All in all, the effect of subsidization policies has been ineffectual. While they resulted in large increases in maize production ever since the last half of the 2000s,[22] this increase appears to have had limited impact on the welfare of the poorest farmers. At the end of MMD dominance, most poor people still resided in rural areas, crippled by the poor state of the infrastructure in those areas and the lack of any serious commitment to land reform.

Beyond Party Politics: Land-Related Issues

Certain structural conditions are impeding further improvements and are the main cause of poverty in rural areas because of poor infrastructure and a tenure system which has led to concentration of the best lands in few hands. Notwithstanding, since 2001 the agricultural sector has shown signs of improvement particularly for cash crop production such as cotton, tobacco, maize and wheat. In 2009 agriculture

---

had promised it special consideration should the party return to power. Ensuing events went differently. UNIP boycotted the election and the PFUZ lost support in the government.

22   In the 1970s maize production ranged from 0.6 to about 1.6 million tonnes per year. In the 1980s production stagnated and the slump continued during the 1990s with production rarely exceeding 1 million tonnes due to a decline in the maize share within the total smallholder crop output. One should note that annual demand for maize is estimated at about 1.6 million tonnes. Production started to recover after 2005 (during the 2006/2007 season production rose as high as 1.4 million tonnes) to reach about 1.9 million tonnes during the 2008/2009 season and booming to an estimated 3.3 million tonnes for the 2013/2014 season (sources: Ministry of Agriculture and Livestock; see also *Lusaka Times*, various years).

accounted for a 21 per cent share of GDP which is an improvement compared to 16 per cent in 1992. That improvement was achieved because of an increased role by the private sector. However, poverty in rural areas remained serious and much potential still needs to be developed. The same subsidies policy has proved to be intrinsically inadequate.

In the last 15 years, the Government of Zambia has sought to fill the vacuum left by the underdeveloped private sector by directly subsidizing farmers through the Farmer Input Support Programme (FISP) while at the same time it has aimed to stabilize prices by purchasing grain through the Food Reserve Agency (FRA). These subsidies, along with improved levels of rainfall, have been responsible for large increases in maize production in the last few years (Burke, Jayne and Sitko 2012). However, this improvement appears to have had limited impact on the welfare of the poorest farmers for several reasons: first, poverty in rural areas tends to concentrate where infrastructure is inadequate or unavailable; second, direct subsidies are expensive and detrimental to other safety nets (they accounted for over 70 per cent of the budget to the Ministry of Agriculture over the past five years); third, difficulties in targeting small-hold farmers (they have received a disproportionately lower amount of subsidies); and, finally, distortion of prices in the market. As Chapoto and Jayne (2009: vi) state, 'Malawi and Zambia have the highest degree of price volatility and price uncertainty.'

Land tenure remains, however, the most crucial issue. While it is true that some farmers who are more commercially orientated than the typical smallholder occupy state land under long-term leases (99 years), most farmers still work the land under the traditional tenure systems. Large commercial farms which occupy land mainly allocated along major transport routes and near population centres, are under long-term leases and use modern technology, irrigation and fertilizers. The latter are responsible for most of the country's agricultural exports and benefit most from the government policy of subsidies.

Today, land is ruled under the 1995 Land Act, which marked a change from the previous tenure system since it opened land to investors. For the first time land became tradable by converting it from customary to state ownership. Land formally belongs to the state (and is vested in the president), but it can be leased for 99 renewable years. This different approach has profoundly altered the tenure system in the last 15 years – unfortunately, with no immediate positive consequences. According to Nolte (2013) nowadays about 80 per cent remains customary land – a reduction compared to the 1980s. However, such conversion of titles has first predominantly involved urban areas and only subsequently the rural areas that are more commercially orientated or touristic. Not surprisingly, the groups that have benefitted most are foreign investors and Zambian elites (Brown 2005).

As for the Zambian elites that have profited most, Brown (2005: 97) points to three social strata: chiefs, district councillors and bureaucrats in the Ministry of Land (MoL). Such groups make up an agricultural middle class that gains by a reform-adverse system, which is marginalizing the poorer producers.[23] While formally chiefs must consult the local community before giving their approval to convert customary to state land – a necessary step before it can be leased – very little consultation is done (Nolte 2013: 16). To this one must add the lack of inspection and transparency on the part of the MoL as to the destination of the land leased, which ought to conform to developmental criteria. If we also remember that small producers' trade unions and organizations are weak, the result is that: a) the land is captured by an elite;[24] b) there are emerging 'intra-community conflicts' (i.e. chiefs vs. common people) (Brown 2005: 96);[25] and c) common resources are being closed, to the benefit of the few.

Furthermore such '(mal)administration of land' (Brown 2005: 97) is strictly linked to the poor implementation of the local governance reform as it was intended by the 1991 Local Government Act. The process is well described by Chikulo (2009). Besides financial problems which hamper the ability of local authorities (LAs) to perform as envisioned, LAs have generally been unable to ensure citizen participation and lacked the mechanisms to directly control or address development planning at the local level. The strength of such decentralized local structures therefore remains limited.

The Urban-Rural Divide and 2011 Elections: New Policy But Not for the Benefit of Rural Poor?

Zambia today produces enough maize to feed itself and its neighbours in Eastern and Southern Africa.[26] This is the most important result of the agricultural subsidies policy in Zambia. However, a series of weaknesses still prevent that policy from having a positive effect on poverty levels in rural areas. According to Sitko and

---

23   On this issue see also Sitko and Jayne (2012). In 1995, the Land Act was passed by parliament following two years of a contentious national debate. An array of civil society organizations (CSOs), church groups and traditional leaders all opposed the reform. Approval of the law did not pass until the government, enjoying a large majority, threatened MMD rural MPs with expulsion (Brown 2005: 85–6).

24   Similar cases have been dealt with by Acemoglu, Reed and Robinson (2013) and Scoones et al. (2010).

25   Although such 'intra-community conflicts' may vary across the country and the attitude by the chiefs towards the 1995 Land Act has been mixed, there is a general agreement in Zambia that the 'boma class' has profited by its special relation with subsequent governments. However, on the extension of such conflict and its social and political impact in Zambia more research is needed. On the importance of understanding more about the class structure of social movements, local actors, conflicts and agrarian change dynamics in agrarian societies, see Borras (2009).

26   The crop production index rose to 170.0 in 2009 from 100.0 between 1999–2001 (IFAD – Rural Poverty Portal, Zambia statistics: www.ruralpovertyportal.org/country/statistics/tags/zambia).

Jayne (2012: 19), Zambia's agricultural development strategy 'has failed to provide a viable pathway out of poverty for the millions of small-scale farmers.' Furthermore, given the burden of the policy on the national budget, it is unlikely to be continued in the long run.[27] Several structural problems also persist: first, crop marketing. The storage capacity of the Government of Zambia, which in the recent past has purchased more than 80 per cent of the marketed surplus through FRA, is inadequate and 32 per cent of the crops stored is lost. The Government buys maize above the market price. As a result (the second structural problem), private business does not play an adequate role in buying or exporting maize,[28] to the detriment of national investments, in a period of growing interest by international investors (Deininger and Byerlee 2011).[29] Third, since 2008 the government has also subsidized the milling industry with a view to reducing the consumer price of maize; however the main beneficiaries have been big miller companies while most of the informal milling sector has not been reached by this scheme and has been squeezed out of the market. Fourth, while the subsidies policy has enlarged the area under maize cultivation at the expense of other crops, productivity has remained the same, since small-hold production does not easily reach the national market because of the poor state of the infrastructure and services available to farmers in much of the country.[30] The effect has been that Zambia is now as heavily dependent on maize production as it is dependent on copper. Fifth, since the land available to smallholder production is not so abundant as policy makers assumed, small-scale farmers will shortly find themselves bottled up in high density areas where the options for profitable use of agriculture will hardly provide them with the opportunity to exit from poverty (Sitko and Jayne 2012: 19). If present land titling and management in customary areas continues as regulated by the 1995 Land Act, small farms will have a limited future, here as elsewhere (Collier and Dercon 2009). Finally, the collective burden of these various subsidies accounts for over 80 per cent of government spending on agriculture, about 2 per cent of GDP

---

27 This remark sums up the outcome of investigations and reports made by the Indaba Agricultural Policy Research Institute (IAPRI) of Lusaka, which can be found at www.africaresearchinstitute.org/blog/agricultural-subsidies-in-zambia.

28 More details on the effects of the higher FRA buying prices are to be found in Nkonde et al. (2011). Two important results are that well-capitalized farmers are more suited to benefit from the higher prices and that millers have found it cheaper to buy maize from South Africa.

29 According to recent reports (see for example Anseeuw et al. 2012) Zambia seems to be one of the most targeted African countries as far as attempts at land acquisition by foreign investors is concerned.

30 In marketing year 2007/08, only 10 per cent of smallholders sold maize to the FRA and these households had larger landholdings, more farm assets and a higher education level than smallholders who did not sell maize to the FRA (Mason, Jayne and Myers 2012). At the same time, only 56 per cent of the total number of smallholders receive FISP fertilizer (smallholders, those who cultivate less than 2 hectares of land, account for 73 per cent of farmers in Zambia). These are the poorest households (Mofya-Mukuka et al. 2013).

in 2011. If we consider that the effects on market prices have been poor – while FISP has caused a drop in retail prices, FRA activities have generally triggered a rise in maize prices – the upshot is that this policy is no longer sustainable after 15 years' implementation.

In 2012, after the elections were won by a party that is considered less favourable to agricultural interests, such policies have not surprisingly been halted. The fact that subsidies were in part delivered according to political determinants (Mason and Ricker-Gilbert 2013) only speeded up the decision.[31] Since 2006 PF has campaigned on a platform centering on urban interests and the mining industry and speaking out aggressively against foreign interests – namely Chinese – in the copper sector (Larmer and Fraser 2007). While in 2006 this strategy failed nationally, PF was able to build a strong base in Copperbelt and Lusaka, which are the main urban areas. By the 2008 presidential elections, the MMD position in Luapula and Northern provinces, which are mainly rural, was eroded by a rampant PF. The PF presidential candidate was Michael Sata, a Bemba, and this helped the party to penetrate such rural areas. National disaffection with the twenty-year period of MMD power also helped PF to win both presidential and parliamentary elections in 2011, though with a small majority (38 per cent against 34 per cent of the vote at the parliamentary elections) thanks to a fall in MMD rural votes. Although still partly affected by the ethnic vote, since 2006 elections have been marked by a growing rural-urban divide (Battera 2013). It was not only PF that moulded its electoral platform around urban interests; MMD also based its campaign issues around fertilizer subsidies and higher maize prices after the death of President Levy Mwanawasa in August 2008 and the elections to replace him (Chapoto 2012: 18). One major reason for that was that the core support for the then ruling MMD party was overwhelmingly comprised of rural farming households.

The decisive PF victory in the 2011 election is even more striking if one considers that macroeconomic conditions on the eve of the election were very encouraging for the incumbent party: in 2010 the real GDP had grown by 7.6 per cent, which was above the target established by the Fifth National Development Plan (FNDP). According to the economic reports, that growth had been driven not only by the rise in metal (mainly copper) exports but by agriculture as well.[32]

Once PF got into power, MMD entered a state of shock, shaken by floor-crossing and subsequent serious defeats in by-elections at the hands of PF. However, notwithstanding the fact that PF has now penetrated rural areas, the party has not

---

31   Once in government, PF ministers and cadres regularly denounced the electoral bias of the previous government's subsidies policy and the way land was allocated, enjoying some support in this from certain rural sectors such as the Zambia Land Alliance (ZLA), which is an NGO umbrella working for reforming land policies. However, the degree of impact by pro-rural CSOs activism on PF policies remains doubtful.

32   Copper earnings in 2010 were 81.6 per cent up from the 2009 figure.

reversed its own priorities.[33] PF stands firm on its previously formulated strategies which are centred around fighting poverty through income redistribution and infrastructure investments. How agriculture and poor rural farmers may benefit from any renewed strategic approach is still a matter for speculation. Two major measures have actually been taken: the reduction of subsidies to farms and the redoubling of mineral royalties. Such measures were intended to free resources for other 'pro-poor' efforts such as increased social spending to improve living standards, especially in urban areas, health and education, and job creation. Some pillars of the PF programme.

Since coming to power, the PF government has been conscious both of the non-sustainability of the FRA-FISP scheme[34] and of the country's dependence on copper revenues. Since the latter is a condition that will not change in the short-medium term, the government decided to increase its profits from copper production. In April 2012, mineral royalties were doubled (from 3 to 6 per cent). As a result, Zambia's tax revenues from copper mining jumped by 46 per cent (Zambia's revenue 2012). Much of the debate around revenues from mining hinged at that time on the implementation of a windfall tax on above-average profits from mines. The option had been considered by the former MMD government but was cast aside because many of the mines were still making losses due to unfavourable contracts signed by former governments with foreign mining firms. The choice of a mineral royalties hike paid off, freeing resources for other priorities. The second aim of the plan was to reduce agricultural subsidies. The thinking behind this measure was later explained by the Finance Minister, Alexander Chikwanda, in August 2013, when he announced that in the period covered by the National Development Plan 2013–2016 the government would remove some of the bottlenecks that had so far inhibited smooth implementation of development (Government Revises 2013). The Zambian government accordingly reduced subsidies for farmers (the cost-sharing is now 50 per cent for government and farmers respectively as against 75–25 per cent) and millers as well, while it continues to provide farmers with free seed and to buy maize for the FRA, paying farmers above the market price but not selling it at a subsidized rate to millers. This measure angered the ZNFU but to no avail (Removing Subsidies 2013). Other critics cautioned that the government was moving too fast. Furthermore, in April 2013 fuel subsidies were likewise removed, leading to a 21 per cent increase in fuel prices. By the beginning of 2013 the double removal of subsidies for farmers and millers had indeed begun to impact on consumers but not as expected,[35] the

---

33   PF has won most of the by-elections held since 2011. Most of these regard rural constituencies outside the Bemba areas previously represented by MMD. This success has largely been due both to the crisis which shook MMD after the 2011 elections and to a band-wagon effect in favor of PF.

34   FISP alone accounted for roughly 39 per cent of the resources allocated to agriculture in the 2011 budget.

35   See interview with Rhoda Mofya-Mukuka (Bhalla 2013).

government having big maize reserves in the FRA by which to control prices. With the same purpose in mind, the PF government also decided to halt cooperation with neighbours in difficulty who were asking cash for maize exports to Zimbabwe (Mashininga 2013). The government was convinced it was on the right path. The timing for reducing subsidies was incidentally considered good for the party in power, since general elections were not expected before 2016.[36] As for job creation, President Sata announced at the end of 2013 that in 2014 the government would prioritize job creation and raising the standard of living among people in rural areas. On the former point, the government intends to re-establish the Industrial Development Corporation (INDECO) which will 'focus on developing labour intensive industries and enterprises in the key areas of agriculture, construction, manufacturing, tourism, science and technology' (Mwenda 2014). As is known, INDECO had been responsible for burgeoning corruption, inefficiency and malpractice in the 1970s. The declaration unleashed controversy between those in favour (former President Kaunda backed the idea) and against (some of them aligned with the MMD). In particular, MMD politicians question to the positive effect of INDECO in rural areas (INDECO Critics 2014). More realistically, plans like that of reviving INDECO could only have a positive impact if governance was improved, as warned permanent secretary for finance, Pamela Kabamba, who underlined the lack of coordination among government departments and the need for a systematic approach to national development planning – problems shared by other underdeveloped countries (Kabamba Urges 2013).

Conclusions

When PF won the 2011 elections, ending the 20-year long interlude of MMD in power, nobody doubted there would be a decisive urban bias to development strategy. So much was clear from the stated intention of Michael Sata's leadership, his political profile, the way PF had campaigned and the location of its strongholds. Backing by former UNIP cadres and by Kaunda himself, the intention of resuscitating INDECO: all pointed to a resumption of 'unipist' developmental strategy. By such a strategy, agriculture is in danger of being viewed essentially within the prism of surplus extraction for industrialization (Kay 2009: 106). PF endorsed Zambia Vision 2030 (adopted in 2006) which indeed envisages the gradual transformation of the economic structure from an agriculturally to an industrially based economy. The modernization of agriculture is mentioned as crucial and 'Secure, fair and equitable access and control of land for a sustainable socio-economic development' is also mentioned by Vision 2030, together with the provision of a safety net policy providing social protection for low-capacity households from periodic shocks (WB 2013: 87). So far, however, the tools are

---

36   In the meantime, Michael Sata died in October 2014 because of a worsening of his health condition. New presidential elections were held on 20 January 2015.

missing to make 'secure, fair and equitable access and control of land' not a dream but a reality. What is lacking is an approach to rural development which breaks with the past. Although the PF government attitude put an end to the patronage approach to farmers' interests (which is positive),[37] no innovative or comprehensive rural agenda tackling the crucial issue of tenure has been forthcoming,[38] leaving the impression that rural areas will again be left out from the established priorities.

Besides copper earnings, the agricultural annual growth rate underlines the importance of agriculture and its potential. The problem is that many key drivers of agricultural growth such as agricultural research, irrigation and infrastructure are still underfunded (Kuteya 2012). If we look at the 2013 budget allocations, agriculture accounts for a mere 5.8 per cent, almost the same as in the 2011 budget under the previous government.[39] This falls short of the CAADP target of 10 per cent[40] and has been hampered by other trends: generally, the real spending on agriculture has been far below planned expenditure; second, most of the actual spending in 2013 was still consumed by FISP/FRA which accounted alone for about 93 per cent of the sums allocated to the Poverty Reduction Programmes (PRPs) (49.2 per cent of all the sums allocated to agriculture).[41] Therefore, apart from formal declarations and commitments as to the importance of agriculture for poverty reduction,[42] it seems that the actual weight of agriculture is all too slight in Zambian development strategy, nor is there any synergy between agriculture

---

37   The government, in particular the Lands Minister, has repeatedly warned local councils to stop the indiscriminate allocation of land and prevent local PF cadres from land grabbing (*Lusaka Times*, 16 July 2013; *The Post*, 15 September 2013).

38   The PF manifesto for the general elections of 2011 did not say much about the place agriculture would take in party development planning apart from mentioning the need to preserve the 'traditional land tenure system in order to enable emerging farmers (especially women) to use their land as collateral for purposes of raising loans through registration of individual parcels of land' (PF 2011: 19). Chiefs are also recognized as crucial in the development process (PF 2011: 17).

39   Though with an increase (from 1,231 billion ZK to 1,865 billion) in the sums allocated, due to increased availability of funds. If we compare the last MMD government budget of 2010 with that approved in October 2013 under the PF, the shares of budget by function remained largely unchanged, although allocations almost doubled thanks to the increase in funds made available by copper earnings.

40   The Comprehensive Africa Agriculture Development Programme (CAADP) is an initiative by African governments under the African Union/New Partnership for Africa's Development (AU/NEPAD) to accelerate growth and eliminate poverty and hunger among African countries. In principle, CAADP seeks to achieve at least 10 per cent allocation of the national budget to the agricultural sector.

41   Agricultural development programs (most of them funded by donors) account for 17 per cent and personal emoluments about another 15 per cent. But if we consider actual spending, agricultural development programs are further curtailed while PRP remains almost untouched.

42   See the final draft of the Zambia National Agriculture Investment Plan (NAIP) 2014–2018 (GoZ 2013).

State, Poverty and Agriculture in Zambia   77

and industry (Kay 2009: 129–30). The condition is unlikely to be reversed in the short term. Weaknesses in the strategic approach to rural land and agriculture are exacerbated by other crucial factors related to organizational limitations: mobilization in rural areas is too localized and national farmers' associations in particular are weak and still too fragmented to be able to voice a common interest. Even when rural areas did enjoy government attention, during MMD rule, interests tended to be regulated through clientelism. Even the re-introduction of the FISP programme in 1997 was more the result of pressure by rural MMD MPs than the work of rural organizations.

References

Acemoglu, Daron, Tristan Reed, and James A. Robinson. 2013. *Chiefs: Elite Control of Civil Society and Economic Development in Sierra Leone*. NBER Working Paper 18691. Cambridge, MA: National Bureau of Economic Research. http://www.nber.org/papers/w18691.pdf.

Anseeuw, Ward, Mathieu Boche, Thomas Breu, Markus Giger, Jann Lay, Peter Messerli, and Kerstin Nolte. 2012. "Transnational Land Deals for Agriculture in the Global South. Analytical Report based on the Land Matrix Database." Bern, Montpellier and Hamburg: CDE/CIRAD/GIGA. http://www.oxfam.de/sites/www.oxfam.de/files/20120427_report_land_matrix.pdf.

Bhalla, Jonathan. 2013. "Maize Dependency and Agricultural Subsidies in Zambia: In conversation with Rhoda Mofya-Mukuka." *Africa Research Institute*, 11 July. http://www.africaresearchinstitute.org/blog/agricultural-subsidies-in-zambia.

Bates, Robert H. 1981. *Markets and State in Tropical Africa: The Political Basis of Agricultural Policies*. Berkeley, CA: University of California Press.

Battera, Federico 2013. "Political Participation and Democratization in Zambia: Do Poverty Levels Affect Voters' Perspectives?" Paper presented at the Fifth European Conference on African Studies, Lisbon, Portugal, 27–29 June.

Baylies, Carolyn and Morris Szeftel. 1982. "The Rise of a Zambian Capitalist Class in the 1970s." *Journal of Southern African Studies* 8(2): 187–213.

Borras, Saturnino M. Jr. 2009. "Agrarian Change and Peasant Studies: Changes, Continuities and Challenges – An Introduction." *The Journal of Peasant Studies* 36(1): 5–31.

Bratton, Michael. 1980. *The Local Politics of Rural Development: Peasant and Party-State in Zambia*. Hanover: University Press of New England.

Brown, Taylor. 2005. "Contestations, Confusion and Corruption: Market-Based Land Reform and Local Politics in Zambia," in *Competing Jurisdictions: Settling Land Claims in Africa*, edited by Sandra Evers, Marja Spierenburg and Harry Wels, 79–107. Leiden: Brill.

Burke, William J., Thomas S. Jayne, and Nicholas J. Sitko. 2012. *Can the FISP More Effectively Achieve Food Production and Poverty Reduction*

Goals? FSRP Policy Synthesis No. 51. Lusaka: Ministry of Agriculture & Cooperatives; Agricultural Consultative Forum; Michigan State University.

Central Statistical Office – Republic of Zambia (CSO-RoZ). 2004. *Living Conditions Monitoring Survey Report 2004.* Lusaka: Central Statistical Office – Ministry of Finance.

——. 2006–2010. *Living Conditions Monitoring Survey Report 2006 & 2010.* Lusaka: Central Statistical Office – Ministry of Finance.

Chapoto, Antony 2012. *The Political Economy of Food Price Policy. The Case of Zambia.* UNU-Wider Working Paper No. 100. http://www.econstor.eu/bitstream/10419/81063/1/731514246.pdf.

Chapoto, Antony and Thomas S. Jayne. 2010. "Maize Price Instability in Eastern and Southern Africa: The Impact of Trade Barriers and Market Interventions." Paper prepared for the Comesa policy seminar on "Variation in staple food prices: Causes, consequence, and policy options", Maputo, Mozambique, 25–26 January.

Chapoto, Antony and Thomas S. Jayne. 2009. "The Impacts of Trade Barriers and Market Interventions on Maize Price Predictability: Evidence from Eastern and Southern Africa." MSU International Development Draft Working Paper 102. December 2009.

Cheeseman, Nic and Marja Hinfelaar. 2010. "Parties, Platforms, and Political Mobilization: The Zambian Presidential Election of 2008." *African Affairs* 434: 1–26.

Chikulo, Bornwell 2009. "Local Governance Reforms in Zambia: A Review." *Commonwealth Journal of Local Governance* 2: 98–106.

Chipungu, Samuel N. 1992. "Accumulation from Within: The Boma Class and the Native Treasury in Colonial Zambia," in *Guardians in Their Time: Experiences of Zambians under Colonial Rule, 1890-1964,* edited by Samuel N. Chipungu, 74–96. London: Macmillan.

Collier, Paul and Stefan Dercon. 2009. "African Agriculture in 50 Years: Smallholders in a Rapidly Changing World." Report prepared for the Food and Agriculture Organization of the United Nations (FAO) Expert Meeting on How to Feed the World in 2050, Rome, Italy, 24–26 June. http://www.fao.org/3/a-ak983e.pdf.

Deininger, Klaus and Derek Byerlee. 2011. *Rising Global Interest in Farmland: Can it Yield Sustainable and Equitable Benefits?* Washington, DC: World Bank Group. http://siteresources.worldbank.org/INTARD/Resources/ESW_Sept7_final_final.pdf.

Erdmann, Gero. 2007. *Ethnicity, Voter Alignment and Political Party Affiliation – an African Case: Zambia.* Giga Working Papers, No. 45. Hamburg: German Institute of Global and Area Studies. http://edoc.vifapol.de/opus/volltexte/2009/1605/pdf/wp45_erdmann.pdf.

Fraser, Alastair and John Lungu. 2006. *For Whom the Windfalls? Winners & Losers in the Privatization of Zambia's Copper Mines.* Lusaka: Civil Society Trade Network of Zambia.

Good, Kenneth. 1986. "Systemic Agricultural Mismanagement: The 1985 'Bumper' Harvest in Zambia." *The Journal of Modern African Studies* 24(2): 257–84.

Government of Zambia (GoZ). 2013. *Zambia National Agriculture Investment Plan (NAIP) 2014-2018. Final Draft.* Lusaka: Ministry of Agriculture and Livestock.

"Government Revises the Sixth National Development Plan." 2013. *Lusakatimes. com*, 23 August. http://www.lusakatimes.com/2013/08/23/government-revises-the-sixth-national-development-plan.

"INDECO Critics." *The Post*, 10 January.

Jackson, Robert H. and Carl G. Rosberg. 1982. "Why Africa's Weak States Persist: The Empirical and the Juridical in Statehood." *World Politics* 35(1): 1–24.

"Kabamba Urges Systematic Approach to Development." 2013. *The Post*, 13 July.

Kay, Cristóbal. 2009. "Development Strategies and Rural Development: Exploring Synergies, Eradicating Poverty." *The Journal of Peasant Studies* 36(1): 103–37.

Kuteya, Auckland. 2012. "Analyzing Zambia's Agricultural Sector Budget 2013." Presentation at the ACF/IAPRI Budget Meeting, Top Floor Limited, Lusaka 1 November. http://fsg.afre.msu.edu/zambia/2013_Zambian_Agricultural_Sector_Budget_Analysis_Auckland.pdf.

Larmer, Miles and Alaistair Fraser. 2007. "Of Cabbages and King Cobra: Populist Politics and Zambia's 2006 Election." *African Affairs* 425: 611–37.

Lolojih, Peter K. 2009. *Bearing the Brunt of a Liberalized Economy: A Performance Review of the Cooperative Movement in Zambia.* ILO, CoopAFRICA Working Paper No. 16. http://www.ilo.org/public/english/employment/ent/coop/africa/download/wp16_bearingthebrunt.pdf.

Mashininga, Kudzai. 2013. "Zambia Backs out of Maize 'Deal' with Zim." *Mail & Guardian*, 25 October. http://mg.co.za/article/2013-10-25-00-zambia-backs-out-of-deal.

Mason, Nicole M., and Jacob Ricker-Gilbert. 2013. "Disrupting Demand for Commercial Seed: Input Subsidies in Malawi and Zambia." *World Development* 45: 75–91.

Mason, Nicole M., Thomas S. Jayne, and Robert J. Myers. 2012. "Zambian Smallholder Behavioral Responses to Food Reserve Agency Activities (revised version)." Policy Brief, No.57. Lusaka: Indaba Agricultural Policy Research Institute. http://citeseerx.ist.psu.edu/viewdoc/download?doi=10.1.1.258.4825&rep=rep1&type=pdf.

Mofya-Mukuka, Rhoda, Stephen Kabwe, Auckland Kuteya, and Nicole M. Mason. 2013. "How Can the Zambian Government Improve the Targeting of the Farmer Input Support Program?" Policy Brief, No.59. Lusaka: Indaba Agricultural Policy Research Institute. http://fsg.afre.msu.edu/zambia/ps_59.pdf.

Mwenda, Joseph. 2014. "Govt to Establish INDECO." *The Post*, 1 January.

Negi, Rohit. 2011. "The Micropolitics of Mining and Development in Zambia: Insights from the Northwestern Province." *African Studies Quarterly* 12(2): 27–44.

Nkonde, Chewe, Nicole M. Mason, Nicholas J. Sitko, and Thomas S. Jayne. 2011. "Who Gained and Who Lost from Zambia's 2010 Maize Marketing Policies?" Working Paper No. 49. Lusaka: Food Security Research Project. http://fsg. afre.msu.edu/zambia/wp49.pdf.

Nolte, Kerstin. 2013. "Large-Scale Agricultural Investments under Poor Land Governance Systems: Actors and Institutions in the Case of Zambia." GIGA Working Papers, No. 221. Hamburg: German Institute of Global and Area Studies. http://www.giga-hamburg.de/de/system/files/publications/wp221_knolte.pdf.

Ollawa, Patrick E. 1978. "Rural Development Strategy and Performance in Zambia: An Evaluation of Past Efforts." *African Studies Review* 21(2): 101–24.

Patriotic Front (PF). 2011. *Manifesto 2011–2016*. Office of the Secretary General and approved by the Central Committee of the Party.

Posner, Daniel N. 2005. *Institutions and Ethnic Politics in Africa*. Cambridge: Cambridge University Press.

Rakner, Lise. 2003. *Political and Economic Liberalisation in Zambia 1991-2001*. Stockholm: The Nordic Africa Institute.

Rakner, Lise, and Lars Svåsand. 2004. "From Dominant to Competitive Party System. The Zambian Experience 1991–2001." *Party Politics* 10(1): 49–68.

"Removing Subsidies in Zambia." 2013. *IRIN Africa*, 30 September. http://www. irinnews.org/report/98849/removing-subsidies-in-zambia-the-way-to-go.

Republic of Zambia (RoZ). 2011. *2010 Census of Population and Housing. Preliminary Population Figures*. Lusaka: Central Statistical Office.

Rotberg, Robert I. 2002. *Ending Autocracy, Enabling Democracy: The Tribulations of Southern Africa 1960-2000*. Washington: Brooking Institution Press.

Scoones, Ian, Nelson Marongwe, Blasio Mavedzenge, Felix Murimbarimba, Jacob Mahenehene, and Chrispen Sukume. 2010. *Zimbabwe's Land Reform Myths and Realities*. Harare: Weaver Press.

Simutanyi, Neo. 1996. "The Politics of Structural Adjustment in Zambia." *Third World Quarterly* 17(4): 825–39.

——. 2008. *Copper Mining in Zambia The Developmental Legacy of Privatisation*. ISS Paper No. 165. Institute for Security Studies. http://www.issafrica.org/uploads/Paper165.pdf.

Sitko, Nicholas J., and Thomas S. Jayne. 2012. "The Rising Class of Emergent Farmers: An effective Model for Achieving Agricultural Growth and Poverty Reduction in Africa?" IAPRI Working Paper No.69. Lusaka: Indaba Agricultural Policy Research Institute (IAPRI). http://fsg.afre.msu.edu/zambia/wp69.pdf.

Tangri, Roger K. 1999. *The Politics of Patronage in Africa: Parastatals, Privatization and Private Enterprise*. Oxford: James Currey.

Taylor, Mike, and Dag Aarnes. 2002. "The 2001 Zambian Elections in the Context of Economic Decline." *African Social Research*, No. 45/46.

United Nations Development Programme (UNDP). 2013. *Millennium Development Goals. Progress Report Zambia 2013*. Lusaka: UNDP.

World Bank. 2013. *Using Social Safety Nets to Accelerate Poverty Reduction and Share Prosperity in Zambia*. Washington: WB, Human Development Department.

"Zambia's Revenue from Mines up 46%." 2012. *The Post*. 4 June.

"Zambia's 2013 debt to reach 37% of GDP." 2013. *Lusakatimes.com*. 24 September. http://www.lusakatimes.com/2013/09/24/zambias-2013-debt-to-reach-37-of-gdp.

Chapter 5

Land and Labour Contestation in Manica, Mozambique: Historical Issues in Contemporary Dynamics

Corrado Tornimbeni

Introduction

The province of Manica stretches along the border with Zimbabwe in central Mozambique. Historically, the ecological and environmental conditions of its territory have been generally good, and favoured a number of economic activities stimulating the development of the region. Its links with neighbouring Zimbabwe, through communications and the people's networks, have been a common feature of the province since colonial times, and comparisons have often been made between the two sides of the border with regard to their political economy and historical evolution.

This chapter intends to discuss issues of land access and rural development within the context of the policies pursued in Manica under the colonial and independent governments of Mozambique. Since it does not claim to offer an exhaustive analysis of the 'land issue' in Mozambique, it focuses on the relationship between land access and rural development on the one hand, and the distinctive element that characterized much of the discussion on Mozambique in the past, labour, on the other.

Drawing on a number of research works centred on this area, and on my own research experience from the late 1990s to mid-2000s, I will explore how far the developments of the last two decades fit in with the history of a country in which labour has always been considered more important than land in shaping local politics and power relations. Certainly, the current context has increased the visibility of issues related to land access and distribution, but these were not missing in previous historical periods; indeed, we need to understand them as part of a history of interdependence between land, labour and rural development.

84 *State, Land and Democracy in Southern Africa*

From the 'Protection of African Peasants' to the 'Promotion of African Farmers': Land, Rural Development and Forced Labour under the Portuguese Colonial Regime

The current province of Manica[1] covers part of the territory that the Companhia de Moçambique governed in central Mozambique on behalf of Portugal from 1892 to 1942, when the colonial state under the Estado Novo of Salazar took on government of the area until Mozambique became independent in 1975.

While the Companhia de Moçambique was asked to participate in the process of 'nationalizing' the colony by promoting immigration and settlement of farmers from Portugal, the latter never reached numbers comparable to Southern Rhodesia and generally their economic situation remained extremely weak (Neil-Tomlison 1978; Newitt 1995; Allina 2012). Even where white farmers settled, real alienation of land from Africans was a fairly rare occurrence (Pfeiffer 1997: 104; das Neves 1998: 89–90). Some sub-concessionary companies were more successful, by contrast, and consolidated their activities over larger terrains. Recently, Bárbara Direito (2013) and Éric Allina (2012) examined the rule of the Company in detail, the former more specifically with regard to its policies on land, the latter to its policies on African labour. However, both confirmed the close relation between the two issues, and also connected them to the international debates on colonial politics that intensely engaged European and American milieus, something that has too often been overlooked in the recent literature and debate over development policies in Africa.

The early Company's rules on land and labour were simply intended to promote white settlement and to show white farmers and sub-concessionary companies that it was ready to provide them with cheap African labour. However, by the first decade of the century it was becoming clear that African agriculture was on the way to being a key economic sector for the Company in terms of revenue from taxation and the labour force employed (Direito 2013: 168). The development of big plantations companies surrounded by settled African agriculture gradually gained ground among colonial policy makers and increasingly influenced subsequent legislation.

For example, the Company's Labour Regulations of 1907 included provisions regarding the 'African farmer' that resembled those already contained in the labour laws (*Regulamento de trabalho indígena* – RTI) issued by Lisbon in 1899. By 1914, on the other hand, 'African reserves' had begun to be established in Manica mainly to accommodate the few claims by white farmers about Africans 'squatting in their lands' and to 'protect' the latter from further expropriation. However, the number of African peasants moving inside the reserves remained very low: these reserves were highly inappropriate for farming, while they were more successful in other parts of central Mozambique, where a few European plantation companies

---

1 The organisation of the administrative divisions of Mozambique has changed over time. For practical purposes, in this chapter I will use the current designations.

with big land holdings were developing and African peasants could produce for the nearby markets (Direito 2013: 274–8).

While early Portuguese policy makers regarded the African populations as mere occupants of the land and only worthy of 'protection' by the state, the approach gradually evolved towards recognition of their contribution to the economic development of the colonies. This happened partly because of, and in reaction to, the international symposiums in which colonial agricultural policies were debated, such as the Congress of Colonial Agriculture held in Paris in 1918 and the various meetings of the International Colonial Institute, which raised the issue of state intervention in rural development policies, indigenous ownership of land and the promotion of 'African farmers' (Direito 2013). Some of these ideas, for example, were reflected in the new land regulations of 1924, which lasted until the end of the Company's rule and presented a number of innovative aspects, including provision for land titles for Africans inside the reserves.

Since only a very small proportion of the lands in theory allocated to white farmers were actually under cultivation (das Neves 1998), African agriculture remained fairly autonomous as long as control of its labour resources (household labour and surplus labour from kin-based communities) was not significantly hindered. While reforms of colonial labour recruiting – addressed below – were pointing in the direction of new ideas (Allina 2012), the Company increasingly found that, in order to secure African labour for white enterprises, it might possibly pay to allow and regulate the presence of African peasants inside 'white lands' rather than concentrate on trying to drive Africans inside unattractive reserves (Direito 2013: 294–5).

During the 1930s, new plans for government intervention in agricultural production reached Manica as well. The Company begun offering incentives to 'African agriculture', recognizing that a number of peasants were producing with profit in both subsistence and commercial agriculture and that some of them were also making use of the local labour force. According to das Neves (1998), by that decade the African peasantry had begun seizing the few opportunities for commercial agriculture: for example, development of the sugar industry by the Companhia Colonial do Búzi (CCB) and the Sena Sugar Estates (SSE) stimulated African maize production for the market, while in the 'white areas' of Chimoio and Manica the need for cheap food for both white farmers and their workers stimulated African producers, who found new markets for their crops across the frontier with Southern Rhodesia as well. Technological advances in African agriculture were visible mainly among households and communities that participated in the regional labour migration system, and, according to das Neves, African agriculture responded with vigour to the stimulus of the new market opportunities even in areas cut off from communications and market infrastructures (das Neves 1998: 134). A measure of economic and social differentiation thus began to appear within the African peasantry.

1944 was a turning point: two years after the end of the Royal Charter of the Companhia de Moçambique, the new *Estatuto do Agricultor Indígena* was issued

86   *State, Land and Democracy in Southern Africa*

and envisaged the creation of progressive African farmers (*agricultores africanos*) (DH-UEM 1993: 88). Under certain conditions, this status dispensed the peasants from a number of provisions regarding the native regime in Mozambique, including taxation and recruitment for public works. According to das Neves, in Manica about 1,192 Africans were registered as progressive farmers (das Neves 1998: 141), and some of them may even have limited their profits from sales in Southern Rhodesia in order to preserve their new status inside Mozambique and thus be exempt from forced provision of labour (O'Laughlin 2002: 521–2). Initially, African progressive farmers were mainly peasants who already enjoyed an advantage from their position in local hierarchies, from alternative skilled occupations or from labour migration abroad. As time passed, however, agriculture became a source of wealth accumulation and social and economic differentiation for a larger group (das Neves 1998: 138, 188–9).

In 1953, Lisbon established its first five-year development plan (*Plano de fomento*) in the colonies. Funds were allocated for creating new infrastructure, extending agricultural areas, increasing commodity production for both the local and Portuguese market and, once again, for stimulating the unemployed Portuguese poor to migrate and settle in the overseas African territories. Great engineering projects, from irrigation schemes to barrages and dams for hydroelectric power, became part of the Mozambican landscape.

The second five-year development plan was launched in 1959. One of its main features was state sponsorship of settlement programmes (*colonatos* and *ruralatos*) aimed at stimulating rural development in selected areas of the country and offering a model of 'social and economic progress' for the African farmers. The *colonatos* were organized irrigated settlements primarily of white farmers in which a small number of African households were allowed to settle in small plots. The *ruralatos* were dedicated only to the African population, generally in areas of cotton production (DH-UEM 1993).

In the province of Manica a number of infrastructures, dams and bridges were built. A *colonato* was established in the fertile district of Sussundenga, where other lands were alienated for forest reserves and plantations, as in the case of the upland territory of TseTserra along the border with Southern Rhodesia (ISANI 1968). It is argued that these projects entailed the first examples of real land expropriation in the region, amounting, for example, to 20 per cent of the territory of Sussundenga, and generating a number of land conflicts over fertile lands (Alexander 1994: 69; Walker 2012). In Sussundenga, I was told that in many cases people combined agricultural work on white farms by day with work on their own household's field (*machamba*) at the end of the day.[2] Other peasants were displaced to more distant territories on the mountains, from where they periodically moved on to enter into labour contracts with white farmers or plantation owners (Alexander 1994; das

---

    2   *Single and group interviews*: Distrito de Sussundenga, Localidade de Monhinga, October 2001. The field work in 2001 was conducted with the technical support of the Arquivo do Património Cultural (ARPAC) – Delegação Provincial de Manica.

Neves 1998, 161; Walker 2012). A few African peasants were included in the *colonato* of Sussundenga, but higher numbers were channelled into the *ruralatos*, which in Manica were mainly designed for cotton production. The latter initially met with some success, but problems of land competition and soil erosion soon emerged (das Neves 1998: 171, 182–4).

Despite these problems, in Manica the 1950s saw a steady consolidation and modernization of large sectors of African agriculture. The colonial administration accordingly formed agricultural cooperatives among groups of progressive African farmers, headed by *agricultores* in traditional leadership positions. The purpose was to keep such progressive Africans within the framework of colonial policy and secure their loyalty to the colonial state.

Apart from a few evictions, as recently recognized by Walker (2012), on the whole the African population retained considerable control over their agricultural lands and natural resources. The majority of the adult male population, however, continued to follow the consolidated patterns of labour migration to Southern Rhodesia and South Africa. Das Neves (1998) has shown in great detail how lack of land seemed not to play any role in the decision to migrate. As shown in my own studies too (Tornimbeni 2003, 2005 and 2007a), avoiding the forced labour regime, earning higher wages, acquiring agricultural implements, as well as education, were good reasons for the African peasants to emigrate and then invest at home in order to enhance their agricultural output.

Eventually, income from labour migration abroad, combined with economic and social differentiation boosted by the Portuguese investments and development projects of the 1950s, produced a certain amount of agricultural and land expansion among the African peasantry; it also produced new patterns in the use of land and natural resources that favoured some African households over others (Schafer and Black 2003). Conflicts over land began to occur in Manica not so much with the settlement programmes for white farmers, as with the expansion of land required by the new progressive African farmers to further develop their agricultural production (das Neves 1998: 164–6). Localized conflicts occurred between African farmers wanting to expand into new lands and white farmers only prepared to allow them into their concessions as tenant labourers; other conflicts saw these African farmers reacting against the colonial government when new projects were established alienating territories where Africans could potentially expand their crop-growing areas, as in the case of the forest plantation projects launched by the colonial government along the border with Southern Rhodesia (TseTserra and Rotanda).

This trend grew more pronounced in the 1960s with the abolition of the *indigenato* system and of forced labour and forced cultivation. Certain local administrators in Manica even favoured the distribution of more land to African households, fearing the escalation of violence after the liberation struggle of the Frente de Libertação de Moçambique (FRELIMO) began in 1964. However, it has been noted that the emergence of a consolidated class of African progressive farmers continued to depend by and large on the household labour that African peasants could control and on the degree of surplus labour force they could

88 *State, Land and Democracy in Southern Africa*

mobilize (das Neves 1998: 149). And this was severely limited by the local power dynamics that characterized the implementation of the forced labour system.

African peasants perceived the yoke of colonial rule not so much with land expropriation as with the labour provisions of the regime and the way in which the latter co-opted their traditional authorities into implementing these rules. The RTI of 1899, by stating the 'moral and legal' obligation to work, paved the way for extensive use of coercion and violence to provide forced labour for white farmers and other private employers. Allina (2012) examines in great detail the brutal and exploitative conditions under which Africans were forced into contract labour by the officials of the Companhia de Moçambique in its territory, the way in which the local African authorities were systematically co-opted into carrying out these measures, and the varying responses by the population. The most effective reaction was often represented by migration strategies, while the colonial authorities strove to identify people and control their movements in order to enforce labour recruitment. As the mines and farms of Southern Rhodesia and South Africa increased their demand for African labour from the region, Manica, and central Mozambique in general, became areas of severe regional labour competition (Newitt 1995).

Following criticisms at the League of Nations, the new Labour Code of 1928 and its 1930 Regulations formally abolished the 'legal obligation to work.' However, the 'moral obligation' was maintained, and informally the standard patterns of forced labour recruitment continued almost unaltered until it was formally reintroduced once the colonial state took over government of the territory from the Company in 1942 (Newitt 1995: 470). That year, the employers' expectations came true when the famous *Circular 818/D-7* re-imposed the forced labour system on paper (GGCM-RG 1942).

The system envisaged by the 1942 Circular dogged labour relations in Manica over the following years.[3] Recruitment generally entailed a well-tried process, involving colonial authorities, private recruiters and traditional African authorities. As noted by certain of the more liberal colonial officials (Moutinho 1944), and as fixed in people's memories,[4] real voluntary labour was always discouraged. In general, I have identified the mechanisms of control over people's mobility established by the Portuguese after 1942 as the crucial strategy by the colonial administration in implementing the forced labour system (Tornimbeni 2003, 2005).

Although colonial reports reveal the degree of flexibility in applying this system,[5] generally a 'native' found outside his/her district without proper authorization signed by the colonial administrators on a personal pass (*caderneta indigena*) could be considered a 'vagrant' and thus conscripted for forced labour. People's memories of colonial recruitment in such conditions leave no doubt as to the coercion: 'when someone returned from contract labour, we had a party,

---

3   For more details, see Tornimbeni (2003).

4   *Single and group interviews*: Distrito de Gondola, Posto de Cafumpe, October 2001.

5   See, for example, PMS-DPAC (1949).

because it was as if he was returning from jail!'.[6] Only a very few prosperous large farmers and certain plantation companies were able of their own accord to offer relatively better labour contracts, improved conditions at work, higher salaries and production bonuses, securing African labour for their needs without coercion.[7]

Moving out of the reach of the colonial administration and emigration to neighbouring countries were the most profitable forms of resistance to contract and forced labour (das Neves 1998; Tornimbeni 2003, 2005), but these movements were often cramped by the influence of the traditional African authorities. I have argued (2003, 2005) that their power *vis-à-vis* the colonial establishment on the one hand, and their own communities on the other hand, was the fruit of constant bargaining playing on their role in controlling the peasants' movements and decisions: that is, either steering their labour force towards the administrative authorities or securing it for the agricultural production of African households. Male surplus labour, in particular, was either employed in foreign countries when people challenged the authority of traditional chiefs by emigrating abroad, or contracted as de facto forced labour inside Mozambique when people were not prepared to flout the recognized traditional hierarchies.

The measures on forced labour and control over people's movements were later complemented by other rules reserving some districts for recruitment by organizations of white farmers or plantation companies (Tornimbeni 2003). Many of the areas of the province once considered as 'land reserves' for the 'protection' of African settlement and subsistence production, such as Mossurize, eventually found a much more effective role in the colonial design as 'labour reserves' for colonial recruiting.

In 1962, the new Código do Trabalho Rural (CTR) abolished the forced labour regime, but the local recruitment practice continued to fuel this system for many years. Furthermore, control on the circulation of people found a further justification in the counter-insurgency tactics employed against FRELIMO. The latter was proposing new forms of rural governance in the liberated areas of the north, while exercising its own control on people's movements for both military and production reasons through new personal passes known as *guias de marcha*.

The Socialist Interlude and War

After independence, the new Constitution (1975) declared state ownership of land. In 1979, the first Land Law included prohibitions of market mecanisms to access land and gave the local organs of the state the role of managing and allocating land in the rural areas through a formal structured process. Furthermore, 'modernization' and 'socialization' of the countryside led to the establishment of communal villages,

---

6   Z.S., *Interview*. Distrito de Gondola, Posto de Cafumpe, October 2001.

7   AHM, FGDB, Cx.629: Governo do Distrito de Manica e Sofala, N°6719/B/11, Beira, 30 de Setembro de 1960.

agricultural cooperatives and state farms. In the province of Manica, the new communal villages were established on abandoned settler lands and in proximity to state farms. Some state farms were created in the former area of the *colonato* of Sussundenga, and these attracted back a significant number of people displaced during the colonial period (Alexander 1994; Pfeiffer 1997; Walker 2012).

Bridget O'Laughlin (1995, 1996) and Mark Wuyts (2001) argued that the new policies of FRELIMO assumed the rural population was a homogenous group of subsistence producers, ignoring the extent to which access to wage labour through seasonal migration had become a crucial component for the reproduction and development of the rural economy of African households. Wage labour was extensively pursued in the countryside through multiple strategies, including contracting out to better-off farmers. Indeed, the rural policies of FRELIMO also ignored the incipient economic and social differentiation that had grown among the Mozambican peasantry and rural producers during the late colonial period. O'Laughlin, in particular, showed how some rural producers were recruiting extra household labour, and thus labour could not be considered purely as a residual resource available to state farms from poor households on a permanent basis (O'Laughlin 1996: 21).

Peasant families were badly affected by the concentration of investments and technical support in the state sector. In Sussundenga, land around the communal villages deteriorated and the rural economy was impoverished (Walker 2012: 711). The introduction of local state authorities, land commissions and village councils into land politics corresponded with the development of multiple land claims based on new sources of legitimacy, and land contestation increased. But the newly elected structures were weak on the ground and, like their colonial predecessors, had to seek help from a range of actors claiming the status of traditional authorities in implementing the new policies. Jocelyn Alexander maintained that, contrary to the national political will, it was a common practice in this period for FRELIMO district officials to include the traditional authorities on local political structures in Manica province (Alexander 1994).

FRELIMO's own misreading of rural society, coupled with the international economic crisis of the 1970s and the regional confrontations of the 'hot' Cold War, allowed the armed rebellion of the Resistência Nacional Moçambicana (RENAMO) to take root in Manica as well as in other central provinces of Mozambique. The communal villages soon turned into a strategic response to impending civil war. In the district of Sussundenga, many people remember that during the war large areas were left almost empty: the majority of households went to Zimbabwe, while others moved to the FRELIMO communal villages of Chirara and Messambuzi, looking spontaneously for shelter and land to cultivate or directed there by government troops.[8] Some communal villages were developed precisely to accommodate displaced people (Alexander 1994).

---

8 *Single and group interviews*, Localities of TseTserra and Mupandeia, district of Sussundenga, October–November 2005. The field work in 2005 was conducted with the

By the early 1980s, for security reasons pressure rapidly mounted on protected terrains around government-held positions and communal villages, while the most marginalized areas and the old colonial labour reserves were de facto taken over by RENAMO. In these emptied territories, new authorities were empowered to manage land distribution and access, investing new generations with new sources of rights on land. The legacy of this experience is very clear in current disputes between individuals and families over the status of legitimate 'traditional authority' in a given area.[9]

As people emigrated en masse, rural markets almost disappeared. Smallholder production nearly vanished: people who took refuge abroad did not return or invest in their home economy, and those who took to the bush just tried under cover of night to reach safe areas which they might cultivate for their own survival.[10] Many young people, who until the previous decade represented the bulk of the surplus labour available to 'progressive' African farmers for expansion of production, were instead increasingly conscripted as guerrilla soldiers by both rebel and government forces. Thus, according to Wuyts (2001) the war impinged on the peasantry even as suppliers of labour by limiting the sustainability of wage employment. Furthermore, especially near the provincial capital Chimoio and other towns, or in the commercial areas under military protection, the war prompted the development of an informal economy that steered many former peasants towards petty trade and smuggling. This situation in part accentuated the economic and social differentiation of Mozambican peasants: in particular, it enabled some wealthier African farmers to draw on cheap labour thanks to their control over 'wage goods' through the parallel (informal) economy (Wuyts 2001: 6–7).

In this war situation, controlling the movement, identity and labour potential of rural people was considered a decisive factor by both sides to the conflict. The Mozambican army and administrators revived the use of the *guias de marcha*: these limitations cramped the peasant's options on settlement and production strategy, and people remember them with bitterness (Tornimbeni 2007a). In 1984, a Circular Note from the Ministry of the Interior officially issued Regulations on control of people's movements, which extended the use of *guias de marcha* to all citizens wanting to move outside their administrative areas (Instituído regulamento 1984). By then, taking advantage of consolidated practice, local *guias de marcha* were also being used by RENAMO guerrillas to control the territory and to negotiate their authority over local people with the alleged traditional leaders.

---

technical support of the Centro de Estudo da População (CEP – Universidade Eduardo Mondlane, Maputo) and of the Manica provincial branch of the NGO Organização Rural de Ajuda Mútua (ORAM).

9   This kind of competition was a common finding in my fieldwork in both 2001 and 2005.

10   *Single and group interviews*, Localities of TseTserra and Mupandeia, district of Sussundenga, October–November 2005.

92   *State, Land and Democracy in Southern Africa*

Just as the traditional leaders were informally involved in land management and local administration in the early years of independence, so access to labour in the rural areas for production or military purposes was eventually negotiated with the same customary authorities by institutional representatives and rebel leaders alike. As in colonial times, this fact became a key factor shaping local politics and power relations.

Peace, Market and Land Deals: Time for a Land Issue in Mozambique?

In Manica disputes over land and every kind of physical, social and political resource soon flared when the war ended in 1992 (Alexander 1994; West and Kloeck-Jenson 1999). With masses of people still abroad, the majority of the chieftaincies got dispersed or fragmented. All local equilibriums over natural resources and labour management had been disrupted, and new contestations over land were generated by privatization as per the economic reforms since 1987. Alexander considered the new land claims as part of the general picture of claims upon authority throughout Manica in this period (1994).

In the post-war period, a number of households were displaced by the new 'owners' of lands valued for their proximity to the few markets, communication infrastructures or new development projects being implemented by the government with the support of international donors (Myers 1994). New conflicts arose over lands previously included in the state farms or 'belonging' to the rural cooperatives, as well as lands now reserved for new conservation projects or for domestic and international investors. Only in a few cases, says Myers (1994), did the state authorities favour smallholders in assigning the new land rights.

In Manica the situation became particularly tense as three distinct waves of people immigrated into the province during the first 10–15 years after the war ended: the return flows of internally displaced people or of Mozambicans who had escaped abroad; white farmers from South Africa and Zimbabwe looking for new areas to settle; and black Zimbabweans responding to deepening economic and social crisis in their home country.

Especially in fertile districts such as Sussundenga and Manica, the resident population swelled as soon as the war ended in 1992 with the return of Mozambicans from abroad or from other provinces. Other immigrants were moving in for the first time. During my interviews, a number of land conflicts were reported: some people said that those who returned first from abroad after the war were favoured by the traditional authorities in land allocation and disputes; others maintained that the rights of the original '*dono da terra*' (the 'owner' of the land) were eventually recognized. However, consensus was always difficult to reach on who enjoyed the status of the original '*dono da terra*', as well as on the very narratives and authorities allegedly legitimizing it. In some cases, when the disputed land was large enough, the traditional authorities decided to divide it between old and

Land and Labour Contestation in Manica, Mozambique   93

new occupiers to settle these disputes.[11] Eventually, as noted in other parts of the province (Pfeiffer 1997; Walker 2012), these competing claims did not produce a generalized situation of land scarcity, but just some shortage of wetland areas for dry season cultivation affecting new arrivals who had often been allocated land to cultivate at a considerable distance from their new settlement.

In the midst of this, after the end of apartheid in South Africa and following the radicalization of the situation in Zimbabwe, a number of white farmers from these countries were granted land concessions in Manica by the local authorities, often on former state farm lands, causing alarm that land grabbing was in the offing (Walker 2012; Hammar 2010). In some cases, formerly displaced people who had occupied those lands during the war and had obtained the status of 'internal refugees', were either forced out of them or dispossessed of access to cultivable plots and water resources (Norfolk 2004: 5). In other cases, the white farmers managed to settle without any significant conflict with local communities. One Zimbabwean farmer confirmed to me that his move to Sussundenga had gone smoothly: his only worry was to follow local '*shona* rules' in relating to his farm workers, though he could not say if these were Mozambicans or Zimbabweans.[12] Indeed, by that time central Mozambique was also hosting immigration by black Zimbabweans fleeing economic hardship and political tensions at home.

In Manica this immigration injected radically new dynamics into a society that was traditionally characterized by emigration abroad. Zimbabweans entered the country in search of new lands to cultivate or trafficked in a number of informal economic enterprises. By the mid-2000s, their presence in the borderland areas had become very common and informally tolerated by Mozambican authorities,[13] and once they decided to move towards the interior of the country they were then able, quite easily at times, to acquire provisional Mozambican certificates or more permanent identity cards,[14] a throw-back to the strategies adopted by many Mozambican migrants in Southern Rhodesia during the colonial period. During interviews, it emerged that Zimbabwean immigrants may have been responsible for cattle raiding in the area, and it was also said that at times they disregarded the local authorities and customary rules.[15]

---

11   *Single and group interviews*, District of Sussundenga, October 2005.

12   Johan Fourie, *Interview*. Comunidade de TseTserra, Localidade de Mupandeia, Distrito de Sussundenga, 21 October 2005.

13   António Consul, Programme Officer of ORAM – Branch of Manica-Tete, *Interview*. Chimoio, 11 October 2005.

14   Johan Fourie, *Interview*. Comunidade de TseTserra, Localidade de Mupandeia, Distrito de Sussundenga, 21 October 2005; I.E., *Interview*. Comunidade de Mussimwa-Rotanda – Munhinga 1, Localidade de TseTserra, Distrito de Sussundenga, 28 October 2005.

15   *Single and group interviews*, District of Sussundenga, October 2005

The borderland areas of the province of Manica were thus under pressure from the above challenges when the Government started to reform its legislation on land, natural resources and local 'traditional' authorities; these policies, in theory, were to recognize and preserve the rights of local communities over 'their' resources as well as presenting them with new development opportunities. The reform of the land title and access system (1997–2000) represented an explicit attempt to couple the recognition of community land rights with a modern system of formal land titles in order to attract foreign and national investments: rural communities could have their traditional land rights guaranteed by a formal title and registered in the official cadaster (Tanner 2002), and recently Carlos Serra (2013) and João Carrilho (2013) have examined the relation between the Mozambican 'mixed' land regime on the one hand, and the local land markets and sustainable development opportunities on the other hand. The Law on Forestry and Wildlife (1999) similarly aspired to preserve the rights of communities over these resources and to link them to nature conservation, complementing a number of Community-Based Natural Resources Management (CBNRM) programmes already under way in the country. Last but not least, in 2000 the Decree Law 15/2000 on 'Community Authorities' de facto officially recognized the traditional authorities as legitimate representatives of the rural communities, and envisaged for them a number of roles as implementing agents of state policies (Kyed and Buur 2006).[16]

By the mid-2000s, in the localities of TseTserra and Mupandeia, District of Sussundenga, where a few communities had accomplished the process of registering their lands, as well as being involved in a CBNRM programme linked to the development of the Chimanimani conservation area, it was generally agreed that the recent land conflicts between old and new occupiers were diminishing, and that the land reform played an important role in 'clarifying the procedures to resolve them'.[17] However, local customary rules did not necessarily coincide with the way in which formal legislation understood them (Schafer and Black 2003), and some people admitted that the new provisions did not adequately cover the legacy of war-related movements and displacements. For example, it was not uncommon for people's fields (*machambas*) to be still quite distant from the place where they lived and in areas now considered as belonging to different 'communities'.[18] Numerous cases of disputes between a number of customary authorities holding the ritual power to regulate distribution of land were another legacy of the war period which the above programmes could not prevent. These

---

16 On the ambiguous conception of the 'traditional rural community' which is implicit in this legislation, above all in the land reform, see Tornimbeni (2007b).

17 *Single and group interviews*, Localities of TseTserra and Mupandeia, district of Sussundenga, October–November 2005.

18 L.A. João Gama, Presidente do Comité de Gestão do Recursos Naturais, Comunidade de Mussimwa-Rotanda, *Interview*. Localidade de TseTserra, Distrito de Sussundenga, 27 October 2005.

disputes at times even intensified, as in the case of the quarrel between Mussimwa and Sembeséa over the collection of taxes (Tornimbeni 2007b).

The framework built up by the new rules represented both an opportunity and a challenge for the peasant communities of Manica with regard to their land-based livelihoods. They could profit from the rights to which they were formally entitled, or they might find their resources limited by a number of authorities in a position to secure new opportunities for a restricted group of people. In this regard, a good test was represented by the development programmes and international land deals of the late 1990s and 2000s, when the prospect of plentiful land and a favourable political environment attracted a number of foreign investors to Mozambique.

The Mozambican authorities, as so often happened in the colonial past, ambiguously used the concept of 'unused' or 'vacant' lands to catch the attention of investors and grant them enough land to start their business. Grazing lands and farmlands for future expansion of production by African smallholders or larger farmers were then under threat from the influx of both white farmers from the region and international plantation companies. The latter included biofuel projects, which had intensified by the late 1990s, and were raising concern from within and outside Mozambique about the phenomenon of land grabbing. Post-war local land conflicts between households and lineages were also inclined to escalate if coupled with new evictions by the state to clear areas for international investors.

There is some debate over the extent to which local communities were really involved by the Mozambican authorities, as prescribed by the land reform, in decision-making over these new concessions. In the mid-2000s, Joe Hanlon reported that in the province of Manica at least in some cases the processes of community consultation were serious and successful (Hanlon 2004: 609), confirming what I was assured by a provincial officer of agriculture and rural development in 2005.[19] However, it was also said that in some cases government authorities considered former colonial farms and *colonatos* or former state farms – as in the case of Sussundenga – as not subject to community rights and thus favoured the commercial farmers' interests over claims by local communities (Virtanen 2005; Hanlon 2011).

The lack of a real agreement about the degree of land granted to foreign investors affected debates on these issues. One of the most quoted sources, the World Bank Report *Rising Global Interest in Farmland*, placed Mozambique among the seven countries with most land available for international land deals, and said that between January 2004 and June 2009 2.7 million ha of land were transferred to investors; however, the report also admitted that some 50 per cent of these lands were unused or not fully used (Deininger et al. 2011, XXXII, 62). The extent to which such figures were often exaggerated was analysed in a report written by Joe Hanlon for The Oakland Institute (2011). In Manica province, by 2010 Sun Biofuels, which took over an abandoned tobacco farm for jatropha production, had 5,000 ha of land, while Mozambique Principle Energy

---

19   Eng. Cremildo Rungo, *Interview*. Chimoio, 10 October 2005.

Ltd, a sugarcane production enterprise integrating plantations with an area for outgrowers, had 18,000 ha (Nhantumbo and Salomão 2010; The Oakland Institute 2011). However, the largest land concessions in Mozambique regarded forest management by national and international companies. In Manica, for example, this refers to Moçambique Florestal and Indústrias Florestais de Manica (Ifloma) (The Oakland Institute 2011). A complex situation of overlapping between a forest concession to Ifloma, a conservation area (Chimanimani), a CBNRM programme and a community land delimitation process of two rural communities involved a portion of territory bordering with Zimbabwe in the district of Sussundenga. In this area, people were clearly interested not so much in nature conservation *per sé*, as in the job opportunities it might bring in connection with the definition of their community lands by the land reform. Jobs and labour-related issues, indeed, probably remained the main concern of the rural population in these areas.

In Manica, the local state authorities often justified the land concessions to white farmers and plantation companies by promising that a number of jobs would be created for local people. Between the late 1990s and early 2000s, the new investors did create new employment opportunities (permanent or seasonal). They also stimulated commercial agriculture by Mozambican small farmers through outgrowing and contract farming schemes; however, mismanagement, together with lack of investment finance, technical inputs and, in general, state support, soon doomed these to failure. By the second half of the 2000s, the 'Manica miracle' – as it was often described – was considered already over, leaving on the ground, Hanlon and Smart argue, a number of small African commercial farmers with the potential to expand if provided with the necessary support (Hanlon and Smart 2008).

In 2009–2010, following country-wide reports of land conflicts and failure by investors to keep promises in terms of production, development of infrastructures and job creation, the government decided to put an unofficial halt to large new land grants (above 1,000 ha); on the same basis, a number of land concessions were cancelled, and delimitation of community lands was also resumed after being stopped a few years before (Hanlon 2011; The Oakland Institute 2011). It seems that this situation coincided with the development of new consensus over the proper development model to be pursued for the rural areas of Mozambique. After recognizing the repeated failure by big foreign investments in Mozambique, says Hanlon, the World Bank shifted its beliefs and started backing small farmers and contract farming (Hanlon 2011: 7). The government of Mozambique, in its turn, following an intense debate within the country that divided the political leadership of the state, apparently changed its perspective with the new policy on agriculture issued in 2011 (Plano Estratégico de Desenvolvimento do Sector Agrário – PEDSA), centred on support for African small farmers rather than large-scale foreign investment (The Oakland Institute 2011). Other observers embraced the idea that the small and medium African peasants should be helped to become more successful farmers and entrepreneurs rather than simply being available as a reserve of labour for plantation agriculture run by foreigners (Hanlon 2011).

Recently, Hanlon and Smart (2014) tried to demonstrate that this is possible if adequate technical advice and finances are facilitated, allowing Mozambique's 'emergent farmers' to fill in the 'missing middle' between big plantations and subsistence farming – the model essentially pursued since the colonial period. According to their data and observations in the field, in Manica there must be about 9,000 emergent farmers (small and medium commercial farmers), whose growth has been made possible in the last few years also by financial and technical support linked to private contract farming with new companies or big farmers, and by agricultural finance provided by a UK-based non-profit development agency (AgDevCo).

Interestingly, the work of Hanlon and Smart also shows that where these 'emergent famers' began developing, a few localized cases of land competition and conflicts with bigger investors or national political elites nonetheless materialized in a region (and country) which remains above all land-abundant (Hanlon and Smart 2014). In my view, this shows a striking similarity with developments in the 1950s and 1960s, when the colonial government began supporting a small sector of African 'progressive farmers' side by side with large plantations and capitalist companies, a fact that has remained unremarked in the recent literature. This calls, for example, for re-assessment of the colonial betterment schemes for African agricultural techniques in connection with development plans dedicated to the rapid modernization of agricultural production.

A second factor that reminds one of the late colonial period is labour. It has been noticed that, as in the past, people's primary concern is with labour opportunities. A rural labour market survey was undertaken in the early 2000s in three provinces of Mozambique, including Manica, by a group of scholars from the School of Oriental and African Studies, London. Cramer, Oya and Sender showed that rural (decent) wage opportunities again represented a key factor in poverty reduction (and even more from a gender viewpoint), and argued for supporting farm enterprises employing large number of rural workers rather than simply 'small' farmers and micro-credit programmes (Sender, Oya and Cramer 2006; Cramer, Oya and Sender 2008). One decade later, Hanlon and Smart note that employment is still at the top of the list of rural people's needs (Hanlon and Smart 2014). Under the colonial government, people came to depend on the big enterprises for the quality of jobs available, and the wages earned became an asset assisting the agricultural production of African households. Apparently, some peasants are still thinking the same way, and the wages earned by working for big companies are still integrated in the structure of rural production. However, Hanlon and Smart suggest that the medium and small African commercial farms could be much larger employers of labour than big plantation enterprises, and contract farming could also represent a way forward (Hanlon and Smart 2014). My argument is that further analyses on the issues of power relations involved in controlling the peasant labour force (and surplus labour) would form a welcome addition to the above remarkable studies on the supply of employment opportunities and the desirable policy options for rural development.

98   *State, Land and Democracy in Southern Africa*

In the 1990s, O'Laughlin (1996) and Wuyts (2001) pointed to the poor peasants and women-headed households who did not have the surplus labour, or did not have the income to hire that labour, to expand production onto the new lands they could claim from the post-war distribution process, and thus were further disadvantaged by the new government policies and donor-funded programmes. As we have seen, in the past the control of the peasant labour force (and surplus labour) was often engineered through relations of power and authority exploiting the control of people's movements. By the mid-2000s, in the neighbourhood of the Chimanimani Trans-Frontier Conservation Area (district of Sussundenga) where I did my fieldwork, it seemed that a revival of old mechanisms was being introduced informally by the traditional authorities keeping tabs on people's identity and mobility in order to control their labour force and settlement patterns, on the one hand, and negotiating power relations at a local level, on the other.[20] According to a number of both traditional authorities and ordinary community members, people wanting to move and settle in a new area needed a written document signed by their traditional authority to be handed to the authority of the new place, a process that recalled, as some people explicitly said, the colonial controls linked to implementation of the forced-labour regime, or the *guias de marcha* under FRELIMO.[21] In my view, the rural authorities of these communities have been making use of old and new instruments to preserve individual and sectional advantages arising in the new context of government reforms and international development projects.

This specific experience cannot be taken as directly symptomatic of more general developments in the whole province or country; nevertheless, it does suggest that localized research at a community level may reveal how the *longue durée* of historical issues concerning local politics in Mozambique is affecting current rural development policies in a country in which labour, more than land, has always been contested. Hence, rather than land access, is it not once again local power relations centred on control of surplus labour that provide the key to understanding the current perspectives on the so-called 'land issue' in Mozambique and on its policies of rural development?

Conclusions

This chapter has addressed land and labour issues in the province of Manica, Mozambique, from a historical perspective stretching from the colonial period to the present day. It started by formulating a number of hypotheses and, admittedly, ends by providing more questions than answers.

---

20   More details can be found in a number of published articles. See, for example: Tornimbeni (2007a).

21   *Single and group interviews*, Localities of TseTserra and Mupandeia, district of Sussundenga, October–November 2005.

The Portuguese colonial governments gave up their historical nationalist support for European small farmers and promoted, instead, a rural development model made up of big companies side by side with a labour reserve of small African peasants and a developing sector of larger African 'progressive' farmers. One crucial factor in this picture was the command that the colonial state tried to exercise over surplus African labour through co-opting African authorities and limiting peasant mobility within the context of the forced-labour system. This last feature shaped local power relations and hindered the full development of African progressive farming.

The early years of independence showed ambitious plans to reverse previous imbalances and exploitations, but also showed some points of continuity with the political practices of the colonial administration at a local level. Then the internal war emptied the rural areas and left new sources of contestation over land, natural resources and political authority. When Mozambique started to address this difficult heritage, it also hosted new investments from abroad, and new development programmes and policy reforms on land and natural resources were launched. In this context, the overall fertile province of Manica has again been the theatre of debate as to land contestation and about development options centring on the promotion of African progressive farmers. However, notwithstanding the fashionable arguments about land grabbing, it appears that, as in the past, land access *per sè* is not such a problem. Rather, in the light of my own specific research experience in a territory bordering on Zimbabwe, it is questioned to what extent local power bargaining on the control of the labour, mobility and settlement of African peasants may still be affecting, today as in the past, rural development prospects centred on the bolstering of medium and small-scale 'advanced' African farmers. Building on the few recent studies on the structure of the labour market in Manica and Mozambique, by throwing light on labour and power contestation from a historical perspective, may be a way forward.

References

Alexander, Jocelyn. 1994. "Terra e autoridade política no pós-guerra em Moçambique: o caso da Província de Manica." *Arquívo* 16: 5–94.
Allina, Éric. 2012. *Slavery by Any Other Name: African Life under Company Rule in Colonial Mozambique.* Charlottesville: University of Virginia Press.
Carrilho, João. 2013. "Poderà, o arrendamento, contribuir para a alocação eficiente de terras em Moçambique?," in *Dinâmicas de Ocupação e do Uso da Terra em Moçambique,* edited by Carlos Manuel Serra and João Carrilho, 169–83. Maputo: Escolar Editora.
Cramer, Christopher, Carlos Oya, and John Sender. 2008. "Lifting the Blinkers: A New View of Power, Diversity and Poverty in Mozambican Rural Labour Markets." *The Journal of Modern African Studies* 46(3): 361–92.

das Neves Têmbe, Joel. 1998. "Economy, Society and Labour Migration in Central Mozambique, 1930-C.1965: The Case Study of Manica Province." PhD Thesis, SOAS, London.

Deininger, Klaus and Derek Byerlee, with Jonathan Lindsay, Andrew Norton, Harris Selod, and Mercedes Stickler. 2011. *Rising Global Interest in Farmland: Can it Yield Sustainable and Equitable Benefits?* Washington, DC: World Bank Group. http://siteresources.worldbank.org/INTARD/Resources/ESW_Sept7_final_final.pdf.

Departamento de História – Universidade Eduardo Mondlane (DH-UEM). 1993. *História de Moçambique. Vol.3. Moçambique no Auge do Colonialismo, 1930–1961.* Maputo: Departamento de História, Universidade Eduardo Mondlane.

Direito, Bárbara Pinto Teixeira. 2013. "Políticas coloniais de terras em Moçambique: o caso de Manica e Sofala sob a Companhia de Moçambique, 1892–1942." Tese de doutoramento em Ciência Política – Política Comparada, Instituto de Ciências Sociais, Universidade de Lisboa.

Governo Geral da Colonia de Moçambique – Repartição do Gabinete (GGCM-RG). 1942. *Circular n. 818/D-7, 7 de Outubro de 1942.* AHM, Fundo do Governo do Distrito da Beira (FGDB), Cx.622.

Hammar, Amanda. 2010. "Ambivalent Mobilities: Zimbabwean Commercial Farmers in Mozambique." *Journal of Southern African Studies* 36(2): 395–416.

Hanlon, Joseph. 2004. "Renewed Land Debate and the 'Cargo Cult' in Mozambique." *Journal of Southern African Studies* 30(3): 603–26.

——, ed. 2011. "Land Moves up the Political Agenda." Mozambique Political Process Bullettin 48, 22 February.

Hanlon, Joseph and Teresa Smart. 2008. *Do Bicycles Equal Development in Mozambique?* Oxford: James Currey.

——. 2014. *Galinhas e cerveja: uma receita para o crescimento.* Maputo: Kapicua.

Inspecção dos Serviços Adminisrativos dos Negócios Indígenas (ISANI). 1968. *Relatório da Inspecção Ordinária ao Concelho de Manica, by António A.S. Borges, 1968.* Arquivo Histórico de Moçambique (AHM) – Fundo da Inspecção dos Serviços Adminisrativos dos Negócios Indígenas (FISANI), Cx 52.

"Instituído regulamento sobre circulação de pessoas." 1984. *Notícias* 1 de Março.

Kyed, Helene Maria and Lars Buur. 2006. "New Sites of Citizenship: Recognition of Traditional Authority and Group-based Citizenship in Mozambique." *Journal of Southern African Studies* 32(3): 563–81.

Moutinho, Abel de Souza. 1944. *Relatório da Inspecão Ordinária às Circunscrições de Buzi, Chemba, Cheringoma, Chimoio, Gorongosa, Manica, Marromeu, Mossurize, Sena, Sofala, 1943–1944. Inspector Administrativo Cap. Abel de Souza Moutinho.* AHM, FISANI, Cx.39.

Myers, Gregory W. 1994. "Competitive Rights, Competitive Claims: Land Access in Post-War Mozambique." *Journal of Southern African Studies* 20(4): 603–32.

Neil-Tomlison, Barry. 1978. "The Growth of Colonial Economy and the Development of African Labour: Manica and Sofala and the Mozambique Chartered Company, 1892–1942," in *Mozambique, Seminar Proceedings*. Edinburgh: Centre of African Studies, University of Edinburgh, 1 –2 December.

Newitt, Malyn. 1995. *A History of Mozambique*. London: Hurst & Co.

Nhantumbo, Isilda, and Alda Salomão. 2010. *Biofuels, Land Access and Rural Livelihoods in Mozambique*. Maputo: Centro Terra Viva; London: International Institute for Environment and Development.

Norfolk, Simon. 2004. "Examining Access to Natural Resources and Linkages to Sustainable Livelihoods: A Case Study of Mozambique." Livelihood Support Programme Working Paper 17. Rome: FAO.

O'Laughlin, Bridget. 1995. "Past and Present Options: Land Reform in Mozambique." *Review of African Political Economy* 22(63): 99–106.

——. 1996. "Through a Divided Glass: Dualism, Class and the Agrarian Question in Mozambique." *The Journal of Peasant Studies* 23(4): 1–39.

——. 2002. "Proletarianisation, Agency and Changing Rural Livelihoods: Forced Labour and Resistance in Colonial Mozambique." *Journal of Southern African Studies* 28(3): 511–30.

Pfeiffer, James T. 1997. "Desentendimento em Casa: Income, Intrahousehold Resource Allocation, Labor Migration, and Child Growth in Central Mozambique." Ph.D. dissertation in Anthropology, University of California, Los Angeles.

Província de Manica e Sofala (PMS) – Direcção Provincial de Administração Civil (DPAC). 1949. *N°8805/B/17, Beira, 26 de Dezembro de 1949*. AHM, FGDB, Cx.683.

Schafer, Jessica, and Richard Black. 2003. "Conflict, Peace, and the History of Natural Resource Management in Sussundenga District, Mozambique." *African Studies Review* 46(03): 55–81.

Sender, John, Carlos Oya, and Christopher Cramer. 2006. "Women Working for Wages: Putting Flesh on the Bones of a Rural Labour Market Survey in Mozambique." *Journal of Southern African Studies* 32(2): 313–33.

Serra, Carlos Manuel. 2013. "Transmissibilidade dos direitos de uso e aproveitamento da terra em Moçambique." In *Dinâmicas de Ocupação e do Uso da Terra em Moçambique*, edited by Carlos Manuel Serra, and João Carrilho, 51–73. Maputo: Escolar Editora.

Tanner, Christopher. 2002. "Law-Making in an African Context. The 1997 Mozambican Land Law." FAO Legal Papers Online 26. Rome: FAO. http://www.fao.org/fileadmin/user_upload/legal/docs/lpo26.pdf.

The Oakland Institute. 2011. *Understanding Land Investments Deals in Africa. Country Report: Mozambique*, edited by J. Hanlon. Oakland, CA: The Oakland Institute.

Tornimbeni, Corrado. 2003. "'Working Boundaries'. Boundaries, Colonial Controls and Labour Circulation in Beira District, Mozambique, 1942–1960s." In *Community & the State in Lusophone Africa*, edited by Malyn Newitt, with Patrick Chabal and Norrie Macqueen. 137–81. London: King's College London.

——. 2005. "The State, Labour Migration and the Transnational Discourse – A Historical Perspective from Mozambique." *Stichproben. Wiener Zeitschrift für kritische Afrikastudien/Vienna Journal of African Studies* Special Issue 8: 307–28.

——. 2007a. "'Isto foi sempre assim'. The Politics of Land and Human Mobility in Chimanimani, Central Mozambique." *Journal of Southern African Studies* 33(3): 485–500.

——. 2007b. "'O cadastro vivo da memória'. Community Mapping, Conservation and State-Making in Mozambique." *afriche e orienti* Special Issue 2007: 156–77.

Virtanen, Pekka. 2005. "Land of the Ancestors: Semiotics, History and Space in Chimanimani, Mozambique." *Social & Cultural Geography* 6(3): 357–78.

Walker, Michael Madison. 2012. "A Spatio-Temporal Mosaic of Land Use and Access in Central Mozambique." *Journal of Southern African Studies* 38(3): 699–715.

West, Harry G., and Scott Kloeck-Jenson. 1999. "Betwixt and Between: 'Traditional Authority' and Democratic Decentralization in Post-War Mozambique." *African Affairs* 98(393): 455–84.

Wuyts, Mark. 2001. "The Agrarian Question in Mozambique's Transition and Reconstruction." Discussion Paper No. 2001/14. Helsinki: UNU/WIDER.

PART II
Land Reform in Zimbabwe: National and International Dimensions

Chapter 6

Proposed Large-Scale Compensation for White Farmers as an Anglo-American Negotiating Strategy for Zimbabwe, 1976–1979

Timothy Scarnecchia

This chapter looks at the diplomatic record to uncover various aspects of how international and local actors dealt with the notion of compensating white Rhodesians for their properties and assets. It may seem at first an odd way of exploring the more recent Fast Track Land Reform and the connected politics of race and land in Zimbabwe, but it is an important historical process to consider. Where did the question of foreign powers paying compensation to whites originate? Why did it become such a central part of the Lancaster House agreement reached in 1979? Most importantly, how and why did such a racialized concept become such a key part of international diplomacy and Cold War strategies starting in 1976? On a more general level, however, this chapter may be useful to help historically examine a much talked about variable since the support of the ruling Zimbabwe African National Union – Patriotic Front (ZANU-PF) for land occupations in 2000. That has been the notion that the British and Americans promised to finance the transfer of farmlands from white to black Zimbabweans at the Lancaster House talks, and that the reason why previous land reform efforts from 1980–2000 had failed could be in part rationalized by ZANU-PF because of these failures of the British and the United States to follow through with their promised funds. This chapter jumps back to a period of intense international focus and negotiations over Zimbabwe, between 1976 and 1979, to address in detail how the notion of compensation of whites entered international diplomacy over the Rhodesian crisis in 1976 and how it played out in the final agreements and talks that led to Zimbabwe's independence in 1980.

Financial Proposals for White Rhodesians in 1976

When Henry Kissinger began in early 1976 to shift American policy in Southern Africa away from support for white minority rule in Rhodesia, he wasn't very caught up on details, so it took him some time to get up to speed on many issues.

106   *State, Land and Democracy in Southern Africa*

New York Times editor Tom Wicker, covering Kissinger's new emphasis on Cubans in Southern Africa after Angola, described Kissinger as a

> maker of empty threats, who could not have found Africa on a four-color map before he perceived it as an arena of big-power rivalry, and who persists in looking at it as a chessboard of global politics rather than a continent with its own problems, political and economic necessities and its own human rights and aspirations. (Wicker 1976: 30)

The British, of course, had no problem finding Rhodesia on a map and at times wished it wasn't on the map of their former colonial responsibilities. The animosity between Ian Smith's UDI government and the British meant that there was little interest on the part of the latter in taking responsibility for any negotiations. The responsibility for negotiations therefore fell on the regional powers, most notably Zambia and South Africa in 1975, and led to a failed negotiation between Ian Smith and Joshua Nkomo, leader of the Zimbabwe African People's Union (ZAPU). Following Kissinger's trip to the region in April 1976, where he gave his speech in Lusaka, the main players in the previous negotiations were somewhat suspicious and cautious of the famous Kissinger's newfound interest in their region. Given the stalemate over Rhodesia and the failure of regional intervention in Angola, they all had their own reasons to hope that Kissinger's attention to Rhodesia could be played to their advantage. The key regional players were the South Africans, the Zambians, and the Tanzanians. The British were closest to the Tanzanians, as President Julius Nyerere had showed his relative regional power by committing Tanzania's military strength in Uganda (Pallotti 2011). Zambia was of lesser importance to the British, and more important to the Americans. Therefore the two most important Front Line States presidents in these early stages of the Cold War Rhodesia negotiations were Zambia's President Kenneth Kaunda, and Tanzanian President Julius Nyerere. Of these two, Nyerere held more weight in terms of what he could do to encourage and support further guerrilla war from bases in Tanzania. Kaunda also played a key role, however, in his personal support for Zimbabwean leader Joshua Nkomo, whose ZIPRA forces maintained bases in Zambia. Samora Machel, Mozambique's new leader after the fall of the Portuguese colonial state in 1975 was much less experienced but given the long eastern border with Rhodesia and his ability to influence and exert control over the guerrilla fighters stationed in Mozambique, he would eventually play a crucial role in the negotiations, particularly at the decisive moment in 1979 when he is credited with forcing Robert Mugabe and ZANU leaders to accept the terms of the Lancaster House agreement that would lead to a ceasefire, a new constitution, and elections that ultimately led to Zimbabwe's independence.

If we think historically, however, the intervention of Kissinger and the Americans into the 'Rhodesian problem' in 1976 offers an interesting window to view the origins of the concept of international compensation for either the purchase of white farms to provide to African farmers, or the compensation of whites more generally to keep them from leaving Rhodesia during a proposed transitional period to majority rule. The origins of the concept came from two very different perspectives. On the one hand, Tanzania's Julius Nyerere first floated the idea of an international fund to 'buyout' the whites in order to have them leave Rhodesia and therefore help to facilitate a peaceful transition to majority rule. On the other hand, British Rhodesian experts in the Foreign and Commonwealth Office (FCO) were simultaneously floating a similar idea of a fund that would 'buyout' those Rhodesians who were viewed as incapable of living in an African majority rule country, but also providing funds for those whites who wished to stay on, and to give them an economic assurance that even if things 'went south' as in the Congo or Mozambique from the perspectives of white property owners, they would be able to receive compensation for their investments.

In June 1976 the Rhodesia department in the FCO, partly in response to the perception that Kissinger was taking too prominent a role over the Rhodesia crisis at a time when the situation for whites was looking increasingly dire, began to make contingency plans for assisting white Rhodesian who might be forced to emigrate. Some thought it would be helpful to leak the existence of such plans through the Commonwealth to put pressure on Smith to negotiate, while others thought it a good way to take some attention away from Kissinger's efforts. While examining the concept, the Rhodesian experts gave some thought to Julius Nyerere's earlier call for a Commonwealth plan to financially assist the emigration of whites from Rhodesia in order to make a transition to majority rule faster and less violent. The Rhodesian Department officials were generally not impressed with the Tanzanian proposal, but before discussing their criticisms, it is worth looking at the logic originally put forward by the Tanzanians.

The main Tanzanian document on the topic was put forward on 30 March 1976, "Memorandum from the United Republic of Tanzania; Rhodesia." The memorandum was 'submitted to the Secretary General of the Commonwealth, who circulated it to the Sanctions Committee' (Tanzanian Government 1976a: 1). The memorandum divides white Rhodesians into three categories. The first 'are the racialists and hardliners like Smith himself. ... Living under majority rule will be ideological impossible for them. And members of this group may be unacceptable to a majority government, because they will never cooperate in building a new Zimbabwe' (p. 3). The second category was defined as 'those who are not necessarily racialists, but whose attitudes towards Africans as servants and inferiors have become fixed by long habit.' This second group, although they 'may be personally kind: they may be paternal in their relationships with Africans whom they meet.' The document deemed these two first groups as incompatible with majority rule, and therefore in need of assistance to leave Rhodesia as soon as possible. The third group is defined as young Rhodesians, who were seen as 'willing and able to adjust to the new reality; who can accept majority rule either happily or as a better alternative than exile from Rhodesia.' The memorandum therefore suggests 'The whole of Africa, and the world, will benefit if those who will leave Rhodesia anyway are persuaded to leave without plunging the country into the misery of protrated [*sic*] liberation war.' The Tanzanians noted

> such compensation to people who might otherwise cause problems by resisting the march of history – and who have the power to create such problems – is not unprecendented [*sic*] in international affairs. And in some ways it is analogous to the manner in which many countries pay compensation to shareholders in industries which have been nationalized. In all cases the purpose is to achieve a socially desirable objective at the least cost in human and material resources.

The implementation of the plan would have involved Commonwealth countries, South Africa, and the United States publically announcing they would accept Rhodesians within a certain window in order to encourage emigration. The memorandum turns to the first person here, indicating that parts of it may have come from a speech by Nyerere: 'If all such countries would publically state their willingness to accept Rhodesians who come within a certain period, I believe that they would be making a contribution to the growth of peace and justice in Southern Africa.' In addition, the document asked for a 'Commonwealth fund to finance the movement and resettlement of those would-be emigrants who have no external resources' (Tanzanian Government 1976b).

This proposal, which came at the end of the failed Zambian and South African brokered negotiations between Smith and Nkomo, reflected the serious conjuncture the Rhodesian conflict was about to enter. With an expanded Eastern front in Mozambique and the training of forces of the Zimbabwe African National Liberation Army (ZANLA) and of the Zimbabwe People's Army (ZIPA) in Tanzania and Mozambique, the threat of an escalated war with the Organization of African Unity (OAU) and Chinese assistance, in addition to the Soviet support for Nkomo's ZIPRA in Zambia, meant that 1976 would be a turning point unless negotiations could be reconstituted with even greater pressure on Smith from the South Africans. Kissinger's role, therefore, was to secure South African commitments to pressure Smith to accept majority rule within two years, and to use American financial aid to pressure the Front Line State Presidents to deliver the Zimbabwean nationalists to the negotiating table as a united front. Kissinger's priorities, however, were not as much about saving lives and lessening the risk of further war. His priority was simply to get the Americans out of the position of supporting white minority regimes in Southern Africa should there be further Soviet and Cuban intervention in the region. The Angolan conflict had ended without success for the United States or the South Africans, and he used this defeat and the Soweto uprisings in June of 1976 to put further pressure on the South Africans to force Smith to concede to accepting majority rule. The pressure to get this done before the 1976 presidential elections in the United States and before the Soviets or Cubans were indeed involved in the conflict was the main motivation for Kissinger's actions. As many scholars have noted, Kissinger negotiated in Southern Africa with a sense of urgency but did so with a certain disregard for

Proposed Large-Scale Compensation for White Farmers 109

specific details that allowed him to deceive and to lie in order to obtain his stated objectives (Stedman 1991; Onslow forthcoming).

An indication of Kissinger's blustering entrance into the world of Anglo-Southern African negotiations can be seen in his initial acceptance of President Nyerere's notion that whites should be paid to leave, and then his relatively quick acceptance of the South African and British notion that whites needed a financial package that would help them to stay.

In June 1976, when Kissinger met with British Foreign Secretary Anthony Crosland, along with French and German foreign ministers in Paris, the topic of Rhodesian negotiations came up.

> Dr Kissinger said that he supposed that South Africa might only be able to bring pressure on Rhodesia if they could at the same time offer a plan for the help of Whites in Rhodesia. *The idea would presumably be to try to entice the Whites to leave* and the Americans would consider favourably the possibility of joining in some such plan but they would like the British to play the major political hand. Mr. Crosland said that it would be very interesting to know whether Dr. Vorster was considering any such ideas. (British Embassy, Paris 1976. Emphasis added by author)

Crosland seems to be telling Kissinger, in a rather polite way, that he doubted South Africa would be behind such a scheme. While Kissinger was pushing this concept in Paris, the FCO and the South Africans were working with their American counterparts in the State Department to develop a financial assistance plan that would try to entice whites to stay on during a transition to majority rule, effectively shelving Nyerere's plan to pay whites to leave. Kissinger told South African Ambassador R.F. Botha, on 12 August, that he was worried about the future talks over Rhodesia as 'things may unravel in Tanzania. We have intelligence information that the Tanzanian Foreign Ministry is hardening its line. They object to guarantees that keep the whites there ... ' (Department of State 1976, 12 August, 2). By the end of August, a Tanzanian High Commission document entitled "The Struggle Must Continue," which circulated in London, concluded: 'Those for whom Zimbabwe has no room should be vigorously encouraged and assisted to leave Zimbabwe now and settle elsewhere. No attempt should be made to encourage or guarantee such racists to stay in Rhodesia' (Department of State, 24 August, 1976).[1]

The FCO's Rhodesian Office had already considered the ramifications of Nyerere's proposal and they recommended a more moderated approach. According to the Rhodesian office, efforts were needed to convince whites with skills to remain in a majority rule Rhodesia. Not to pay them to leave.

> Moreover, as Mr. Nkomo has constantly pointed out, an independent Zimbabwe will, for some years to come, need white skills and expertise to maintain the

---

1   Thanks from Arrigo Pallotti for bringing this file to my attention.

110 *State, Land and Democracy in Southern Africa*

economy. It is essential that the largely white dominated agricultural sector should remain efficient: Rhodesia is at present self-sufficient in basic foodstuffs and could play an important role in satisfying the requirements in this field of certain neighbouring countries. If the white farmers left en bloc, it would be a calamity. (FCO 1976, 5 July)

The idea put forward was for farmers and other skilled whites 'to accept the risk of agreeing to early majority rule while at the same time giving Smith's white political opponents a basis on which to rally opposition to his continued refusal to negotiate' (FCO 1976, 5 July). The Rhodesian office hoped to approach the Americans and the South Africans for assistance in such a plan. They then criticized Nyerere's proposal to finance emigration of whites:

Our difficulties about this proposal can be summarized as follows:

a. A mass exodus of Europeans from Rhodesia would be likely to lead to a break down of the administration, the disruption of the economy and, perhaps, to civil war, between the tribally-based factions of the nationalist movement. At the end of the day, as in Mozambique and Angola, an extreme, radical African government would preside over a ruined country.

b. It would be totally impracticable to make an offer of compensation to the whites in Rhodesia which would come anywhere near to providing them with a sufficient inducement to leave: on very rough estimates, the total value of European owned assets in the country amount to between $R 1 and 2 billion. (or between £800 and £1,600 million)

Any global figure for compensation that we can offer, even taking into account a likely American contribution, would be regarded by the Europeans as derisory; and the effect of the offer, therefore, would be counter-productive. (FCO 1976, 5 July)

Even given all of the suggestions that such a plan would be too expensive, the Rhodesian Office was not completely opposed to working on a large-scale scheme to help white Rhodesians remain in a future majority rule country.

During Kissinger's shuttle diplomacy leading up to the Geneva conference in 1976, he met with South African Prime Minister Vorster in Zurich, Switzerland, on 4 September 1976 in order to develop the strategy to use in dealing with Ian Smith. Kissinger, in his typical fashion, did his best to stress that the United States was most concerned with possible Cuban and Soviet intervention, and most importantly that his entire strategy was to keep the United States out of any possibility of having to militarily intervene on behalf of Ian Smith and the white minority. Kissinger therefore hoped to push South Africa to pressure Smith into accepting the concept of 'majority rule' in order to get the United States out of the dilemma of potentially supporting white rule. Economic leverage was one of

Proposed Large-Scale Compensation for White Farmers 111

his main tools in this, and the proposed plans to create a fund for whites was one such tool. It still remained vague to Kissinger in this meeting exactly how it would work, as he vacillated between promoting the economic incentives as a way of paying whites to leave, and alternatively a fund to help keep whites in the country after majority rule.

The following passage from Kissinger in his meeting with the South Africans encapsulates his thinking. He emphasizes that he is not concerned with who ultimately 'wins' in the Rhodesian struggle, but more that should the Cubans and Soviets become directly involved and the United States responds, it would not be viewed as a 'morally' bankrupt position to take. Hence the need for a quick shift to majority rule in Rhodesia.

> Kissinger: ... These guarantees, I hate to say ... What we're doing is preventing Communist foreign penetration into Rhodesia. With luck ... We might be terribly lucky; I'm not doing it with illusions.
>
> If the war continues, even a Rhodesian victory has the paradoxical consequences that it brings nearer foreign intervention, which we won't be able to resist, given our domestic situation. I personally think, even in defense of the whites, that foreign intervention must be resisted. But I must tell you I am the only senior official who feels that way – even in this Administration. I can't even get the Pentagon to do contingency planning. Just to show you the framework in which we're operating. A Carter Administration would not resist.
>
> Rogers: He might.
>
> Kissinger: I believe Cuban and Soviet intervention has strategic consequences that must be resisted, on behalf of everybody. If we do this and the blacks reject it, the moral situation is different. (Department of State 1976a)

Typical of Kissinger's negotiation style, he wanted the South Africans to know that he and the United States were not particularly concerned with the outcome in Rhodesia, as long as it remained outside of a Cold War conflict. The use of American power in this instance was therefore directed at gaining the cooperation of the Front Line States Presidents on the one hand and South Africa on the other to push the African nationalists and the Smith regime to the table in a manner that would either close the door for future Cuban and Soviet intervention, or at least change the terms of the conflict away from the defence of white rule.

Kissinger and Vorster discussed the issue of foreign aid in any settlement plan. Kissinger suggested that 'No one is against economic assistance to the Rhodesian blacks' to which Vorster added 'If money was available to buy out land owned by whites, it will make a tremendous difference. The same in South-West Africa.' Rogers said that this is 'one of the features of this program.' And Kissinger then, now aware of the error of his earlier acceptance of Nyerere's plan of paying whites

112   *State, Land and Democracy in Southern Africa*

to leave, states: 'But it would be a mistake to present the plan as a plan to buy out the whites and send them out of Rhodesia.' Rogers added, 'It's bad politics and bad economics.' To which South Africa's Ambassador to the United States and Permanent Representative to the United Nations, R.F. Botha, replied: 'Make it available but don't force it' (Department of State 1976, 6 September, a: 24).

After working out this strategy with Vorster and the South Africans, Kissinger and his team met with the South Africans again in Pretoria on 11 and 17 September, and then Ian Smith and his team on 19 September, five days before Smith would make his speech accepting the concept of future majority rule. The financial incentive plan was not a prominent topic in these discussions, although Kissinger and his team left Smith and the Rhodesians with the impression that financial support would be forthcoming from a number of donors. At their first of two meetings on 19 September with the Rhodesians, David Smith brought up the topic of financial compensation, reiterating the point that such a fund should be designed ' ... Not to buy people out; I'd like to get away from that idea. But to inject development capital.' Kissinger replied 'That is our idea. We have the assurances of the British, French probably, and Germany. Probably Canada.' (Department of State 1976, 19 September, 30). Responding to the larger point of a fund for whites, Ian Smith replied 'This is important, because the last thing we want to do is force people out.' Kissinger replied, 'No, we want to keep people in, and it's morally important to us too.' Kissinger was well aware that such sympathy for whites would be the best strategy to get Smith to publically accept majority rule within a two-year timeframe. Smith's immediate response showed this to be the case: 'Young people will want to know what kind of life they have before them, or else they'll leave.' Kissinger agreed and then Smith vocalized a consistent theme of his through this period: 'If we're asked to commit suicide, people will pack up and go.' Kissinger responded with humour: 'Are you going to tell the Rhodesians the U.S. asked you to commit suicide?' After some laughter, Ian Smith replied, 'I hope I'll be more tactful than that' (Department of State 1976, 19 September, 31). The overall feeling from these conversations is that Kissinger was willing to offer Smith more than what either the Front Line State Presidents or the British thought to be the starting points of negotiations (Stedman 1991: 119; Onslow, forthcoming).

The financial plan, officially called an "International Economic Support for A Rhodesian Settlement," that Kissinger presented to Smith and his colleagues consisted of the following points (Department of State 1976, 6 September, b). It was to be run by the British during the interim government, and it would provide a 'major international effort to respond to the economic opportunities and effects of the political transition.' The proposal then turns to financial assistance and guarantees to protect white economic interests, 'in order to enhance the sense that majority rule does not mean financial disaster.' This section covered three main areas: pensions, housing, and farms. Specific language on farms stated:

Proposed Large-Scale Compensation for White Farmers 113

> as to farms, again as a safety net, by which a public authority would for five years purchase improvements to farms (buildings, tractors, crops, cattle, roads, fencing, etc.) at a fraction (say 80%) of their value at the time of the inauguration of the new government. (Department of State 1976 b, 6 September)

Two elements are important to note. First, this document worked out between the British and the Americans, and approved by the South Africans before given over to Smith was meant to be only 'illustrative" and the finer details would be worked out in a 'tripartite' meeting between the United States, the United Kingdom and South Africa at a later date. The percentages and amounts offered to whites were therefore not fixed at this date. However, it is also important to note that the financial assistance plan did not specify any direct compensation for farmland, as had been warned against previously by British and American officials. It appears that the Americans had removed the idea of compensating white farmers for land, as a telegram from Assistant Secretary of State for African Affairs, William Schaufele to Under Secretary of State for Economic Affairs, William D. Rogers, of 7 September, regarding the comments made by British officials on the revised economic paper that was ultimately provided to Smith. Their first point was that 'There is no provision for farm land as opposed to farm improvements' (Department of State 1976, 7 September). Apparently there was no major objection to leaving out the compensation for land from the British, as there was no change in the language in the draft submitted to Smith on 19 September by Kissinger.

The decision to play up the imprecise nature of any possible financial aid, to emphasize that such figures were 'illustrative', was reiterated on 16 September in a discussion between the British and the Americans. They mutually agreed to tell Vorster 'that it would be better not to be too precise about the kind of figures to which the Americans and Europeans might commit themselves' and that Vorster

> ... should certainly not intimate to Smith that the Western governments could be relied upon to come up with financial proposals in specific terms. Any figures would, in other words, be merely illustrative, designed to show that if the Rhodesians were prepared to commit themselves politically in the direction we wished, we too would look sympathetically at the financial problems with which they might be faced (FCO 1976, 16 September).[2]

In other words, Kissinger and Vorster agreed not to promise Smith any fixed amounts in aid for whites. This, as argued in the next section, would be the very same strategy used by the British and Americans with the Patriotic Front leaders at the Lancaster House talks in 1979.

The proposed 'financial plan' ruled out the direct purchase of farmland from Europeans both because it would be too costly and because, it was suggested,

---

2   Thanks to Arrigo Pallotti for sharing this file.

' ... a mass exodus of European farmers would lead to severe food shortages.' The report did, however, realize that something had to be done, as 'the advent of a black government will be followed by insistent demands for rapid progress towards a redressment of the current gross disparity in land apportionment in Rhodesia.' In order to work through this contradiction, the authors offered the following plan to both keep white farms productive while also buying land to give to African farmers:

> A possible solution aimed at reconciling these requirements would be a package deal comprising:
>
> (a) a guarantee by the Rhodesian Government of a 20 or 25 year free lease of land to all bona fide European farmers, up to a maximum of 4,000 acres of land per farmer only; and
>
> (b) the establishment of an Agricultural Land Commission which would carry out a phased purchase of European farms over a period of, say, 10 years. The purchase scheme would not offer the full 'market value' of the farms; one possibility would be to offer 45% of the market value in year 5, increasing to 75% in year 15 after independence. The purchase price would, of course, be paid in convertible currency.
>
> The maximum cost of such a scheme would be between £400–550 million, depending on the assumptions made about "market value". The benefit would be to offer a substantial inducement to a large number of European farmers (since nearly 90% of them farm less than 50% of European-owned land), while leaving aside a large area of land which is generally of low productivity, usually adjoining Tribal Trust Lands, and which Africans could rapidly take over. Much of this land is at present farmed by large ranching concerns (often in multinational ownership) which are probably discounting for early nationalization by a black government in any case ... The drawbacks of a scheme on these lines would include the cost, and the fact that there is no provision in it for remittance of profits abroad pending purchase by the Commission. (FCO 1976, 2 July: 7–8)

For as detailed a plan as this was, it would in fact take on a very low priority in the subsequent Geneva talks. It was rarely if ever raised in the discussions there, and when it was raised, it was the Patriotic Front representatives who characterized compensation for whites as an insulting concept. The Geneva negotiations failed for too many reasons to elaborate here, but Kissinger and his team did manage to steer the ship in the right direction, that is, towards a negotiated settlement. Unfortunately, it would take another three years of difficult and tragic fighting, killings, and massacres before the two sides would agree at Lancaster House in London to a new constitution and a ceasefire. It was during the crucial period of the Lancaster House negotiations, however, that the question of compensation for white farmers, or more specifically funds to help a new majority rule government finance a land reform programme that included compensation to white farmers, would once again be part of the agenda. There was a plan put forward in 1977 by Ivor Richards, and then by David Owen, when he took over as Britain's Foreign Secretary, to create a trust fund for whites as part of the Anglo-American Plan. The amount of money offered in this "Zimbabwe Development Fund" was stated as between US$500 million and US$1 billion (Department of State 1977). The Anglo-American plan failed to bring the opposing sides to the table. The inclusion of a trust fund did however indicate that the Rhodesians still thought international guarantees to protect white financial assets would help gain support for any potential negotiated settlement back in Rhodesia.

Lancaster House, 1979

The 1979 Lancaster House negotiations achieved what was impossible in 1976, forcing the Smith regime to finally accept universal suffrage as the basis for majority rule and, given the pressures on Mozambique's economy and people, forced Mugabe and his comrades in ZANU-PF and ZANLA to agree to a ceasefire and participation in elections. Had Samora Machel not forced Mugabe's hand, the Lancaster House agreement may not have come to fruition. Still, the African nationalists came close to walking out during the talks once they realized that the proposed independence constitution presented to them by the British contained provisions to protect white farm owners from state expropriation of their land. As Michael Bratton has recently described:

> On the critical issue of land, the Lancaster House Agreement favoured the Status quo. Contrary to ZANU-PF's preference for confiscation of commercial farms without compensation, the constitution mandated that land could only change hands on market terms – that is, between willing sellers and willing buyers. Although a new African government would lack the financial resources to buy and develop much land, the British and US governments remained vague about promises of foreign assistance for land purchases. In this way, the independence settlement deferred a fundamental problem that would later come back to haunt the country. (Bratton 2014: 52)

Zimbabwean Fay Chung also describes the dilemma the land clause in the Lancaster House constitution created for the ZANU-PF leaders:

> A more serious disagreement occurred over the Bill of Rights, which would ensure that ownership of land remained in white hands after independence. Land could not be confiscated from whites, but would have to be bought on a 'willing seller, willing buyer' basis. The British government made vague promises to provide some money for the purchase of farms, and argued that the United States

116 *State, Land and Democracy in Southern Africa*

and other countries could provide more money for this purpose. ... However, despite their virulent objections, the Patriotic Front was forced to accept this part of the independence agreement. (Chung 2006: 245)

Diplomats who took part in the Lancaster House negotiations have subsequently noted the important role played by American and British promises of financial aid to purchase white farmland. A 2007 BBC interview by Martin Pluat with Sir Shridath Ramphal, the former Commonwealth Secretary General during the Lancaster House talks, reported that Ramphal worked with then American Ambassador to the United Kingdom, former Yale University President Kingman Brewster, to obtain last minute promises from President Jimmy Carter that the United States would financially support land reform. Ramphal told Pluat: 'Brewster was totally supportive. We were at a stage where Mugabe and Nkomo were packing their bags' he explains.

> He came back to me within 24 hours. They had got hold of Jimmy Carter and Carter authorised Brewster to say to me that the United States would contribute a substantial amount for a process of land redistribution and they would undertake to encourage the British government to give similar assurances.
>
> That of course saved the conference. (Pluat 2007)

Ramphal also gave an interview to the Africa Research Institute on the topic of "Sleights of hand at Lancaster House." At one point in the interview, the Africa Research Institute interviewer (unidentified) asked Ramphal why there wasn't a fixed amount agreed on at Lancaster, and whether 'Given how vexed and difficult those issues had been up until that point, wouldn't you have expected a bit more detail?' Ramphal replied:

> No, I don't think so. You are dealing with the government of the United States, the government of Britain. Solid assurances were recorded in the documents of the conference and notified to all Commonwealth countries. It wasn't a little thing. It didn't specify a sum, but specifying a sum would have been very difficult in the context of Zimbabwe. (Ramphal n.d., 162)

Pluat argues that the 'unwritten deal worked' for eight years: 'White farmers were paid around \$35m by the UK for their land, which was then redistributed' (Pluat 2007). Jeffrey Davidow, a US diplomat involved in the Lancaster House talks, corroborates Ramphal's emphasis on the role of Kingman Brewster, the US Ambassador to Britain, 'President Carter authorised Brewster to convey to the British, the Front Line States, and the Patriotic Front a pledge of US assistance should Lancaster House result in a success' (Davidow 1984: 65). Davidow was quick to point out, however, that there was no actual commitment of US funds when this offer was made to the Patriotic Front: 'The wording of the US commitment was convoluted and cautious, reflecting the Carter administration's concern that it might face Congressional criticism for participating in a "buyout" of white landlords or for opening the US Treasury to land-hungry peasants' (Davidow 1984: 65).

Sue Onslow has written an excellent article on the diplomacy over the land issue at the Lancaster House talks. Her work gives much more context and detail than is possible in this chapter. Although, as she points out, she did not then have access to the classified documents that have since been declassified by the British government when writing (Onslow 2009: 72). So what can we learn from the archival sources about why promises were made but without specific commitments? And how did this process at Lancaster House fit with similar issues brought up in 1976? On 11 October 1979, the talks reached an impasse as Nkomo and Mugabe issued a joint statement that they would not be able to move forward because of their reservations over major issues in the draft constitution, which included the land issue. The statement conceded that it was time to move on to the next stage of the negotiations, but the number of issues that the document identified as still possible stumbling blocks forced Carrington to call a recess in the talks. The statement of the Patriotic Front (PF) on the constitution read:

> Except for such major issues as land, the unalterability of the Declaration of Rights in so far as it affects land and pensions, and the provisions of the four principal institutions of government (the army, the police, the public service and judiciary), over which we cannot but reserve our position because they have a vital connection with transitional arrangements, we are now satisfied that the conference has reached a sufficiently wide measure of agreement on the independence constitution to enable it to proceed to the next item on the agenda. If we are satisfied beyond doubt as to the vital issues relating to transitional arrangements, there may not be need to revert to discussion on the issues we have raised under the constitution. (Patriotic Front 1979: 366)

Carrington therefore adjourned the meeting until the following Monday, giving the PF this time to sort out their objections. Roderic Lyne, who reported on the Conference to the Prime Minister's office, summed up the impasse as follows:

> There were clear signs of strain between ZAPU and ZANU at today's session. Nkomo appears to be looking for a way out, while Mugabe seems determined not to accept the points in the Constitution covering land and pensions, as well as maintaining general reservations about the Army, Police and Public Service.

> There is a possibility that ZAPU will look for a way out of the dilemma. But, if we have to face a breakdown of the Conference, we will, in Lord Carrington's view, have a fully defensible position, and we would lose the support of Bishop Muzorewa and his delegation if we give way on this issue. (Lyne 1979: 338)

118   *State, Land and Democracy in Southern Africa*

Lyne's statement indicates that Carrington thought it quite possible that the conference would come to an end on this issue, but as Kissinger had felt in 1976, he was convinced that should the PF walk out, he and his colleagues would not be to blame. It is also interesting that Muzorewa's position is considered to rest on the ability to placate white fears of either losing their British state pensions or their farms.

To understand why, by 1979, the guarantees given to whites had become so important and, in a sense, non-negotiable, it is necessary to see how Ian Smith and his colleagues were threatening the talks as well. The British High Commissioner in Nigeria at the time, Mervyn Brown, who had worked on the 'Rhodesia problem' in the FCO before leaving for his posting in Lagos, made the following point to Carrington on 15 October:

> Ian Smith was still a problem and he had just been in Rhodesia trying to rally
> white opposition to the constitution. If we were now to give way on the question
> of pensions or of expropriation of land without compensation, this would rally
> virtually the whole of white opinion behind Smith and destroy any hope of
> agreement on the constitution. (Brown 1979: 233)

That same day, 11 October, Carrington and the British issued a statement on land and compensation in order to alleviate the criticisms from the PF of the clauses in the draft constitution's Bill of Rights that protected white-owned land from expropriation. The first statement made it clear that the British could not establish a specific amount to financially support the purchase of land from white farmers.

> If an Agricultural Development Bank or some equivalent institution were set
> up to promote agricultural development including land settlement schemes, we
> would be prepared to contribute to the initial capital. The costs would be very
> substantial indeed, well beyond the capacity of any individual donor country,
> and the British government cannot commit itself at this stage to a specific share
> in them. We should however, be ready to support the efforts of the government
> of independent Zimbabwe to obtain international assistance for these purposes.
> (Carrington 1979 October 11: 341)

The following day letters were sent to the High Commissions in Lusaka and Dar es Salaam to help explain the impasse and to ask for the assistance of Kaunda and Nyerere in convincing the PF to accept the Draft Constitution. The letter to Nyerere was slightly different than the one to Kaunda, as it included reference to Nyerere's prior advice to the British that they should try to assuage the PF's concerns:

> As you suggested, we have tried to help the Patriotic Front over the question
> of land. We recognize the very great importance of this problem to both sides.
> But the independence constitution does make fully adequate provision for the
> government to acquire land for settlement. What it also does is to provide for

Proposed Large-Scale Compensation for White Farmers 119

adequate compensation, and that is what the Patriotic Front are at present unable to accept. Peter Carrington made a statement in the Conference on 11 October which was designed to help them even over this hurdle. He promised that we would help, with the limits of our financial resources, with technical assistance for land settlement schemes and capital aid for agricultural development projects and infrastructure. We shall also be ready to help the new government obtain international assistance for these and other purposes. (FCO 1979, 11 October: 282)

A few days later, on 14 October, the British High Commissioner in Dar responded with Nyerere's reading of the situation on land and the PF's unwillingness to accept that clause in the Bill of Rights. Nyerere downplayed the importance of land compensation as a stumbling block.

Nyerere was grateful for the message, he really did not believe that there was now any major issue between us and the PF, and he was seeking to persuade the PF of this. He welcomes the fact that it had come down to the land question and compensation, because he thought this was soluble 'It was not a constitutional issue at all.' (FCO 1979a, 14 October)

Nyerere also indicated that Nkomo had told the BBC that the amount necessary for land reform stood at £55 million. Nyerere

considered this was very reasonable: in fact rather small. He did not know but he thought that Nkomo, who was very shrewd, might deliberately have named a figure at this juncture with the negotiation in mind. He wanted to suggest that we should take Nkomo up on this figure. He was going to say to the PF that they 'should be able to get the kind of money Nkomo was speaking of', and should settle with us on that basis. (FCO 1979 a, 14 October)

As time progressed, this amount would indeed be a very low-ball figure. A week later, for example, Mugabe, in a discussion with the Dutch that was reported to the British, is recorded to have added to his list of concerns with the talks: 'On the question of land, Mugabe's reluctance to see Zimbabwe begin its independence with "a debt of £500 million"' (FCO 1979, 22 October).

In any event, Nyerere, Kaunda, and Machel did manage to persuade the PF not to leave London and continue the negotiations. There are indications that the Mozambican government's pressure on Mugabe played a central role in dropping their objections to the protection and guarantees offered white Rhodesians in the new constitution. The land question was therefore resolved in terms of PF 'reservations' over the independence constitution, and by 22 October Prime Minister Thatcher was informing interested parties that the new constitution had been agreed to and all that was left were the details of the ceasefire, elections, and the transition of power.

The extent to which promises of funding to pay compensation to white farmers entered into the equation at the time is still hard to assess without more evidence from PF sources. Ramphal makes mention of papers presented by the PF indicating American and British guarantees, but so far such documents have not appeared in the British files on the subject. Perhaps they will materialize in the files of the PF or other participating parties at Lancaster. Of course, the devil is in the details, and as argued above and below, both the British and Americans were careful to avoid making any firm and specific commitment to compensation – much the same as they had deliberately avoided any firm amounts when putting forward guarantees to whites in the 1976 period. A hint at the lack of financial commitment by the Americans in 1979 compared to earlier large sums thrown around during and after the Geneva talks comes from a comment made by Anthony Lake, Vance's director of Policy and Planning in the State Department at the time, as described in a FCO telegram. Apparently, at a meeting in Washington on 17 October, Lake told Robinson from the FCO that the US

> Administration was very conscious of the need to avoid giving the impression that its purpose was to buy out whites, or that it would compare in size to the old 1977 Zimbabwe development fund. The sort of thing that they [Carter Administration] had in mind would be for the whole region, perhaps with a figure nearer to the bottom end of the Zimbabwe Development Fund than to the 55 million pounds attributed to Nkomo in a Speech in Oxford for development purposes generally. It would be easier to get money from Congress for a regional fund, and it would certainly be difficult to get money to buy out whites. (FCO 1979, 17 October: 205)

Even Ramphal seemed to equivocate on the issue of funding when he met with Lord Carrington on 16 October 1979. In a heated meeting where Carrington pressed Ramphal to be more supportive of British efforts, Carrington told Ramphal how 'he wished people (including the Americans) would realize that we are not simply negotiating with the Patriotic Front; but that we were dealing with people who were in and in possession of Salisbury.' This came after Ramphal had described to Carrington how 'he had just seen the Patriotic Front, who were in a state of surprise and bemusement. They were hoping to meet the Americans on the question of land, and he was trying to encourage them to continue working for a settlement on this issue.' He said he realized that the Front Line States 'were also urging the Patriotic Front to move' on the question of the independence constitution.

> But Mr Ramphal was worried lest the Patriotic Front should be too humiliated. ... Meanwhile he was continuing to urge them to devise a form of words (he himself had produced a draft) designed to register their unhappiness about aspects of the Constitution, but to accept it all the same. It was vital that this should be done without too much loss of face.

Lord Carrington replied that 'there was no reason for the Patriotic Front to feel surprised ... When he had seen the Patriotic Front yesterday they had simply asked what we were intending to do. Yet they had known that it was not possible for us to move any further on land' (FCO 1979 October 16: 228).

The closest direct evidence of the British turning to the Americans for financial support and promises at the time, as Sir Ramphal would later suggest happened, is Secretary Cyrus Vance's message of 14 October to Carrington, where Vance demonstrates US support:

> ... to help gain agreement on constitutional proposals. I [Vance] have requested Ambassador Brewster to back up your October 11 statement by indicating privately to Front Line Representatives that we believe a multi-donor effort would be appropriate to assist in the agricultural and economic development of an independent Zimbabwe within the framework of a wider development concept for Southern Africa as a whole and we would be prepared to cooperate in such an effort. We cannot of course make a specific commitment and will point out that this effort would be contingent both on reach[ing] a successful outcome at Lancaster House and on gaining Congressional Support for the concept at a time of severe budgetary constraint. (FCO 1979, 14 October: 241)

After the successful conclusion of the Lancaster House agreement, the Americans would continue to point out that the language of such promises had been purposely designed to be non-committal. It was during February 1980, as the elections were underway in what was soon to become Zimbabwe that the British FCO began to ask the Americans about their ability to fulfil the promises made to the PF for financial assistance. The most specific reference by an American diplomat came from Richard Moose, Carter's Assistant Secretary of State for Africa, who had the following to say about American promises:

> Moose said that the original American aid proposals had been designed to overcome specific Patriotic Front (PF) objections to the draft constitution during the Lancaster House conference. These proposals had provided a means by which the PF could escape from the corner into which they had painted themselves, and it had been stressed at the time that they should not read more into the carefully worded proposals than they actually contained. (FCO 1980, 21 February)

To make matters worse, the Americans reported that only $2 million was available for Zimbabwe in 1980, given the extremely tight foreign aid budget for 1979–1980 (FCO 1980, 21 February). In fact, on the day the voting began in Zimbabwe's first election, the director of the United States Agency for International Development (USAID) told a 'shocked' Congressional panel that none of the $120 million in foreign aid for Southern Africa in 1980 had been earmarked for Zimbabwe (Reuters 1980).

122   *State, Land and Democracy in Southern Africa*

Lord Carrington was already aware of the lack of commitment from the Americans after a meeting with US State Department representatives on 31 January 1980. Carrington describes that the Americans left a 'clear implication that little or no aid would be offered in Fiscal 1980 or 1981 except from Southern African Regional Funds.' Carrington noted that this 'would contrast sharply with our and the Rhodesian interpretation of assurances by American officials during the Lancaster House conference ... ' (Carrington 1980, 29 February).

Conclusion

What is perhaps most important to this discussion is to remember that the land issue was not in itself the major stumbling block at Lancaster House, it was one of many and certainly not the most important, as security during a future ceasefire and transitional period, as well as the ability to hold 'free and fair' elections were on the top of the list for both sides. Mugabe and Nkomo were willing and ultimately did accept the clause on protecting white farmland included into the Lancaster constitution as a guarantee for Smith and Muzorewa's cooperation. The extent to which they were 'duped' by the carefully worded promises from the Americans, or that they were willing to go along with these certainly vague commitments to 'save face' as Ramphal suggested at the time, is a question that Mugabe and others would later indicate had more to do with the latter, as they rationalized that they would be able to change the constitution in the future after gaining power through elections (Onslow 2009: 71). Another useful conclusion from the above investigation is just how much race and property (or perhaps racialized property) became so integral to notions of a negotiated 'morality' in a Cold War context. Equally important to note is how little real concern there was, certainly on the part of the US government and to a lesser extent the UK government, for specific financial guarantees in either 1976 or 1979. The UK had a much greater stake in the issue, first because many whites in Zimbabwe were also British citizens who could make real demands on their government, and also because powerful groups in the UK were also owners of land in Rhodesia, so the question of compensation was more than academic to this group who feared expropriation of their properties should the PF act on promises to nationalize land. This group also had ties to Lord Carrington, himself a member of the wealthy land-owning elite in the UK. The Thatcher government took heavy criticisms in 1979 for not supporting Smith and Muzorewa earlier before the Lancaster talks, so the pressure to show tangible evidence of support for whites was an important element of Carrington's political strategy – perhaps more important for the right wing of his party than for white farmers in Zimbabwe. While Americans had mining and other interests in the region, land ownership in Zimbabwe was not a high priority or one with a vocal constituency in the United States. The main driver of this issue for the US was to find some leverage to work with Smith and Muzorewa to guarantee a settlement given Cold War interests to limit Soviet and Cuban involvement

Proposed Large-Scale Compensation for White Farmers 123

in Zimbabwe and Southern Africa more generally. The PF, therefore, found it necessary to find a way to 'save face', as Ramphal put it, and asked for promises from the US and UK for international compensation in return for accepting the guarantees for white farmers in the independence constitution. The Americans and British then engaged in a carefully worded subterfuge in order to help the PF 'out of a corner' and to bring the Lancaster House talks to a successful conclusion. Beyond that, as the record shows, there was very little sincere interest on the part of the US government in financing the transfer of farmland from white to black Zimbabweans. For the British, as long as there was not wholesale expropriation of land without compensation or a mass exodus from Zimbabwe to the UK of British citizens, there was no need to spend beyond the amounts pledged for land reform during the 1980s. If anything, the comparison here between the approach to white financial compensation or guarantees at both the Geneva and Lancaster talks demonstrates the extent to which diplomats used a smoke screen of large-scale financial packages (without specific details) in hopes of pushing one side or the other to a negotiated settlement. Beyond this basic element of Cold War diplomacy, there appears to be little more that can be read into promises to white farm owners or Zimbabwean nationalists once the ink had dried on the Lancaster House agreement.

References

Bratton, Michael. 2014. *Power Politics in Zimbabwe.* Boulder, CO: Lynne Rienner.
British Embassy, Paris. 1976. "Record of Quadripartite Ministerial Meeting at Paris (British Embassy) on 21 June between 6 PM and 7.30 PM. In attendance: 'Dr. Hans Genscher Germany: Herr Gunther van Wall, France: M Jean Sauvagnargues, M Francois de Laboulaye, USA: Dr. Henry Kissinger, Mr Helmut Sonnenfeld. UK: Rt Hon A Crosland, MP.'
Brown. Melvyn. 1979. "From Lagos to FCO telno 859 of 15 October [1979] 'Rhodesia Constitutional Conference.'" PREM 19/113.
Carrington, Lord. 1979, October 11. "Statement on Land (for use if necessary in reply to the Patriotic Front)." PREM 19/113.
——. 1980, 29 February. "Telegram from Carrington to Washington from ODA London, 19 Feb 1980." FCO 36/2874 US Aid to Rhodesia.
Chung, Fay. 2006. *Re-living the Second Chimurenga: Memories from the Liberation Struggle in Zimbabwe.* Stockholm: Nordic Africa Institute.
Davidow, Jeffrey. 1984. *A Peace in Southern Africa: The Lancaster House Conference on Rhodesia, 1979.* Boulder, CO and London: Westview Press.
Department of State. 1976, 12 August. "Memorandum of conversation with Henry Kissinger and R.F. Botha, Sec of States office, State Dept." Henry Kissinger Memcons, Box 18 Folder 1, August 1976. NARA II.
Department of State [US]. 1976, 24 August. "Embassy London to SecState Wash DC 4823. Tanzanian Note on Southern Africa".

Department of State. 1976a, 6 September, "Memorandum of Conversation, Kissinger, Vorster, 6 September, Zurich Switzerland." Henry Kissinger Memcons, Box 18 Folder 2, September 1976.

Department of State. 1976b, 6 September, "International Economic Support for A Rhodesian Settlement" Annex B to Memcon, Kissinger, Vorster, 6 September, Zurich Switzerland. Henry Kissinger Memcons, Box 18 Folder 2, September 1976. NARA II.

Department of State. 1976, 7 September. "Schaufele to Rogers 7 September 1976"

Department of State. 1976, 19 September. "Memorandum of Conversation, Kissinger, Ian Smith, et al." RG 59 General Records of the Department of State, Records of Henry Kissinger 1973-1977, Box 18, Memcons, September 76 Folder 4, USNA College Park.

Department of State. 1977. "Telegram from Davidow 'Rhodesia: Approaches to Host Countries' 9 August".

Foreign and Commonwealth Office (FCO). 1976, 2 July. "Europeans and European Assets in Rhodesia." FCO 36/1883 1976.

——. 1976, 5 July. "1976 Item 6, To Mr Aspin 'Policy on Rhodesia.'" FCO 36/1883 1976 British Policy towards a Settlement in Rhodesia (Including Economic Guarantees to Europeans).

——. 1976, 16 September. Tel no 339 of 16 September 1976 Prem 16/1095 File 15.

——. 1979, 11 October. "Draft Letter to Nyerere." PREM 19 113.

——. 1979a, 14 October. "'Rhodesia: Constitutional Conference'. Dar es Salaam to FCO, 14 October 79. telegram 804 of 14 October." PREM 19 113.

——. 1979b, 14 October. "FM FCO to Washington telno 1406 of 14 October 1979" PREM 19/113.

——. 1979, 16 October. "Call by the Commonwealth Secretary General on Lord Carrington. Notes by G G H Walden." PREM 19/113 16 October 1979.

——. 1979, 17 October. "FM Washington to FCO telno 3234 of 17 October." PREM 19/112

——. 1979, 22 October. "From Hague 22 October 79 To FCO Telegram 323 of 22 October. Reports of Mugabe's meeting on Oct 22 with Van Gorkum, Director General of International Cooperation at the [Dutch] MFA." FCO 36/2408 Rhodesia Political Parties: The Patriotic Front (ZANU Mugabe) Part A – 45 1979 item 85.

——. 1980, 21 February. "Washington to Priority FCO, Telegram number 792 of 21 February 1980, from Henderson." FCO 36/2874 US Aid to Rhodesia.

——. 1980 20 March. "Telno 1175 of 20 March 1980 'U.S. Aid for Zimbabwe.'" FCO 36/2874 US Aid to Rhodesia 1980.

Lyne, Roderic. 1979. "Rhodesian Constitutional Conference" PREM 19/113, 11 October.

Onslow, Sue. 2009. "Zimbabwe: Land and the Lancaster House Settlement." *British Scholar* II(1): 40–74.

——. Forthcoming, "'Dr Kissinger, I Presume?' The US, Britain, South Africa and the Rhodesia Issue in 1976: South Africa, Rhodesia and the Anglo-American Initiative of 1976." *South African History Journal.*

Pallotti, Arrigo. 2011. "Tanzania and the Decolonization of Rhodesia." *afriche e orienti* Special issue II: 215–31.

Patriotic Front. 1979. "Patriotic Front Reply to Chairman's statement of 11th October 1979." PREM 19/113 no date (likely October 11, 2).

Plaut, Martin. 2007. "US Backed Zimbabwe land reform." BBC News, 22 August. http://news.bbc.co.uk/2/hi/africa/6958418.stm.

Ramphal, Shridath. Nd. "Sleights of hand at Lancaster House." http://www.africaresearchinstitute.org/files/book-downloads/docs/Sleight-of-hand-at-Lancaster-House-5ANGIJ6NAH.pdf.

Reuters. 1980. 28 FCO 36/2874 "US Aid to Rhodesia 1980" Kew Day 8 Washington, 27 February.

Stedman, Stephen. 1991. *Peacemaking in Civil War: International Mediation in Zimbabwe, 1974–1980.* Boulder, CO: Lynne Reiner.

Tanzanian Government. 1976a. "Memorandum from the United Republic of Tanzania; Rhodesia." Britain Tanzania Society Bulletin No. 2, July 1976. http://www.tzaffairs.org/wp-content/uploads/2011/10/Issue-2-1.jpg.

Tanzanian Government. 1976b. "Memorandum from the United Republic of Tanzania; Rhodesia." FCO 36/1883 British Policy towards a Settlement in Rhodesia [Including Economic Guarantees to Europeans Part A 1976].

Wicker, Tom. 1976. "Kissinger Out on a Limb." *New York Times*, 26 March.

Chapter 7

Land Reform, Livelihoods and the Politics of Agrarian Change in Zimbabwe[1]

Ian Scoones

Introduction

Misperceptions about the outcomes and implications of Zimbabwe's land reform persist even 15 years after the major redistribution of land took place in 2000. Perspectives have been dominated by images of chaos, destruction and violence. While these have been part of the reality, there is also another side of the story. This chapter argues that the story is not simply one of collapse and catastrophe; it is much more nuanced and complex, with successes as well as failures. The processes of social differentiation that have occurred following land reform have resulted in a new politics of the countryside.

This chapter reports on work carried out in Masvingo province in the southeast of the country since 2000. It updates and extends the story presented in the book *Zimbabwe's Land Reform: Myths and Realities* (Scoones et al. 2010). The question posed for our research was simple: what happened to people's livelihoods once they got land through land reform from 2000? We can also add: what have been the implications for rural politics? Yet, despite the simplicity of the questions, the answers are extremely complex.

The research has involved in-depth field research in 16 land reform sites located in four research 'clusters' across the province, involving a sample population of 400 households. The study area stretched from the relatively higher potential areas

---

1 This chapter draws on work stretching over nearly 15 years. It has been funded by various sources, including during the 2000s by the 'Livelihoods after Land Reform' project, and more recently by the 'Space, Markets, Employment and Development' project, both hosted by the Institute for Poverty, Land and Agrarian Studies at UWC, Cape Town and funded by the UK Economic and Social Research Council and Department for International Development. Over this period the work has been developed by a team, including Blasio Mavedzenge, Felix Murimbarimba, Jacob Mahenehene, Nelson Marongwe, Chrispen Sukume, Joseph Chaumba and Will Wolmer, among others. This chapter offers a synthesis of findings, updating the book, *Zimbabwe's Land Reform: Myths and Realities*. Different sections of the chapter builds on Scoones et al. (2010, 2011) and Scoones (2014b), with new data from recent survey work. This work would not have been possible without the involvement of many farmers across our sites in Masvingo, as well as the support of Agritex officers in Masvingo as well as the districts.

near Gutu to the sugar estate of Hippo Valley to the dry south in the lowveld, offering a picture of diverse agro-ecological conditions (Figure 7.1).

Most commentary on Zimbabwe's land reform insists that agricultural production has almost totally collapsed, that food insecurity is rife, that rural economies are in precipitous decline, that political 'cronies' have taken over the land and that farm labour has all been displaced. The reality however is much more complex. In our research we asked: which aspects of agricultural production have suffered? Who is food insecure? How are rural economies restructuring to the new agrarian setting? Who are the new farmers and farm labourers? And what class and political positions do they adopt, and what alliances and conflicts are evident?

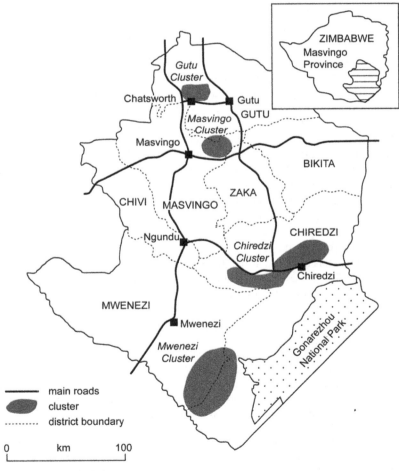

Figure 7.1   Map of Masvingo province, showing study areas
Source: The author.

Of course a focus on Masvingo province gives only a partial insight into the broader national picture. With most land being previously extensive ranch land, with pockets of irrigated agriculture outside the sugar estates, it is clearly different to the Highveld around Harare, where highly capitalized agriculture reliant on export markets did indeed collapse and where labour was displaced in large numbers (Sachikonye 2003). But the picture in the new farms of Masvingo is broadly representative of broad swathes of the rest of the country, as research across multiple districts is now showing (Moyo et al. 2009; Cliffe et al. 2011; Matondi 2012; Mkodzongi 2013; Mutopo 2014).[2]

A Radical Change in Agrarian Structure

Across the country, the formal land re-allocation since 2000 resulted in the transfer of land to nearly 170,000 households by 2010 (Moyo 2011: 496). If the 'informal' settlements, outside the official 'fast track' programme are added, the totals are even larger.

Events since 2000 have thus resulted in a radical change in the nation's agrarian structure (Table 7.1). At independence in 1980, over 15 m hectares was devoted to large-scale commercial farming, comprising around 6,000 farmers, nearly all of them white. This fell to around 12 m hectares by 1999, in part through a modest, but in many ways successful, land reform and resettlement programme, largely funded by the British government under the terms of the Lancaster House agreement (Gunning et al. 2000).

The Fast Track Land Reform (FTLR) programme, begun in 2000, allocated to new farmers over 4,500 farms making up 7.6 m hectares, 20 per cent of the total land area of the country, according to (admittedly rough) official figures. This represented over 145,000 farm households in A1 schemes and around 16,500 further households occupying A2 plots (Rukuni, Nyoni and Matondi 2009).

Overall, there has been a significant shift to many more, smaller-scale farms focusing on mixed farming, often with low levels of capitalization. This is not to say that large-scale commercial units no longer exist. Especially important in Masvingo province is the estate sector, including for example the major sugar estates in the lowveld. These largely remained intact following land reform, without-grower areas being transferred to subdivided A2 plots. Today, there are still around 3.4 m hectares under large-scale farming, some of it in very large holdings. There are, however, perhaps only 200 white-owned commercial farmers still operating across 117,000 ha nationally, complemented by 950 black-owned large-scale farms on 530,000 ha (Moyo 2011: 514). Most white-owned farms were taken over, with a substantial number of farm workers displaced (Scoones et al. 2010: 127; Chambati 2011).

---

2   See also the Zimbabwe working papers at www.lalr.org.za.

Table 7.1   Changes in the national distribution of land, 1980–2013

Land category	1980 Area (million ha)	2000 Area (million ha)	2013 Area (million ha)
Communal areas	16.4	16.4	16.4
Old resettlement	0.0	3.5	3.5
New resettlement: A1	0.0	0.0	4.1
New resettlement: A2	0.0	0.0	3.5
Small-scale commercial farms	1.4	1.4	1.4
Large-scale commercial farms	15.5	11.7	3.4*
State farms	0.5	0.7	0.7
Urban land	0.2	0.3	0.3
National parks and forest land	5.1	5.1	5.1
Unallocated land	0.0	0.0	0.7

Note: Includes all large commercial farms, agro-industrial estate farms, church/trust farms, BIPPA farms and conservancies.

Source: Derived from various government sources, as presented in the 2013 ZANU-PF manifesto (p. 57).

Two main 'models' have been at the centre of the land reform process since 2000 – one focused on smallholder production (so-called A1 schemes, either as villagized arrangements or small, self-contained farms) and one focused on commercial production at a slightly larger scale (so-called A2 farms). Much larger A2 farms, replicating the large-scale farms of the past, have also been created, many later in the land reform process (Moyo 2011).

In practice, the distinction between these models varies considerably, and there is much overlap, with some self-contained A1 schemes, for example, being very similar to smaller A2 schemes. Processes of land allocation, rather than their administrative definition, have more importance in understanding who ended up on the land and what happened next. Most A1 schemes, and all 'informal' land reform sites, were allocated following land invasions starting from 2000. These had diverse origins, but were usually (but not always) led by war veterans and involved groups of people from surrounding communal areas and nearby towns (Chaumba, Scoones and Wolmer 2003; Moyo 2001). More formal allocation of plots happened later, with the pegging of fields and settlement sites as part of the FTLR programme and the issuing of 'offer letters'.[3]

---

3   These are documents providing a permit to occupy the land, but no formal title or lease.

Depending on the pressure on the land, the local demands and often the discretion of the planning officers, A1 sites were demarcated as villages (with shared grazing and clustered homesteads) or 'self-contained' plots, with houses, arable fields and grazing within a single area. The 'informal' A1 sites, by contrast, were usually organized in line with local preferences. A1 sites, mostly with their origins in land invasions, took on a particular social and political character, organized initially by a 'Seven Member Committee', often with a war veteran base commander in the lead. Later these became village committees, and were incorporated into chiefly authorities and local government administrative systems (Scoones et al. 2010).

By contrast, A2 schemes were allocated later (from around 2002) as a result of business plan applications to the Provincial and District Land Committees. Many who applied were civil servants, often linked to the agriculture ministry, who had few strong political connections if any; although in some instances were able to manipulate the administrative procedures in their favour.[4] The most obvious, and often blatant, corrupt practices linked to political patronage were associated with the later allocation of larger A2 farms, especially around the time of the 2008 elections when the struggle for power and the deployment of political patronage by the ZANU-PF (Zimbabwe African National Union – Patriotic Front) elite was at its height. There are large-scale A2 farms in Masvingo province across 110,719 ha (Moyo 2011: 514).

In sum, the land reform has resulted in a very different farming sector, with a radically reconfigured agrarian structure. The following sections of this chapter explore the patterns of production, investment and accumulation of the 'new' farmers over the past 15 years, and the implications this has for patterns of social differentiation. In the final section, I turn to the implications for rural politics.

Changing Livelihoods: Investment, Accumulation and Social Differentiation

This focuses on Masvingo province and explores the outcomes of land reform across our research sites in the period 2000–2013. This was a time of variable rainfall, and periodic droughts (Figure 7.2). It was also a period of extreme economic stress, particularly from around 2005 to 2009 when hyperinflation took hold. Since 2009, there has been relative stability following the establishment of a Government of National Unity (2009–2013), and from July 2013 a return to a ZANU-PF government. Pressures on the economy through withdrawal of international finance has persisted, and this has had impacts throughout the economy. While 2014 saw a bumper harvest, both of maize and of other crops, notably tobacco, the recovery of the agricultural economy following land reform has been slow.

Across the province about 28 per cent of the total land area was transferred as part of the FTLR programme, according to official figures. Much of this land was previously cattle ranches, with limited infrastructure, low levels of employment

---

4   Political manipulation of allocation processes was more common in areas close to towns (Marongwe 2011) and where high value crops were at stake (Zamchiya 2011).

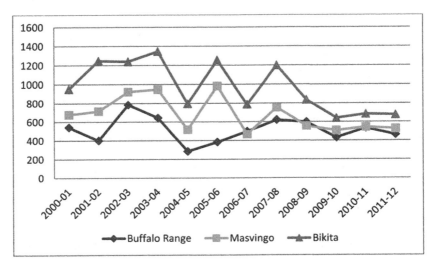

Figure 7.2   Annual rainfall totals (mm) across three stations in Masvingo province

Source: The author.

and only small patches of arable land outside the irrigated lowveld areas. This was taken over by over 32,500 households on A1 sites (making up 1.2 m hectares) and about 1,200 households in A2 areas (making up 371,500 hectares), alongside perhaps a further 8,500 households in 'informal' resettlement sites where 'offer letters' had not been issued. Although there is much variation, the average size of new A2 farms is 318 hectares, while that of A1 family farms is 37 hectares, including crop and grazing land. At the same time one million hectares (18.3 per cent of the province) remains as large-scale commercial operations, including some very large farms, wildlife conservancies and estates in the lowveld that remained largely intact (Scoones et al. 2010: 32–3).

Table 7.2 offers an overview of the socio-economic characteristics of the different sites in our study, presented in relation to the four districts and the four different types of resettlement 'scheme', highlighting the diversity of contexts, livelihood assets and strategies. The data come from 2010–11, after the stabilization of the economy and a decade after the land reform, but at a time of low rainfall and sequential droughts (cf. earlier 2009 data in Scoones et al. 2010).

This radical transformation of land and livelihoods has resulted in a new composition of people in the rural areas, with diverse livelihood strategies. This has major implications for rural politics as explored in the final section of this chapter. In 2008 we undertook a 'success ranking' exercise in all 16 sites. This involved a group of farmers from the area ranking all households according to their own criteria of success. A number of broad categories of livelihood strategy emerged from these investigations – following Dorward (2009) and Mushongah (2009). These are listed in Table 7.3.

Table 7.2　A socio-economic profile of the study sites (average amounts across survey households)

| Cluster | Gutu | | | Masvingo | | | Chiredzi | | Mwenezi | | |
Scheme type	A1 self-contained	A1 villagized	A2	A1 self-contained	A1 villagized	A2	A1, previously Informal	A2	A1 villagized	A1 informal	A2
N=	42	29	14	39	116	4	53	29	22	23	7
Age of household head	50	47	56	52	50	53	53	55	45	42	45
Educational level of household head	Form 2	Form 2	Form 3 or higher	Form 2	Form 2	Form 3 or higher	Grade 7	Form 3 or higher	Grade 7	Grade 7	Form 2
Land holding (ha) per household	13.3	2.3	95.1	35.1	8	80.5	7.4	37.6	7.4	8	868.7
Area cropped/ploughed (ha) 2010 per household	3.6	2.7	4.1	9.2	3.7	20.5	4.7	10.4	6.2	6.1	1.7
Area cropped 2011 per household	3.5	2.5	3.6	8.2	3.6	2.5	4.3	9.1	6.2	6.1	2.1
Cattle owned (nos) per household	6.3	6.6	30.1	12.8	5.7	13.3	4.91	13.2	9.5	9	63.9
Maize output in 2011 kg per household	1158	1267.2	1185.7	2911.5	718.5	4550	85	853.5	413.6	60.9	35.7
Sales (GMB and local) in kg in 2011 per household	126.2	143.1	35.7	928.2	81	2737.5	2.8	115.5	50	0	71.4
Maize output in 2010 kg per household	1349	1210.3	1764.3	4202.6	971.6	4525	1476.4	1405.2	418.2	420.4	500
Sales (GMB and local in kg in 2010) per household	1349	1210.3	1764.3	1485.9	234.1	2150	544.3	965.5	63.6	3.9	0
Percent owning a scotch cart	40.5%	44.8%	28.6%	79.5%	51.7%	75.0%	54.7%	55.2%	50.0%	39.1%	14.3%
House type (percent with tin/asbestos roof)	35.7%	55.2%	71.4%	59.0%	44.0%	50.0%	47.2%	86.2%	27.6%	4.3%	71.4%
% receiving remittance	19.1%	6.7%	0%	20.5%	28.0%	0%	10.5%	27.6%	51.8%	34.6%	33.3%

Source: Sample census, 2011–12 across 400 households.

134 *State, Land and Democracy in Southern Africa*

Table 7.3   Livelihood strategies in Masvingo province

Category	Livelihood Strategy	Proportion of Households
Dropping out (10.0%)	Exit – leaving the plot	4.4%
	Chronically poor, local labour	3.3%
	Ill health affecting farming	2.2%
Hanging in (33.6%)	Asset poor farming, local labour	17.8%
	Keeping the plot for the future	10.3%
	Straddling across resettlement and communal areas	5.6%
Stepping out (21.4%)	Survival diversification	2.8%
	Local off-farm activities plus farming	5.3%
	Remittances from within Zimbabwe plus farming	5.0%
	Remittances from outside Zimbabwe plus farming	4.4%
	Cell phone farmers	3.9%
Stepping up (35.0%)	*Hurudza* – the 'real' farmers	18.3%
	Part-time farmers	10.6%
	New (semi-)commercial farmers	4.7%
	Farming from patronage	1.4%

Source: Summarized from Scoones et al. (2010: 228–9); see also Scoones et al. (2012a).

Over half the 400 sample households – across A1, A2 and informal resettlement sites – were either 'stepping up' – accumulating assets and regularly producing crops for sale – or 'stepping out' – successfully diversifying off-farm. These households were accumulating and investing, often employing labour and improving their farming operations, despite the many difficulties being faced. But not everyone has been successful. Some were really struggling and only just 'hanging in'; others were in the process of 'dropping out', through a combination of chronic poverty and ill health.

Others without start-up assets have been unable to accumulate, and have continued to live in poverty, reliant on the support of relatives and friends. Some have joined a growing labour force on the new farms, abandoning their plots in favour of often poorly paid employment. Within the 'stepping out' category, some are surviving off illegal, unsafe or transient activities that allowed survival but little else. Still others are straddling across two farms – one in the communal area and one in the new resettlement – and not really investing in the new areas, while some are simply keeping the plot for sons or other relatives.

Overall, in our study sites there is thus a core group of 'middle farmers' – around half of the population – who are successful not because of patronage support,

Land Reform, Livelihoods and the Politics of Agrarian Change in Zimbabwe   135

but because of hard graft. They can be classified as successful 'petty commodity producers' and 'worker peasants' who are gaining surpluses from farming, investing in the land from off-farm work and so are able to 'accumulate from below' (Scoones et al. 2010; cf. Cousins 2010). This is, as discussed below, having a positive impact on the wider economy, including stimulating demand for services, consumption goods and labour. This group is also significant in terms of political dynamics, as new farmers on the resettlements become a potentially important political force.

Who Got the Land?

Who got the land and what is the profile of the new settlers? Our study from Masvingo province showed by far the majority of the new settlers are 'ordinary' people (Table 7.4); those who had little or very poor land in the communal areas or were unemployed or with poorly paid jobs and living in town. About half of all new settler households were from nearby communal areas and another 18 per cent from urban areas. These people joined the invasions because they needed land, and thought that the new resettlements would provide new livelihood opportunities. As discussed further below, this was not a politically organized grouping with strong connections to ZANU-PF. The remaining third of household heads was made up of civil servants (16.5 per cent overall, but increasing to around a quarter of all settlers in A1 self-contained and A2 sites), business people (4.8 per cent overall, but again proportionately higher in the A1 self-contained and A2 sites), security service personnel (3.7 per cent overall, employed by the police, army and intelligence organization) and former farm workers (6.7 per cent overall).

Table 7.4   Settler profiles across schemes

	A1 villagized	A1 self-contained	Informal	A2	Total
"Ordinary": from other rural areas	59.9	39.2	69.7	12.2	49.9
"Ordinary": from urban areas	9.4	18.9	22.6	43.8	18.3
Civil servant	12.5	28.3	3.8	26.3	16.5
Security services	3.6	5.4	3.8	1.8	3.7
Business person	3.1	8.2	0	10.5	4.8
Former farm worker	11.5	0	0	5.3	6.7
N	192	74	53	57	376

Source: Census data, 2007–08 (N=376), including all sites (Scoones et al. 2010: 53).

Former farm workers made up 11.5 per cent of households in the A1 villagized sites, with many taking an active role in the land invasions. In one case a farm worker organized and led the invasion of the farm where he had worked. This reflects the extent and nature of labour on the former large-scale farms in Masvingo province. Unlike in the Highveld farms, where large, resident labour forces existed without nearby communal homes (Chambati 2011), our Masvingo study sites were often formerly large-scale ranches where labour was limited, and workers came, often on a temporary basis, from nearby communal areas.

Across all of these categories are 'war veterans.' As household heads they make up 8.8 per cent of the total population. The category 'war veteran' is however a diverse and again perhaps a misleading one. Prior to the land invasions, most were farming in the communal areas, a few were living in town, while some were civil servants, business people and employees in the security services. At the time of the land invasions in 2000, many indeed had long dropped their 'war veteran' identity and had been poor, small-scale farmers in the communal areas for 20 years since the end of the liberation war. Those who led the land invasions were often able to secure land in the A1 self-contained plots, but many were sidelined in the allocation of larger A2 farms. However, most were not well connected politically before 2000, although through the Zimbabwe National Liberation War Veterans Association, they became so and part of the political drive towards land reform, although with multiple disputes with the party leadership (Sadomba 2011).

Land was allocated unevenly to men and women. In most cases it is men whose names appear on the 'offer letters', the permits originally issued to new settlers by the government. Yet women were important players in the land invasions, providing support to the base camps during the '*jambanja*' land invasions period, and subsequently investing in the development of new homes and farms. However, across our sample only 12 per cent of households had a woman named as the land holder on the permit. The highest proportion of female-headed households was in the informal settlements, as women often saw the land invasions as an opportunity to make a new independent life and escape abusive relationships or accusations of witchcraft, for example.

Who amongst these groups are the so-called 'cronies' of the ruling party, well-connected to the machinery of the state and able to gain advantage? Those able to gain land through patronage included those who grabbed often large farms around the elections in 2008, as well as some of the A2 farmers able to manipulate the system. Many are absentee land owners – so-called 'cell phone farmers' – presiding over often underutilized land, perhaps with a decaying new tractor in the farmyard. Yet, despite their disproportionate influence on local politics (see below), they are few and far between, making up around 5 per cent of the total population in our study areas (Table 7.3) on around 10 per cent of the new resettlement land area.

How much land did each of these groups get? Table 7.5 shows land allocated, cleared and ploughed in 2011 for each of the scheme types. For the A1 villagized and informal sites, the area measurements refer only to arable land, while for the other sites it represents the whole allocation to the households. The data shows

Land Reform, Livelihoods and the Politics of Agrarian Change in Zimbabwe 137

that, for each of the scheme types, so-called 'ordinary' settlers did not receive any less land than other groups; in some cases more. Business people and civil servants were able to clear more land in most instances, due to access to resources to hire labour. Those linked to the security services – the group most likely to be associated with the political-military elite – received marginally more land than the average in the A1 self-contained and informal sites, but less in other sites.

Table 7.5   Land owned and cleared

Scheme type	Area allocated Average/household (ha)	Area cleared 2011 Average/household (ha)	Area ploughed 2011 Average/household (ha)
A1 villagized	4.42	3.42	3.80
A1 self-contained	23.72	7.77	5.74
A2	64.18	18.63	8.79
Informal	7.45	5.27	5.05

Source: Census data 2011–12.

The land reform has thus involved diverse people with multiple affiliations. Being influential in the land invasions, war veterans often managed to secure better plots, although not always larger ones.[5] While the land invasions clearly became highly politicized, and the atmosphere of the 'base camps' on the invaded farms was tightly ordered and politically controlled (Chaumba, Scoones and Wolmer 2003), those who ultimately benefitted were much more diverse than those with close political ties. Again, as discussed above, who got the land in the A1 sites very much depended on the very particular dynamics of an individual invasion, who was leading it and how contested the farm was.

The large group of civil servants, particularly on the A2 plots – and in our sample especially in the sugar estates – were often teachers, agricultural extension workers and local government officials. While not being poor and landless from the communal areas, most could not be regarded as elite, nor particularly well-connected politically. Indeed, in simple financial terms many were extremely poor, as government wages had effectively ceased during the economic crisis to 2009.

The net result is a new mix of people in the new resettlements. In the A2 schemes, for example, 46.5 per cent of new farmers have a 'Master Farmer' certificate,[6] while in the A1 self-contained schemes 17.6 per cent do. 91.6 per

---

5   War veterans had land areas above the average in the A1 villagized schemes only (at 6.8 ha). In all other instances their land holdings were actually on average marginally lower than the average.

6   A quite rigorous agricultural qualification, the result of training by the Ministry of Agriculture's extension arm.

138 *State, Land and Democracy in Southern Africa*

cent of A2 farmers had at least three years of secondary schooling, while this proportion is 71.6 per cent and 44.8 per cent in the A1 self-contained and villagized schemes respectively. The new resettlements are dominated by a new, younger generation of farmers. On settlement most were under 50 in the A1 schemes. A2 schemes are dominated by the over 50s, but often include people with significant experience and connections. That overall 18.3 per cent of households came from urban areas (increasing to 43.8 per cent in the A2 schemes) is significant too, as connections to town have proved important in gaining access to services and support in the absence of official programmes in the rural areas. These backgrounds, experiences, educational profiles, affiliations and connections have major influences on the new politics of the countryside, as discussed below. The new resettlements are therefore not a replication of the 1980s resettlement schemes or an extension of the communal areas, nor are they simply scaled-down version of large-scale commercial farms. Instead, a very different social, economic and political dynamic is unfolding, one that has multiple potentials, as well as challenges.

Investment on the Land

In developing their farms, most new farmers have had to start from scratch. For the most part the Masvingo study sites were ranches: large expanses of bush grazing, with limited infrastructure. There were scattered homesteads, a few workers' cottages, the odd dip tank, small dam and irrigation plot, but not much else. But, within a remarkably short time, people began to invest in earnest. There was an urgency: fields had to be prepared for planting, structures had to be built for cattle to be kraaled in, granaries had to be erected for the harvests to be stored, and homes had to be put up for growing numbers of people to live in.

A peopled landscape of houses, fields, paths and roads soon emerged. Human population densities increased significantly and livestock populations grew. Stocking densities on beef ranches were recommended to be around one animal per ten hectares; now much larger livestock populations exist, combining cattle with goats, sheep, donkeys, pigs and poultry. Investment in stock has been significant, with cattle populations in particular growing rapidly, especially in the A1 sites.

One of the major tasks facing new settlers has been clearing land (Table 7.5). In addition, people have constructed numerous gardens, all of which have required investment in fencing. In addition, people have dug wells, built small dams, planted trees and dug soil conservation works. Investment in fields was complemented by investment in farm equipment, with ploughs, cultivators, pumps and scotch carts purchased in numbers. Building has also been extensive in the new resettlements. Some structures remain built of pole and mud, however, after a year or two, when people's sense of tenure security had increased, buildings using bricks, cement and

Land Reform, Livelihoods and the Politics of Agrarian Change in Zimbabwe 139

tin/asbestos roofing increased. Some very elaborate homes have been built with the very best materials imported from South Africa.

Transport has been a major constraint on the new resettlements. With no roads and poor connections to urban areas, there were often no forms of public transport available. This was compounded by the economic crisis, as many operators closed down routes. This had a severe impact. Lack of access to services – shops, schools, clinics – and markets meant that people suffered. Investing in a means of transport was often a major priority. Bicycles in particular were bought in large numbers, but also cars, pick-ups and trucks.

What is the value of all this investment? A simple set of calculations that compute the cost of labour and materials used or the replacement cost of the particular item show that, on average, each household had invested US$2,161 in a variety of items in the period from settlement to 2008 and a further $1,491/$2,293 in the period to 2012 (Table 7.6).

Table 7.6   The value of investments in the new resettlements: from settlement to 2008, and from 2008 to 2012

Focus of investment	Settlement to 2008 Average per household (US$) at standardized 2009 prices	2008–2012 Average per household (US$) at standardized 2009 prices
Land clearance	385	–
Housing/buildings	631	684
Cattle	612	247 (purchase), all increases 961
Farm equipment	198	271
Transport	150	320 (232 excluding tractors)
Toilets	77	51
Garden fencing	29	–
Wells	79	57
Total	**$2,161**	**$1,491 to $2,293**

Source: Scoones (2014a)

This is of course only a small subset of the total, as such private investment does not account for investments at the community level. Across our sites, churches have been established, schools have been built, roads cut and areas for shops carved out as part of community efforts. Labour and materials have been mobilized without any external help. In the A1 sites in particular this highly-motivated and well-organized pattern of self-help has dominated (cf. Murisa 2011). While the state has been present, it has not always provided assistance. The re-planning of village and field sites was resented by many, as the land use

140 *State, Land and Democracy in Southern Africa*

planning models dating from the 1930s were re-imposed, with fields removed from near rivers and streams and villages placed on the ridges far from water sources. Planning laws were also invoked in the destruction of nascent business centres as part of Operation Murambatsvina (Potts 2008).

Thus with limited state support and without the projects of donors and NGOs – and significantly without formal title or leasehold tenure – the new settlers have invested at scale.

Farm Production

A recurrent myth about Zimbabwe's land reform is that it has resulted in agricultural collapse, precipitating widespread and recurrent food insecurity. There is little doubt that the agricultural sector has been transformed, as discussed above, but our data show that there has been surprising resilience in production.

We tracked maize production on all 400 farms in our sample now over 11 seasons from 2002–03. Table 7.7 indicates the proportion of households who produced more than a tonne (sufficient to feed a family). The data shows an increase in output in the early years, as farms became established, and draft power and other inputs were sourced, but variability since then as droughts hit and the economy collapsed (especially in the mid-2000s). Production levels of maize are inevitably lowest in the drier regions, although food security is enhanced by a greater production of small grains, such as sorghum and millet.

To complement grain production, cotton production has boomed in some sites. This is particular so in Uswaushava in the Nuanetsi ranch. Here cotton production has increased significantly (Figure 7.3). Cotton sales provide significant cash income for nearly all households. Six different private cotton companies operate in the area, supplying credit, inputs and marketing support – allowing cotton producers to access inputs and other support through other means. New cotton gins have opened up too, creating employment further up the value chain.

Table 7.7   Percentage of farmers harvesting greater than a tonne of maize

District	Scheme Type	2002–3	2003–4	2004–5	2005–6	2006–7	2007–8	2008–9	2009–10	2010–11	2011–12	2012–13	Average
Gutu	A1 self-contained	18.4	50.0	45.5	75.0	63.4	28.6	61.5	38.1	42.9	48.8	34.1	46.0
	A1 villagized	13.3	39.1	24.0	79.3	63.3	36.7	78.6	37.9	48.3	34.5	24.1	43.6
	A2	0.0	0.0	44.4	75.0	66.7	n.d	63.6	71.4	42.9	58.3	33.3	45.6
Masvingo	A1 self-contained	55.3	63.2	56.4	100.0	100.0	51.3	100.0	74.4	64.1	50.0	44.7	69.0
	A1 villagized	28.0	38.1	45.8	95.7	91.2	15.8	77.9	21.7	16.5	26.5	22.2	43.6
	A2	0.0	25.0	25.0	n.d	75.0	75.0	100.0	100	50	0	0	45.0
Chiredzi	A2	14.3	38.5	46.2	50.0	66.7	50.0	88.9	24.1	6.9	21.4	14.3	38.3
	Informal	18.8	10.2	3.9	86.5	51.0	24.5	62.5	48.2	0	1.9	18.5	29.6
Mwenezi	A1 villagized	26.9	8.0	0.0	4.8	0.0	0.0	0.0	9.1	9.1	0	9.6	6.1
	Informal	11.5	11.5	0.0	0.0	26.7	6.7	n.d.	0	0	0	11.5	6.8

Source: Maize census, 2003–13 (N=400).
Note: n.d. – no data.

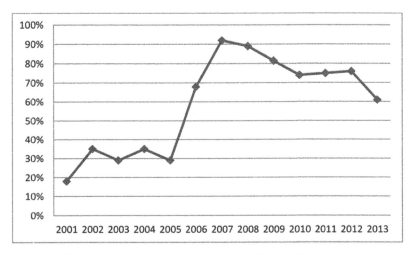

Figure 7.3 Percentage of farmers growing cotton in Uswaushava, 2001–2013

Source: Annual crop census, 2009 data estimated.

Investment in cattle has been particularly important across the sites, but particularly in the A1 schemes, and for certain 'success groups'[7] (Table 7.8). Cattle numbers are increasing in the new resettlement areas, providing an important source of draft power, milk, meat and cash sale and savings. Accumulation has been most evident in the A1 self-contained sites and in the top success groups; in recent years extending from the top group to others, as they establish themselves. A2 farmers were accumulating less in the economic crisis period, but investment in cattle has picked up since.

Table 7.8 Mean cattle holdings: changes by scheme type and success group

Scheme type	Success Group 1			Success Group 2			Success Group 3		
	At settlement (2000–02)	2008	2012	At settlement	2008	2012	At settlement	2008	2012
A1 villagized	6.3	10.4	11.0	4.5	4.5	5.7	1.9	2.6	3.4
A1 self-contained	11.2	16.2	10.7	1.3	10.9	8.2	0.9	3.7	9.0
A2	18.9	20.5	34.6	13.6	14.8	22.9	11.1	4.4	13.8
Informal	7.5	12.5	10.8	4.5	3.8	6.3	0.0	0.5	2.7

Source: Census data 2007–08, 2011–12.

---

7   This is the local characterization of 'success' used in the study to differentiate settlers, with success group 1 being the most 'successful' according to local criteria. Cattle ownership and accumulation was, unsurprisingly, one of the key indicators.

Land Reform, Livelihoods and the Politics of Agrarian Change in Zimbabwe   143

While across our research sites there are of course some who produce little and have to rely on local markets or support from relatives, overall, and especially in the wetter sites of Gutu and Masvingo districts, we did not find a pattern of production failure, widespread food insecurity and lack of market integration. We found a highly differentiated picture, but one that has at its centre smallholder agricultural production and marketing; one that could, given the right support, be the core of an agricultural revolution in Zimbabwe. By contrast to the previous boom in smallholder production in the early 1980s following independence, the Masvingo sample suggests a larger proportion of farmers is involved. Around half are succeeding as 'middle farmers' and a third as highly commericalized producers, compared to only 20 per cent in the 1980s (cf. Stanning 1989); and of course at a much larger scale than the rather isolated successes of that earlier period (Eicher 1995; Rohrbach 1989).

Local Economies and Linkages

On-farm success can result in off-farm economic growth, as linkages are forged in local economies. This is an important dynamic in the new resettlement areas, given the geographical juxtaposition of new resettlement areas of different types, with old communal and resettlement areas. Since 2000, the rural economy has been radically spatially reconfigured, with the old separated economic spheres of the large-scale farms and the communal areas being broken down. The result is a shift to new sites for economic activity, connected to new value chains and new sorts of entrepreneur, linking town and countryside.

The dynamic entrepreneurialism resulting should not be underestimated and represents an important resource to build on. Across our sites, we have small-scale irrigators producing horticultural products for local and regional markets; we have highly successful cotton producers who are generating considerable profits by selling to a wide number of competing private sector companies; we have livestock producers and traders who are developing new value chains for livestock products, linked to butcheries, supermarkets and other outlets; we have traders in wild products, often engaged in highly profitable export markets; and we have others who are developing contract farming and joint venture arrangements, for a range of products, including wildlife. We also have an important group of sugar producers with A2 plots on the lowveld estates who, very often against the odds due to shortages of inputs, unreliable electricity supplies and disadvantageous pricing, have been delivering cane to the mills, as well as other diverse markets, alongside diversification into irrigated horticulture production on their plots.

Off-farm employment was important in 2012 for 58 per cent of households surveyed, resulting in important flows of remittance. Other off-farm activities include trading (27 per cent), building and carpentry (12 per cent), pottery and basket-making (11 per cent), brick-making and thatching (11 per cent), as well as involvement in fishing, tailoring, grinding mills and transport businesses.[8]

Resettlement farmers are also employing labour (Table 7.9). This is often casual, low-paid employment, often of women, but it is an important source of livelihood for many – including those who are not making it as part of the new 'middle farmer' group identified above. The new resettlements sites have become a magnet for others, and households on average have grown by around three members since settlement through the in-migration of relatives and labourers (cf. Deininger, Hoogeveen and Kinsey 2004 for discussion of a similar dynamic in the old resettlement areas). Comparing this level of employment with what existed before on the former cattle ranches, where perhaps one herder was employed for each 100 animals grazed over 1,000 ha, the scale of employment generation afforded by the new resettlement farms is considerable.

Table 7.9   Farm labour: temporary (temp) and permanent (perm)

	A1 self-contained		A1 villagized		Informal		A2	
	Temp	Perm	Temp	Perm	Temp	Perm	Temp	Perm
Percentage of households employing workers	42%	16%	12%	17%	4%	1%	63%	78%
Nos of male workers	76	18	56	32	13	1	239	193
Nos of female workers	28	2	30	4	6	0	114	64

Source: 2011–12 census.

There is frequently a sense of optimism and future promise amongst many resettlement farmers. SM from Mwenezi district commented: 'We are happier here at resettlement. There is more land, stands are larger and there is no overcrowding. We got good yields this year. I filled two granaries with sorghum. I hope to buy a grinding mill and locate it at my homestead.' Comparing the farming life to other options, PC from Masvingo district observed: 'We are not employed, but we are getting higher incomes than those at work.' Despite the hardships and difficulties – of which there are many – there is a deep commitment to making the new resettlement enterprises work.

---

8   Source: 2011–12 census.

Agrarian Change, Social Differentiation and the New Politics of the Countryside[9]

As previous sections have shown for Masvingo province, the reconfiguration of land and economic activity following land reform has resulted in a new politics of the countryside. Yet this politics is contested: especially between the interests of new 'middle farmers' who are 'accumulating from below' and politically-connected elites.

Our analyses of the socially differentiated patterns of production, investment and accumulation show how a new emergent middle farmer group is potentially a key political force. In a rough calculation, this group represents about a quarter of the rural electorate, around a million voters (Scoones 2014b). Indeed, it is this group that showed its influence in the 2013 elections. The new 'middle farmers', now with land, have connections in town, they often have other jobs, they are relatively asset rich, and they have connections, both political and economic. They are very different to the mass of rural people in the communal areas.

Alongside the middle farmer accumulators, in small numbers on smaller land areas in the A2 farms there is the military-business-party elite, well connected to the ruling party, ZANU-PF. Extractive, corrupt and dependent on patrimonial relations, they are using land as one of a number of resources to extend their political-economic hold (along with mines, wildlife, business networks and so on). As noted earlier, in our study areas we estimate they represent around 5 per cent of the households on around 10 per cent of the new resettlement land (Scoones et al. 2011).

Overall, the A2 farmers who were allocated the larger farms were not classic elites. They were more a richer, middle class group of (former) civil servants (including lots of agricultural extension workers), business people and others (Table 7.4). Patronage was unquestionably important in some allocations (Marongwe 2011), but the A2 schemes certainly cannot be described only in terms of patronage-driven elite capture.

Those who did 'grab' land, especially around the time of the 2008 elections, were widely resented, and often shunned by the more legitimate beneficiaries. Other forms of resistance have occurred too (see Scoones 2014b). Some A2 farms have been subject to further invasions by local people. Many of course did not benefit from the land reform in 2000, particularly the youth, and demand for land is increasing once again.

In this chapter there has been a focus on the patterns and processes of social differentiation, highlighting differential patterns of asset ownership, styles of accumulation and dependence or involvement in labouring. It shows how a class of petty commodity producers or 'middle farmers' with a mix of origins – from the peasantry but also from the urban middle classes, including business people and civil servants in particular – are emerging as a potential political and economic force. These people are not the classic rural peasantry of populist land reform

---

9   This section builds on Scoones (2014b).

146   *State, Land and Democracy in Southern Africa*

are renditions, nor are they by and large the elite 'cronies' of the many critics of Zimbabwe's land reform. Instead they are a well-connected, entrepreneurial group, with clear political demands.

The focus of attention on party-connected elites has meant that most analysis has missed this new political dynamic, emergent from the processes of production, accumulation and social differentiation that have unfolded over the last 15 years. It is playing out in different ways in different places, and even with Masvingo there are contrasts between the core land reform areas, and the lowveld periphery (Scoones 2014b; Scoones et al. 2012b). This does not mean such elite capture and party patronage is not important. It is, but must be put in context, and seen as part of a wider struggle for political control in the post-land reform setting.

There is therefore an intense political struggle in the countryside that has emerged since land reform. This is between a small group of well-connected elites plagued by factional politics, and a variegated grouping of poorer smallholder farmers, farm labourers, and a new class of 'middle farmer' petty commodity producers. Electorally, if representative democracy is upheld, any party must rely on the latter to supply the votes, while the rich pickings of land and resources as patronage are to be gained by alliances with the former. As the Masvingo studies show, it is currently a fine balance.

The dynamics of production, investment and accumulation that have been the focus of this chapter will be crucial to the longer-term outcomes, as political fortunes and alliances will turn on the economic basis of different positions. Currently the 'middle farmer' group looks to be on the ascendancy, while corrupt elites are under fire. Key will be bargains that are made with political parties and the state, and as the opposition reforms after their demolition in the 2013 elections, and ZANU-PF contemplates a post-Mugabe era, these political calculations and alliances will be crucial. Land reform has created a dramatically new politics, and new analyses must focus on the complex intersections of economy and politics in the countryside to assess options and ways forward for a more stable, productive and just future in Zimbabwe's rural areas.

References

Chambati, Walter. 2011. "Restructuring of Agrarian Labour Relations after Fast Track Land Reform in Zimbabwe." *Journal of Peasant Studies* 38(5): 1047–68.

Chaumba, Joseph, Ian Scoones, and William Wolmer. 2003. "From *Jambanja* to Planning: The Reassertion of Technocracy in Land Reform in South-Eastern Zimbabwe?" *Journal of Modern African Studies* 41(4): 533–54.

Cliffe, Lionel, Jocelyn Alexander, Ben Cousins, and Rudo Gaidzanwa. 2011. "An Overview of Fast Track Land Reform in Zimbabwe: Editorial Introduction." *Journal of Peasant Studies* 38(5): 907–38.

Cousins, Ben. 2010. "What is a 'Smallholder'? Class Analytical Perspectives on Small-Scale Farming and Agrarian Reform in South Africa." Working Paper 16, January. PLAAS, University of the Western Cape.

Deininger, Klaus, Hans Hoogeveen, and Bill H. Kinsey. 2004. "Economic Benefits and Costs of Land Redistribution in Zimbabwe in the Early 1980s." *World Development* 32(10): 1697–709.

Dorward, Andrew. 2009. "Integrating Contested Aspirations, Processes and Policy: Development as Hanging in, Stepping up and Stepping out." *Development Policy Review* 27(2): 131–46.

Eicher, Carl K. 1995. "Zimbabwe's Maize-Based Green Revolution: Preconditions for Replication." *World Development* 23(5): 805–18.

Gunning, Jan, John Hoddinott, Bill Kinsey, and Trudy Owens. 2000. "Revisiting Forever Gained: Income Dynamics in Resettlement Areas of Zimbabwe, 1983–1996." *Journal of Development Studies* 36(6): 131–54.

Marongwe, Nelson. 2011. "Who Was Allocated Fast Track Land, and What Did They Do with It? Selection of A2 Farmers in Goromonzi District, Zimbabwe and Its Impacts on Agricultural Production." *Journal of Peasant Studies* 38(5): 1069–92

Matondi, Prosper. 2012. *Zimbabwe's Fast Track Land Reform*. London: Zed Books.

Mkodzongi, Grasian. 2013. "Fast Tracking Land Reform and Rural Livelihoods in Mashonaland West Province of Zimbabwe: Opportunities and Constraints, 2000–2013." PhD Thesis, University of Edinburgh.

Moyo, Sam. 2001. "The Land Occupation Movement in Zimbabwe: Contradictions of Neoliberalism." *Millennium: Journal of International Studies* 30(2): 311–30.

——. 2011. "Three Decades of Agrarian Reform in Zimbabwe." *Journal of Peasant Studies* 38(3): 493–531.

Moyo, Sam, Walter Chambati, Tendai Murisa, Dumisani Siziba, Charity Dangwa, Kingstone Mujeyi, and Ndabezinhle Nyoni. 2009. *Fast Track Land Reform Baseline Survey in Zimbabwe: Trends and Tendencies, 2005/06*. Harare: African Institute for Agrarian Studies (AIAS)

Murisa, Tendai. 2011. "Local Farmer Groups and Collective Action within Fast Track Land Reform in Zimbabwe." *Journal of Peasant Studies* 38(5): 1145–66.

Mushongah, Josphat. 2009. "Rethinking Vulnerability: Livelihood Change in Southern Zimbabwe, 1986–2006." DPhil thesis, University of Sussex.

Mutopo, Patience. 2014. *Women, Mobility and Rural Livelihoods in Zimbabwe Experiences of Fast Track Land Reform*. Leiden: Brill.

Potts, Deborah. 2008. "Displacement and Livelihoods: The Longer Term Impacts of Operation Murambatsvina." In *The Hidden Dimensions of Operation Murambatsvina in Zimbabwe*, edited by Maurice Taonezvi Vambe, 53–64. Harare: Weaver Press.

148 *State, Land and Democracy in Southern Africa*

Rohrbach, David D. 1989. "The Economics of Smallholder Maize Production in Zimbabwe: Implications for Food Security." International Development Papers, no. 11. East Lansing, MI: Michigan State University.

Rukuni, Mandivamba, Joshua Nyoni, and Prosper Matondi. 2009. *Policy Options for Optimisiation of the Use of Land for Agricultural Productivity and Production in Zimbabwe.* Harare: World Bank.

Sachikonye, Lloyd M. 2003. *The Situation of Commercial Farm Workers after Land Reform in Zimbabwe.* London and Harare: Catholic Institute for International Relations and FCTZ.

Sadomba, Zvakanyorwa Wilbert. 2011. *War Veterans in Zimbabwe's Revolution.* Oxford: James Currey.

Scoones, Ian. 2014a. "How Have the 'New Farmers' Fared? An Update on the Masvingo Study IV." *Zimbabweland blog*, 21 April. https://zimbabweland. wordpress.com/2014/04/21/1049/.

——. 2014b. "Zimbabwe's Land Reform: New Political Dynamics in the Countryside." *Review of African Political Economy* Published online 3 December. DOI: 10.1080/03056244.2014.968118.

Scoones, Ian, Nelson Marongwe, Blasio Mavedzenge, Felix Murimbarimba, Jacob Mahenehene, and Chrispen Sukume. 2010. *Zimbabwe's Land Reform: Myths and Realities.* Oxford: James Currey; Harare: Weaver Press; Johannesburg: Jacana.

——. 2011. "Zimbabwe's Land Reform: Challenging the Myths." *Journal of Peasant Studies* 38(5): 967–93.

——. 2012a. "Livelihoods after Land Reform in Zimbabwe: Understanding Processes of Rural Differentiation." *Journal of Agrarian Change*, 12(4): 503–27.

Scoones, Ian, Joseph Chaumba, Blasio Mavedzenge, and William Wolmer. 2012b. "The New Politics of Zimbabwe's Lowveld: Struggles over Land at the Margins." *African Affairs* 111(445): 527–50.

Stanning, Jayne. 1989. "Smallholder Maize Production and Sales in Zimbabwe: Some Distributional Aspects." *Food Policy* 14(3): 260–67.

Zamchiya, Phillan. 2011. "A Synopsis of Land and Agrarian Change in Chipinge District, Zimbabwe." *Journal of Peasant Studies* 38(5): 1093–122.

Chapter 8

Women and Land in Zimbabwe: State, Democracy and Gender Issues in Evolving Livelihoods and Land Regimes

Rudo B. Gaidzanwa

Introduction. State, Democracy, Gender and Land: A Historical Overview

The land question in Zimbabwe has occupied a central place in pre- and post-independence Zimbabwean politics. On colonization in 1893, the bulk of the native peoples were forcibly moved out of the prized areas that had minerals, high rainfall and good soils to support agriculture. By 1902, Pass and Labour laws had been institutionalized to restrict the movements of the native peoples in the colony which was officially granted self government status in 1923 and renamed Southern Rhodesia. The native labourers needed a pass to secure paid work in the towns. They were allowed to stay in the towns as long as they had paid work and their passes were stamped to reflect their status as wage workers. However, their wives and children were not allowed to visit and male workers were expected to exercise their conjugal rights during their holidays from work (Barnes and Win 1992). Only the few natives who were church and state functionaries such as teachers, court interpreters and policemen were able to access housing for married couples at police camps, government compounds and church properties. In colonized Zimbabwe, land holdings were skewed in favour of predominantly white, large-scale commercial farmers who comprised less than 0.5 per cent of the population while owning, through private title, at least 50 per cent of the arable agricultural and ranching land in Zimbabwe. The three million peasant farmers held about 45 per cent of land under customary tenure, predominantly in the drier parts of the country. In both the privately held land and in the customarily held land, men predominated as holders of land titles while women accessed land as wives or dependents of land holders. In the privately held land for black people in the former purchase areas where an elite of blacks were allowed to hold land by private title, there were very few women who held land through private title (Cheater 1984).

When independence occurred in 1980, agriculture comprised the backbone of the Zimbabwean economy. At least 75 per cent of the Zimbabwean population earned their livelihoods through agriculture. As described above, landholding was racially skewed since about 4,500 white commercial farmers and a few hundred

150   *State, Land and Democracy in Southern Africa*

blacks owned at least 25 per cent of the country's total land, comprising 11 million hectares. Commercial agriculture provided 25 per cent of the country's total employment while earning 40 per cent of Zimbabwe's total foreign exchange. By independence in 1980, commercial farmers produced 40 per cent of the country's maize, the staple crop.

On the other hand, the bulk of the one million black families in the communal areas, farmed and lived on 16 million hectares of land. Most of the black communal areas were in semi-arid areas with poor infrastructure. This resulted in poor yields and very low standards of living, nutrition and incomes for the bulk of the communal populations. Thus, the major thrust in struggles over land has been on agricultural and ranch land in Zimbabwe although commercial, residential and industrial land have become increasingly important as the economy diversified and pressure on agricultural and ranch land increased over the 20th century.

State, Land and Democracy in Zimbabwe

Zimbabwe has functioned pre- and post-independence with a variety of land regimes which have coexisted, often with contradictory results for land holders and users. This chapter aims to propose and advocate an alternative way of conceptualizing existing land policy regimes and practices, taking into account their benefits and impacts on men and women as well as on poor people in Zimbabwe. The present discourses on land in Zimbabwe tend to be structured primarily and explicitly around race, expressing racially charged grievances around land. However, in this approach, class, gender, age and other issues tend to be muted in the discourses around land, with many writers on land such as Moyo (1999), Sukume, Moyo and Matondi (2003), Marongwe (2011) and others focusing attention on land claimants as peasants and on the privileged, predominantly male and white actors in the discourses and struggles around land. Only a few writers such as Mutopo (2011), Munyuki-Hngwe (2011) Muzvidziwa (1998) and Gaidzanwa (1995 and 2004) differentiate land claimants by gender, and/or race and class.

Issues of class and gender within the racial groups, tend to be muted or ignored altogether. Furthermore, there is a tendency to dismiss the arguments of women's groups, the poorer peasants and working class members of the populace, partly because their proposals are potentially radical and far-reaching for the bulk of the present land policy makers, beneficiaries and stakeholders to deal with. The land lobby groups, men's and women's, in contemporary Zimbabwe also tend to focus on issues around rural arable communal land available through the Fast Track Land Reform (FTLR), especially the A1, small scale land holdings without addressing other types of land that are also available and contested for livelihoods and commercial purposes in contemporary Zimbabwe. Commercial, industrial and to some extent, ranch land, tends to be less contested in Zimbabwe.

The horizons of Zimbabweans with respect to the land debates, have been contracted to focusing on arable rural land and inputs for cropping, thereby legitimizing the land claims and benefits realized by the black, male, middle class in the larger A2 farms and those of the poorer blacks in the A1 farms. Thus, most of the black poor are focused on claiming rural arable land while the white and black middle classes are increasingly moving into another arena of struggles over land in the industrial and residential arena in urban Zimbabwe. In these struggles, the black poor are deployed strategically to threaten and effect the initial occupations which are or were then defended through the government or the ruling party Zimbabwe African National Union – Patriotic Front (ZANU-PF), which mediates their possession and retention of such land. Using gender as the entry point to debates on land, democracy and the state in Southern Africa widens the scope of the debates on land and land reform in rural and urban spheres.

Arable rural and urban land could be worked to produce incomes on which people depended. However, urban land tends to be much harder to access because of titling and private ownership regimes which have predominated in urban areas. Since colonial settlement, most urban spaces have been the preserve of the white minority until 1980 when the bulk of the other racial groups were legally enabled to purchase urban land for residential, industrial, commercial and arable use. Only a few urban areas were designated for use by relatively affluent blacks who were accorded the privilege of holding titles to their urban homes. A gendered analysis of land legislation and practices helps to indicate the internal dynamics of land politics in Zimbabwe.

Gender and the Land Apportionment Act (1930)

The Land Apportionment Act (LAA) of 1930 institutionalized the practice whereby the best agricultural land, the mineral-rich areas and the urban areas were designated 'white areas' which were out of bounds for native peoples. Through the Urban Areas legislation, 'townships' were set aside in urban areas for housing the black, male working class that was needed to work in the colonial economy in the railways, public works, domestic, farm and mining areas of the colony. Trading stores run by colonists were established in rural areas along the railway lines to facilitate the consumption of new types of clothes, food and other products of the colonial economy. The bulk of the black natives were compartmentalized and moved into what were called Tribal Trust Lands while the better-off blacks, most of whom were colonial functionaries such as agricultural advisers, court interpreters, policemen, clerks and teachers were permitted to acquire freehold land in the Native Purchase Areas which were more marginal for agriculture. A significant proportion of the marginalized natives whose land had been appropriated were recruited to work as poorly paid labour on white farms, mines and urban households. Through wage labour, they were able to survive and pay various taxes such as hut, poll and other taxes that were imposed on the native populations.

152   *State, Land and Democracy in Southern Africa*

According to Barnes and Win (1992) by 1946 Africans in Southern Rhodesian cities grew to over 99,000 and most of the town dwellers were in the cities illegally because they had no permits to be in the urban areas according to the LAA (1930) which did not allow undocumented blacks to be in white areas, namely, the towns and cities. Due to demands for black labour in urban areas, the LAA was amended to allow blacks to seek wage work in the towns. Barnes and Win (1992) hold that in 1946 local authorities were allowed to develop 'native' urban areas to house the black working population. In 1946, the Native (Urban Areas) Accommodation and Registration Act, requiring urban employers to provide free housing for their African employees within the native urban areas, was passed. Together with pass laws, this legislation sought to control the movement of black populations between rural and urban areas.

The gendered impacts of the LAA need to be understood. The act itself defined men as 'owners' of land and 'wife/wives or minor children and/or dependents of a native' as 'family.' Colonization introduced rigidities in land available for rotational cultivation and the internal individualization of land rights within households. Prior to colonization, women, whether single, married, divorced or widowed, were responsible for feeding themselves. This obligation became more pronounced as labour migration for wages among black men increased, strengthening women's roles as 'providers' on whom children, the aged and the infirm, depended. In any case, Africans could only own freehold land in the Native Purchase Areas. By 1933, the colonial government had already passed legislation, namely the Native Wills Act, whose enforcement was used to discriminate against wives and daughters as farm inheritors in African Purchase Areas where blacks could purchase land on freehold. Studies by Cheater (1984) showed that only 8.3 per cent of the farmers in Msengezi African Purchase Area allocated portions of land to their wives as expected in tradition. Most of the polygynists in Cheater's study did not make any allocations of land to all their wives save for a few who allocated bits of land to their senior wives. Weinrich (1975) noted that daughters of farmers in the African Purchase Areas preferred to marry poor peasant men from the neighbouring reserves where customary land tenure was more closely adhered to than richer men from the purchase areas. Thus, women's land rights were more secure in the 'backward' reserves than in the more modern areas where blacks could purchase land on freehold. The workloads of women in the reserves were lighter than those of women in the purchase areas. Thus, males literally reproduced farm labour through polygyny and women and their children in purchase areas worked as the farm labourers with very tenuous land and other rights in comparison to their counterparts in the 'reserves'.

Gender and the Native Land Husbandry Act (1951)

In Shona communities, customary land rights were more pronounced and individualized over arable land which was not worked communally. Common land on which resources such as flowers, firewood, wild vegetables, water, clay and thatch were found, was not individualized and these resources were accessed on an equitable basis. Within this area of communal access, individual rights and access to resources particularly by women, the children, poor people and the elderly, were safeguarded. Within households, land rights were individualized and women's land rights were secondary to those of men. Women did not have rights of allocation or disposition of land since their use rights were mediated through men who headed patrilineages and households. Daughters accessed land through their fathers prior to marriage or when they did not marry and when they divorced. As wives, women accessed land through their husbands after marriage. As pressure on reserved land increased as a result of white appropriation and settlement of land, land quality deteriorated fast in the reserves. The political pressure and agitation amongst blacks was related to land hunger and resulted in the passing of the Native Land Husbandry Act (NLHA) in 1951. Through this act, the settler government instituted settlement schemes and land preservation programmes to avoid provision of more land to blacks and payment of living wages in industry and agriculture. The NLHA closely paralleled the Kenyan Swynnerton Plan of 1955. The NLHA had three phases, the agronomic, the administrative and the legislative phases. The agronomic phase focused on arresting soil erosion, presumed to be a result of bad land tenure by Africans. The solution that was developed was the introduction of individualized tenure, presumed to preclude land fragmentation and land disputes and to foster economic growth. The legislative phase was developed to protect individual tenure, presumably providing support to the middle peasantry who were expected to develop a stake in the system devised by the settler state.

The NLHA defined the farmer as 'a native who is a married man with one wife' thereby ignoring the secondary rights to land of wives, sisters, mothers and daughters in patrilineages. Since the 'standard' person was a man with one wife, single men and women, divorced, widowed women and polygynous men were regarded as deviations from the standard. Thus, when destocking was instituted to satisfy agronomic criteria, the stocking rights of polygynous men, single men and women, divorced and widowed women were ignored and thereby eroded or prejudiced. With respect to grazing rights, married women's grazing rights were granted only if their husbands' whereabouts were unknown or if the husbands lived outside Rhodesia. Widows and widowers' grazing rights were equal under the NLHA. Male divorcees were eligible for grazing rights while female divorcees had to have custody of their dependent children to be availed grazing rights. In Shona custom, children over the age of six or seven are normally given to the custody of their fathers if bridewealth has been paid for the children. Divorced women normally return to their patrilineal homes where they are assured of land and grazing rights. Under the NLHA, such rights would be lost to divorced women if their children were customarily claimed by their husbands. Women can own cattle in their own right regardless of marital status and the NLHA eroded these rights by taking away women's grazing rights on divorce. Single men could exercise grazing rights at 21 years of age while single

154   *State, Land and Democracy in Southern Africa*

women could only do so at 25, showing the gender-based discrimination of colonial authorities with respect to issues of majority between men and women. The lower age of majority of men was also designed to make them eligible to pay taxes as land and livestock holders since women were not taxed. Thus, in order to narrow the base of land holders who did not pay taxes, women's eligibility for arable and grazing land and other rights was deferred. Thus, land could be allocated to younger men who were eligible to pay taxes and could also become labour migrants providing labour to farms, mines, factories and white households. For women, membership by birth or marriage in given lineages was no longer enough to entitle them to grazing rights under the NLHA.

The NLHA had the same provisions for men and women on farming rights as grazing rights. Women could own livestock as mothers, wives and daughters but most large stock could be amassed by men through bridewealth payments for sisters and daughters and through wage labour. Women were not welcome in the towns as indicated by Barnes and Win (1992) and others because they were supposed to safeguard the land, grazing and other rights of men who were involved in wage labour in mines, towns and commercial farms. Thus, women were less able to build up wealth through amassing cattle, land and other goods through wage labour. In any case, the NLHA was used by the colonial administration to move 'unsuccessful' farmers out of agriculture into wage labour. Since secondary holders of land rights had lost their land rights through the NLHA, there was growing insecurity for non-inheriting sons, wives in polygynous marriages, widows who refused to be inherited or those with young children or no sons to fight for their rights. Thus, colonization marginalized women in agriculture in rural areas by legally undermining their customary access to land rights in the rural economy while constricting their participation in the urban wage economy. This situation continued until independence in 1980.

Gender and Land Resettlement after 1980: Model A Schemes

Nearly one million people who had been displaced intra and extra territorially were resettled at independence in 1980. The Lancaster House constitution stipulated that land reform was to be based on willing buyer-willing seller principles and the government was to select beneficiaries who could use the land effectively. Initially 18,000 households were to be resettled over five years but this number was increased to 162,000 households. However, only 52,000 households had been resettled on 3.7 million hectares of land by 1989. Only 500 farmers had purchased freehold land or acquired leases to state land for commercial farming when the resettlement programme faltered.

The Model A scheme, the most common model, comprised intensive village settlements with individual household arable and residential allocations in a communal village with shared water, gardens and other amenities. The same assumptions underlying the LAA and the NLHA were replicated in the Model A schemes. Male headship of households was assumed and women's secondary rights were ignored. Very small proportions of female heads of households, between 2 and 15 per cent in various schemes studied by Sunga (1990) and Gaidzanwa (1985), were allocated land. Thus, women's economic rights were undermined by successive land resettlement programmes, resulting in women's increased emigration from rural Zimbabwe. Polygyny rates in the A1 resettlement schemes were higher than in communal areas because resettled male heads of household used marriage as a means of recruiting and reproducing labour on the farm. By 1990, the Zimbabwean economy was faltering and equal numbers of men and women were moving out of agriculture in a process of de-agrarianization. Sithole-Fundire (1994) argued that housing deprivation was rife for both men and women in Marondera, a town neighbouring Harare. Schlyter (1989) indicated that more males than females returned to rural areas permanently following long periods of wage employment. Schlyter observed that significant proportions of women-headed households in Chitungwiza and Kuwadzana, in Harare, were households of divorced and widowed women who had left the rural areas and had no intention of returning. These observations have been validated by censuses since 1990 which show that young women are emigrating at rates equal to those of young men. It appeared that women were more impoverished, landless and more marginalized than men in the rural areas and when they moved from rural areas as a result of divorce, widowhood or other social and marital breakdown, they were less likely to return to the rural areas. Thus, men and women under 30 were equally represented in rural to urban migration in Zimbabwe by 1991. Thus, the crisis developing in communal areas, characterized by the emigration of succeeding generations of women who considered the lifestyles of wives of migrant workers unacceptable, needs to be noted since it indicates the decline of a peasant farming sector based on the exploitation of female household labour.

Successive censuses in Zimbabwe since 1980 have shown growing numbers of young adult female emigration from rural areas. For example, data from the Zimbabwe Demographic Health Survey 2005–2006 (CSO 2007: 10) showed that, despite AIDS-related deaths, females in the age bands between 15 and 19, 20 and 24 and 25 and 29 comprised a larger proportion of the urban population than men in corresponding age bands. By 2010–2011, females in the age bands between 15 and 19, 20 and 24, 25 and 29 and 30 to 34 showed that this trend was continuing as the 15–19 age band of females in urban areas comprised a larger proportion of the population in comparison to males, consolidating the trend.

Quality of life indicators illustrate the reasons for female emigration from rural Zimbabwe. In 2010–2011, the Demographic Health Survey (ZIMSTAT 2012) showed that 70 per cent of urban households, compared to 25 per cent of rural households, had water piped into their premises. At least 28 per cent of rural households had to make trips of 30 minutes or more to access drinking water and this was usually a chore performed by women and girls. 43 per cent of urban households were connected to a sewer system or flushed waste into a septic tank and 25 per cent had improved shared toilets, while in rural areas only 16 per cent of households had improved non-shared toilets and most of these were pit latrines. 39 per cent of rural households had no toilet facility. Since women carry the highest burden of care for the sick, the aged and the young, access to hygienic waste disposal facilities eases women's care burdens by reducing infections and sicknesses due to insanitary practices resulting from inadequate waste disposal facilities. 83 per cent of urban households are connected to electricity power lines whereas only 13 per cent of the rural population enjoy this facility. Given that women perform the bulk of cooking, cleaning and other chores requiring clean energy, their dependence on firewood and less convenient sources of energy absorbs their time used in the procurement of firewood and cooking on open hearths. Women are also exposed to smoke inhalation throughout their lives because a significant proportion of rural households cook on open hearths. 87 per cent of urban households live in premises with cement floors while 58 per cent of rural households surveyed had cement floors. 41 per cent of rural households had sand, dung or earth floors which need more maintenance and renewal than cement floors. 73 per cent of urban households use electricity for cooking while only 6 per cent of rural households enjoy this facility. Urban households own more modern conveniences such as radios with 41 per cent urban and 32 per cent rural households owning or using a radio. 74 per cent of urban households use television sets while only 17 per cent of rural households have access to television sets. 16 per cent of urban households own or use a car while only 3 per cent of rural households own or use a car. 40 per cent of urban households had a bank account while only 12 per cent of rural households had a bank account. These statistics show the differences in the quality and ease of life in urban and rural areas because of the modern conveniences that are available and accessible in urban and rural areas.

There is significant emigration from rural areas by both young women and men in these age bands and it is important to understand that the access to modern conveniences and the land regimes that privilege men in Zimbabwe do not make rural life very attractive for women throughout their life stages. Makura-Paradza (2010) explored and analysed the livelihood vulnerabilities of women in communal areas in Zimbabwe. She analysed the coping strategies of women in a communal area and found that women moved between communal areas, commercial farms, growth points and urban areas to maximize the returns from their activities at specific points in their lives. Makura-Paradza (2010) also established that those women who were able to secure urban property were able to diversity their livelihoods and managed to accumulate incomes and wealth through retaining rural homesteads, land and other resources while also undertaking trading activities and renting out rooms in their urban dwellings. Some of these households were able to develop multi-spatial livelihoods that enabled them to support dependent children and relatives. According to Makura-Paradza (2010: 88) the difficulties in asserting land claims by young, divorced and widowed women, the growing vulnerability of communal area livelihoods, recurring droughts, withdrawal of able-bodied young male labour, the disruption

Women and Land in Zimbabwe 157

of commercial farming by the FTLR beginning in 1999, HIV and AIDS, and economic stagnation, have disrupted the continuity of rural-urban linkages that had been built over generations. Thus, the state and international organizations have stepped in to distribute food as droughts became more frequent and coping strategies failed or proved inadequate. Mudimu (2003: 19) cited by Makura-Paradza (2010: 89) indicates that soil exhaustion has resulted in the under-utilization of agricultural land in communal areas and the declining use of land as an agricultural asset. Thus there is an increase in the importance of livelihood diversification. It is in this context that young people, particularly women, migrate out of communal areas because of declining options.

By 1990, budget deficits, shortage of foreign exchange and technical capacity problems forced the government of Zimbabwe to scale down resettlement initiatives, resulting in suspension of British funding for the resettlement programme worth three million pounds. In September 1996, land redistribution to benefit the rural poor and to resettle between 25,000 and 35,000 households at a cost between £95 million and £145 million was on the agenda. A donor's conference was to be organized to facilitate funding of this initiative. However, in 1997, the new British government, through its Secretary of State for International Development, Clare Short, indicated to the Zimbabwe government that the new Labour government did not consider the UK to have a special obligation to fund land purchase in Zimbabwe. This soured relations between Zimbabwe and the British government, derailing the donors' conference. It was only in January 2000 that the British government indicated that it would avail £5 million for land resettlement through non-government organizations in Zimbabwe. This annoyed the Zimbabwe government which was defeated in the February 2000 referendum on a new constitution by an opposition coalition of non-governmental organizations. When in late February 2000, war veterans, ZANU-PF youths and supporters violently invaded predominantly white commercial farms, the land crisis started in earnest.

The Fast Track Land Reform Programme

The FTLR was characterized by two models. The A1, small scale farm model, whereby farmers produced for subsistence with small surpluses for the market in good seasons; this model was intended to de-congest the communal areas. The A2, large-scale commercial farm model, aimed to create a new cadre of black commercial farmers who would use their own resources, with some concessionary financing, to grow commercial crops and enhance Zimbabwe's food self-sufficiency, generate foreign currency and support agro-industry in Zimbabwe. Table 8.1 shows provincial land allocations by gender.

Table 8.1   Provincial land allocations by gender

Province	Model A1				Model A2			
	Males	%	Females	%	Males	%	Females	%
Midlands	14,800	82	3,198	18	338	95	17	5
Masvingo	19,026	84	3,644	16	709	92	64	8
Mash. Central	12,986	88	1,770	12	1,469	87	215	13
Mash. West	21,782	81	5,270	19	1,777	89	226	11
Mash. East*	12,967	76	3,992	24	n/a	n/a	n/a	n/a
Mat. South	7,754	87	1,169	13	215	79	56	21
Mat. North	7,919	84	1,490	16	574	83	121	17
Manicaland	9,752	82	2,190	18	961	91	97	9
TOTAL	106,986	82	22,723	18	6,043	88	796	12

Source: Provincial profiles, Presidential Land Committee, 2003.
Note: The breakdown of A2 land allocations by gender for Mashonaland East province was not available at the time of reporting.

Although, nationally, 35 per cent of households are headed by women, land allocations fell way below this proportion in both A1 and A2 schemes. The proportions of women, former farm workers and landless in communal areas who were allocated land under the FTLR country-wide is low. Women comprised only 18 per cent of recipients of the A1 plots and 12 per cent of recipients of A2 allocations in those provinces with the highest allocations to women. The Presidential Land Review Committee (PLRC 2003) noted that the FTLR programme had failed to de-congest the communal areas.

State, Democracy and Land in Contemporary Economic and Political Policies

There has been little departure from the colonial assumptions about commercial, large and small scale farming, peasant agriculture and survival in Zimbabwe. The gender relations that are assumed to obtain have changed dramatically but land policies and practices of successive states have stayed static. Problematic aspects of land in small scale agriculture have been linked to labour and its procurement, largely effected through marriage of additional wives and reproduction of labour on the farm (Cheater 1984; Chenaux-Repond 1993; Weinrich 1975). The bulk of the male black famers have not been able to pay market wages for farm labour resulting in polygyny, land fragmentation generationally, disputes over inheritance of land and the insecurity and vulnerability of women and children in small scale farm households. Younger sons, daughters and wives have increasingly reduced their investment in labour and incomes on land they cannot control, own or inherit at the death of the father or husband who is the head of household. Historically, these categories of people have migrated out of the farming sector diminishing the labour available in the rural farm sector. The Chavunduka (Chavunduka Land Commission 1984) and Rukuni Land Commissions (Rukuni 1994) raised this issue but it has never been tackled effectively in agricultural and land policy in Zimbabwe. In the absence of affordable tillage services, resettled farmers and land holders have not been able to utilize their land maximally since the Land Apportionment Act was passed. Polygyny in resettlement areas has also been higher than the national rural average, sponsored by allocations that land holders cannot utilize effectively due to land and agrarian policies that assume the exploitation of women and children's labour with very few rights to incomes and control commensurate with their input. Studies by Matondi (2012), Munyuki-Hungwe (2011), Mutopo (2011) and Gaidzanwa (2004) indicated that the allocations of relatively high proportions of land to civil servants, wage earners and other absentee farmers has replicated and perpetuated the absentee male farmer model in the new larger scale commercial farmland. Given the poor productivity registered so far in most of the resettled areas and Zimbabwe's inability to produce maize and other crops for local domestic consumption, it is fair to argue that the land and agrarian system still needs major review. Matondi (2012), and Munyuki-Hungwe (2011) indicated that poor provision of financing, poor choice of settlers, problems regarding legal frameworks for land holding and the devolution of land generationally, all converge and make workable agriculture problematic. There has been a tobacco boom in the small scale farm sector but it has occurred at the cost of the environment and the production of food crops and food security in Zimbabwe. There has also been growing indebtedness among small farmers to contract financiers who pay farmers set fees for their tobacco in exchange for input provision. Its sustainability still has to be seen. The Rukuni Land Commission (Rukuni 1994) researched the fragmentation of land and its degradation generationally in the small farm sector as settlers died, married more wives and sired maternally differentiated sets of children. According to the Rukuni Commission, the average disputed farm was tied up in litigation for nine years during which time farm operations ceased and farm assets were dissipated or destroyed. White farmers did not have these problems because their land was held through registered companies or monogamous marriages and they wrote wills determining and guiding the devolution of land after the death of the registered owner/s. As the new black farmers enter the commercial farm sector, their cultural and marital dynamics have come to the fore and they will most likely impact negatively on the devolution of land.

The most worrying development is the desertion of rural areas by young, widowed and divorced women. While Weinrich (1975) noted 'marriage resistance' by young women in small scale commercial farm areas to small scale commercial farmers, in contemporary Zimbabwe there is growing general resistance to agricultural pursuits by young people and marriage in the rural areas by young women. This was noted in the GEMINI survey of 1994, where it appeared that rural micro enterprises employed women in vending, retail, bars, pubs and unlicensed *shebeens*, the last three being the enterprises with the highest profits. Munyuki-Hungwe (2011) also indicated that some young men were deserting the

A1 settlements in Mazowe because of age and other dynamics that resulted in undemocratic land allocations, decision-making over inputs and farm machinery and governance in the schemes. As the economic crisis in Zimbabwe unfolded in the wake of the FTLR, a boom in trade and commerce in imported clothes, textiles and other cheap manufactured goods provided rural and urban women with new opportunities beyond agriculture. Mutopo (2011) noted that cross-border trade boomed as these women went into this easy-entry sector requiring low investment and offering relatively high profit. As the crisis deepened, the migration into towns by women increased, resulting in the feminization of cross-border trade in the new millennium. While male migration tended to be cyclical with men going into wage labour during their productive years and then retiring to or re-joining their families on the farms as soon as they have accumulated enough funding to invest in small trade or commercial enterprises in rural areas, increasingly, young, divorced, widowed or dissatisfied women and men are deserting the rural areas for good and setting up permanent residences in urban areas.

This trend was observed by Schlyter (1989) in her research on the difficulties divorced and widowed women face in making homes in small scale farming areas. The *Moving Zimbabwe Forward Survey* (MZF) on poverty in Zimbabwe, conducted by the University of Zimbabwe in 2012 (Manjengwa, Feresu and Chimhowu 2012), found that of sampled rural households, 95 per cent lived below the food poverty line and 68 per cent were classed as very poor whereas only 8 per cent of urban households were classified as very poor. Women-headed households had 64 per cent incidence of poverty while male-headed households had a poverty incidence of 62 per cent in urban areas, while in rural areas women-headed households comprised 72 per cent of very poor in comparison to 67 per cent for men. Thus, there appears to be a concentration of very poor women in rural areas. The *Zimbabwe Demographic and Health Survey* (CSO 2007) indicated that widows between 20 and 29 were the most vulnerable to dispossession of property, with rural widows (47 per cent) almost twice as likely to be dispossessed of their property on widowhood than urban widows (26 per cent). There is more awareness of property rights in urban areas because of the activities of human rights organizations, particularly those focusing on women, and better law enforcement than in rural areas where police posts are few and far between. Rural poverty is related to lack of access to land, livestock, farm implements, draught power, legal assistance and state organs that enforce law and order. The MZF survey also found that a higher percentage of female-headed (53 per cent) than male-headed households (32 per cent), owned their houses (Manjengwa, Feresu and Chimhowu 2012). The rate of polygyny in Zimbabwe is around 11 per cent (CSO 2007). However, rural women (15 per cent) are three times as likely as their urban counterparts to be in polygynous unions. Polygynous unions tend to be characterized by strife when a husband dies and property, such as land, has to be shared amongst several wives and sets of children. In urban Zimbabwe, Ministry of Justice data show that 95 per cent of divorces are initiated by women. These divorces are dealt with in predominantly urban courts and they indicate growing dissatisfaction amongst women with inequitable and exploitative marriage relationships.

The statistics above show why young women are increasingly moving into urban areas. Young women desert the rural areas for trade and commercial opportunities and freedom from strictures of rural life and drudgery. They move to pursue better urban residential housing and lives free of constraints by village kin. Schlyter (1989) found that in Zengeza 5 and Kuwadzana, women who were heads of households or owners of residential land, completed building their houses faster than married couples despite that female household heads earned lower incomes than male-headed households. Women-headed households gave higher priority to housing investment so that they could accommodate siblings, children and kin from rural areas. Housing in urban areas also provided more secure retirement income through letting than rural land and housing. Makura-Paradza (2010) indicated that women with urban houses could use them as business premises for trade and commerce and to shelter families. An urban house also allowed a woman to diversify her income sources and to use rental income to pursue profits in the agricultural sector. Rural women also move in pursuit of better income earning opportunities and education for their children. In urban areas, women comprise a significant proportion of applicants for residential land but councils tend to prioritize males, making women vulnerable to political opportunists. Urban housing policies have not evolved to take into account urban and rural immigrant women's growing demand for housing.

The hunger for residential land and housing has resulted in women allying themselves with political parties that offer housing stands in urban areas through cooperatives and other schemes. These cooperatives group people and procure land through ZANU-PF for residential purposes. The process may be long and, in many instances, opaque. However, the point is that young women are abandoning rural areas at the same rate as young men and, in some instances, middle aged women move into towns on widowhood or divorce. Thus, the focus on arable rural land ignores women's evolving realities and needs for residential and commercial land in urban areas, based on their life trajectories which tend to be different from those of men.

Case Study of Three Sisters, Two of Them Widowed and One Divorced

Three sisters, Mary, Martha and Salome, married men in different parts of Zimbabwe.

Mary's Story

The eldest, Mary, had a husband who worked in Harare as a semi-skilled industrial worker. He acquired a house in a Harare high density township and installed three lodgers to supplement their income. He also built a homestead in their rural home and raised a herd of five cattle before he died in Harare. He had only one son and was buried at his rural home. Mary, his widow, opted to stay in Harare and took all the furnishings from the rural homestead and stored them at her natal home where her widowed mother stayed. Mary gave her son the option to take over his father's homestead if he wished to do so. So far, Mary's son has expressed no interest in the rural homestead which has become dilapidated. The cattle that Mary's household acquired during her husband's lifetime are being tended by a neighbour who has access to them for ploughing. Mary prefers to live with her son and his wife who pay her rent for one of the rooms in her house than to relocate to the rural areas to live in her deceased husband's village away from her son who prefers to live in Harare. She is active in her church and does not want to sever her ties with her neighbourhood and church family because she can earn money from renting five rooms on her premises.

Martha's Story

Martha, the middle sister was divorced from her husband because his family abused her and her children physically and emotionally. She had been a temporary teacher before she married. However, her husband's family were very controlling and abusive to the point where she took her three small children in the dead of night and returned to her natal home where her widowed mother stayed and helped her to raise her children while she worked in Harare as a domestic worker. She built a three bed-roomed brick house with her earnings and became the primary carer for her brother's son whose parents had both died. As her children completed their secondary schooling, her eldest daughter by a previous relationship managed to get to Britain before visa restrictions for Zimbabweans were imposed. Martha's eldest daughter worked and sent her money and Martha decided to buy some residential land and pay for vocational training for her three children who were in Zimbabwe. Her justification was that as her brother's son grew into adulthood and her mother died, her children would never be allowed to own the house she had built or to build their own home at their maternal grandmother's home. She said she knew that, in their clan, the men would tell her sons to go back to their father's home to claim land for housing, farming and other purposes. She said she had no option but to leave the three bed-roomed house in the family homestead to her nephew (her deceased brother's son because he was the one who would be accepted by the clansmen and women as the rightful heir to the house despite that she had built it). Martha pointed out that she could stay in the house until her death but she knew that her children would be thrown out as soon as she died. Martha's ex-husband has since died and his sisters and brothers have been asked to pay bridewealth to assert patrilineal rights and 'redeem' Martha's three children and give them their family name. Martha has bought a residential stand in a high density suburb in Harare and another one in a middle density suburb for herself and her daughter who is still single. Her second daughter has had a child and moved in with the father of her child in Harare. Martha lives in her partially completed house and has bequeathed her village house to her nephew (her deceased brother's son). Martha travels to her natal village to supervise a young man and woman who stay at her home because they do not have land or a house of their own. She buys seed and fertilizer for this young man and his wife to plant and grow maize for her so she does not have to pay for maize meal in Harare. She also gives some of the crops such as maize, pumpkins and sweet potatoes to her son and daughter, both of them married and living in Harare. Her son helps to supervise the caretaker couple who tend Martha's natal homestead *(matongo)* in the fashion described by Makura-Paradza (2010) in her study of single women, land and livelihoods in a communal area in Zimbabwe.

Salome's Story

Salome married a policeman and lived with him in the Midlands. They had four children, two boys and two girls. Salome was not diligent in keeping touch with her natal family after she married. She reconnected with her sisters after her two brothers and then her husband died. Salome never wanted to go back to her natal home after widowhood because she felt that her husband's family would castigate her for taking her children to her people. Salome had resisted relocating to her widowed mother-in-law's rural homestead because she would be cut off from her friends and natal family and would be a domestic drudge to her late husband's aged mother and sisters. Salome was aware that her husband's sisters wanted to make her caregiver for their aged mother while they lived in town free of responsibility for their mother. She borrowed money for rent and school fees from her sisters to survive until they got tired of supporting her and found her a job as a domestic worker in Harare. Salome is now working for an expatriate family and she has joined a cooperative that helps women to secure cheap land for housing in exchange for supporting the political party (ZANU-PF) that organizes access to this land.

***

The shift in focus to residential, commercial and arable land is a result of the strife and uncertainty relating to white-owned farmland that is still subject to compensation by the Zimbabwe government. Thus, women and the poor and others who are lacking security in communal and resettlement land, have opted to secure urban land with more secure title. Urban land is also claimed by an emerging elite which has diversified its portfolios beyond farmland. Urban land, indeed, is not as contentious as previously white-owned farmland for which the majority of farmers still have to be compensated. For example, the parcelling out of land as part of political patronage is described in the following three articles. In the first article that appeared in *Bulawayo 24*, an online newspaper (Zanu-PF Embarks 2012), a staff reporter described the problems that ZANU-PF Harare provincial officials were experiencing in distributing residential stands to their members who desired to acquire urban housing. In another incident, Nelson Sibanda (2013), writing for *The*

Zimbabwean, on 9 October 2013, described how over 300 families had sold assets to acquire land around Norton, a small town near Harare, only to be moved out when it transpired that the land had been improperly acquired and the families illegally resettled on it to boost the votes for a ZANU-PF candidate in that constituency. In a third example, a staff reporter for *NewsDay*, a daily newspaper, wrote an article on the 9 September 2013 (ZANU-PF Parcels 2013) describing how ZANU-PF was taking advantage of desperate home-seekers by claiming to be addressing housing and land shortages amongst poor Zimbabweans by parcelling out council and other land illegally all over Harare to dilute the influence of the opposition Movement for Democratic Change (MDC) which dominates the urban areas.

The importance of the votes of the urban high density suburb population is growing as ZANU-PF desires to displace the opposition party MDC from urban areas. In addition, elites have recognized the security accruing from freehold urban land which is less contestable in comparison with rural farmland. This has resulted in a rush for urban commercial land as demonstrated in an article which appeared in an online website, *Zimbabwe Situation*, in February 2014 (Musarurwa 2014). Given the favourable positioning of elites and senior council employees, their access to industrial, commercial and residential land is easier and they are able to manipulate the situation to their advantage, often without the knowledge of rate and tax payers. Increasingly, various categories of women are growing disenchanted with rural farm life and are moving into the towns but the discourses on land prefer to lock women into the colonial land regimes based on the unpaid labour of poor black rural women. There is very little focus on urban land and its access on equitable bases between men and women. The FTLR programme has failed to move to address the need for a land model based on small peri-urban and urban intensive land use through horticulture, industrial and commercial activity especially by the poor, particularly women.

Amongst the elites, there is growing hunger for urban commercial and industrial land and this has been demonstrated by court cases and revelations through scandals regarding divorce settlements, salaries and perks in parastatal bodies and local authorities in Harare and other towns. The most sensational ones involved the Minister of Local Government and National Housing, Dr Chombo, whose assets were alleged to include over 87 plots of residential, commercial and agricultural land (Messy Divorce Exposes 2010). Dr Chombo, who served as Minister of Local Government in successive ZANU-PF governments, was sued for divorce by his wife and the portfolio of properties that was presented by Mrs Chombo caused consternation amongst Zimbabweans because of its vastness, given the costs of buying urban land in Zimbabwe. The immovable properties that she listed were spread all over the country and the opposition MDC issued a statement indicating that in their opinion, such a portfolio of properties could only have been acquired through illegal means since the salaries and benefits of public servants could never have supported such acquisitions.

In another case, another ZANU-PF member who is related to President Mugabe, Philip Chiyangwa, had properties comprising over 100 plots of farmland, residential and commercial land and other assets listed in an article in *Nehanda Radio*, an online newspaper, on the 29 November 2013 (Full List 2013). His estranged wife listed his properties comprising millions of acres of urban residential, commercial, industrial and rural land. Another ZANU-PF luminary is the Commander of the Defence Forces of Zimbabwe, General Constantine Chiwenga, whose assets were listed in an article by Wilbert Mukori (2014) on *Bulawayo 24* on 19 September 2014, in the wake of the divorce petition by Mrs Jocelyn Chiwenga. Mrs Chiwenga listed a property portfolio including urban, residential, commercial and rural farmland, jewellery and other property. These three men were embroiled in divorce cases which involve vehicles, land holdings, both rural and urban as well as houses, jewellery, motor vehicles and other forms of property. Managers in the City of Harare were also embroiled in land-related scandals whereby they were leased cheap commercial land with options to buy the land while city residents have no access to such land and also have no water, refuse removal and other services. These cases have discredited the government and indicated how elites have cushioned themselves against the uncertainties and conflicts surrounding rural land holdings by acquiring both rural and urban land in all parts of Zimbabwe.

In the absence of a transparent model for accessing residential, commercial and industrial development, poor claimants for land for residential purposes, especially women, have to depend on political patronage to access residential, industrial and commercial land.

Industrial and commercial land is very expensive and has historically been inaccessible to the bulk of Zimbabwe's population desiring involvement in commercial, residential and industrial land activities. This explains why rural women, increasingly aware of the benefits of owning urban land, are using political parties, namely ZANU-PF, to attempt to access urban residential and commercial land. They have recognized that in the current deadlock over land reform and compensation to former owners of large-scale freehold land, they are more likely to reap greater benefits from residential land to which they are able to exercise freehold title. There are huge unplanned urban settlements around most major towns in Zimbabwe due to the recognition that rural land presents problems. In contemporary Zimbabwe, land wrangles within and between black elites and ordinary people have increased as black-on-black land wrangles and seizures escalate.

In the cases described in *The Financial Gazette* of 28 June 2012, the reporter Francis Bere (2012), analyses the wrangles between two High Court judges and other citizens over farm boundaries and land as well as another case involving the Minister of Home Affairs, Kembo Mohadi, and the running battles he was involved in, against war veterans over land in Matebeleland South.

In another case, Bridget Munanavire (2014) reported in the *Daily News* on 24 March 2014 that an aide in President Mugabe's office was involved in a row over land with three other farmers, all former state employees. She also reported that President Mugabe's wife was also embroiled in a row over farmland and was accused of evicting over 100 families from their land in order to establish a game park. In a similar vein, Clement Moyo (2012), in an opinion piece in *ZimEye*, an online news site, on 28 August 2012, argued that future land wrangles would involve blacks against blacks. He cited the growing numbers of land disputes such as that between the late Vice President, John Nkomo, and Mr Masunda, over a safari lodge on 611.79 hectares of land. In that dispute, Mr Masunda's brother was shot and wounded by Vice President Nkomo's bodyguard.

Ian Scoones (2014), in a blog on 18 August 2014, also describes the violence that was unleashed on black freehold land owners who had purchased their farms prior to the land invasions that started in 1999.

In an article serialized on 26 and 27 April 2012, in the *Daily News*, ' ZANU PF elites in land dog fights' Everson Mushava (2012) described the wrangles between ZANU-PF elites over commercial farmland in post FTLR in Zimbabwe. In this article, he described the contradictions arising in the FTLR programme, the privileging of elites in accessing land and the dispossession of poor land holders by politically connected and more affluent blacks in Zimbabwe.

The cases cited in this chapter and the issues raised indicate that the land reform programme in Zimbabwe still has many unresolved problems. The gender-based inequalities relating to land use and the difficulties experienced by young, middle aged divorced and/or widowed women and poor people in rural Zimbabwe, have pushed a significant proportion of women out of rural areas. Both women and men have recognized the insecurity of rural-based living and livelihoods and increasingly seek to diversity their livelihoods by acquiring freehold land and property in urban areas. It is no longer possible to ignore the trajectory of land struggles which have gone beyond struggles for rural communal, commercial and resettlement land. This chapter will hopefully broaden the land debate in Zimbabwe beyond its current focus on gendered farmland and consider gendered industrial, commercial and residential urban land use as equally deserving of policy attention.

References

Barnes, Teresa A. and Everjoyce J. Win. 1992. *To Live a Better Life: An Oral History of Women in the City of Harare, 1930–1970*. Harare: Baobab Books.

Bere, Francis. 2012. "Black-On-Black Farm Wrangles Dog Land Reform." *The Financial Gazette*, 28 June. Accessed 13 October 2014. http://www.financialgazette.co.zw/black-on-black-farm-wrangles-dog-land-reform.

Central Statistical Office (CSO) Zimbabwe. 2007. *Zimbabwe Demographic and Health Survey 2005–06*. Calverton, Maryland: CSO and Macro International Inc.

Chavunduka Land Commission. 1984. *Report of the Chavunduka Land Commission*. Harare: Government of Zimbabwe.

Cheater, Angela P. 1984. *Idioms of Accumulation: Rural Development and Class Formation among Freeholders in Zimbabwe*. Harare: Mambo Press.

Chenaux-Repond, Maia. 1993. *Gender-Biased Land Use in Model A Resettlement Schemes of Mashonaland*. Harare: Rudecon Zimbabwe Ltd.

"Full List of Philip Chiyangwa's Properties." 2013. *Nehanda Radio*, 29 November. Accessed 12 February 2014. http://nehandaradio.com/2013/11/29/full-list-of-philip-chiyangwa-property.

Gaidzanwa, Rudo B. 1985. "Women's Land Rights in Zimbabwe: An Overview." Occasional Paper 13, Rural and Urban Planning Department. Harare: University of Zimbabwe.

——. 1995. "Land and the Economic Empowerment of Women: A Gendered Analysis." *SAFERE* 1(1): 1–12.

——. 2004. "Emerging Challenges in Zimbabwe's Land Reform Program." *OSSREA Bulletin* 1(2): 39–54.

Makura-Paradza, Gaynor. 2010. "Single Women, Land and Livelihood Vulnerability in a Communal Area in Zimbabwe." African Women Leaders in Agriculture and the Environment (AWLAE) Series No. 9. Wageningen: Wageningen Academic Publishers.

Manjengwa, Jeanette, Sara Feresu, and Admos Chimhowu, eds. 2012. *Moving Zimbabwe Forward. Understanding Poverty, Promoting Wellbeing and Sustainable Development. A Sample Survey of 16 Districts of Zimbabwe*, Harare: Institute of Environmental Studies, University of Zimbabwe.

Marongwe, Nelson. 2011. "Who Was Allocated Fast Track Land and What Did They Do with It? Selection of A2 Farmers in Goromonzi District, Zimbabwe and its Impacts on Agricultural Production." *Journal of Peasants Studies* 38(5): 1069–92.

Matondi, Prosper. 2012. *Zimbabwe's Fast Track Land Reform*. London: Zed Books.

"Messy Divorce Exposes Minister Chombo's Mega Riches." 2010. *Nehanda Radio*, 5 November. Accessed 11 January 2014. http://nehandaradio.com/2010/11/05/messy-divorce-exposes-minister-chombo%E2%80%99s-mega-riches.

Moyo, Clement. 2012. "Zimbabwe Future Land Wars – Black on Black." *ZimEye*, 28 August. Accessed 13 October 2014. http://www.zimeye.org/future-land-wars-black-on-black.

Moyo, Sam. 1999. "The Political Economy of Land Acquisition and Redistribution in the 1990s." *Journal of Southern African Studies* 26(1): 5–28.

Mukori, Wilbert. 2014. "Chiwenga Amassed Wealth is Undeserved and Explains his Blind Loyalty to Mugabe." *Bulawayo 24*, 19 September. Accessed 10 October 2014. http://www.bulawayo24.com/index-id-opinion-sc-columnist-byo-54254.html.

Munanavire, Bridget. 2014. "Mugabe Aide in Messy Row." *DailyNews*, 24 March. Accessed 13 October 2014. http://www.dailynews.co.zw/articles/2014/03/24/mugabe-aide-in-messy-row.

Munyuki-Hungwe, Mabel. 2011. "In Search of Community in Zimbabwe's Fast Track Resettlement Area of Mazowe District." PhD thesis. Lund: Lund University.

Musarurwa, Charlotte. 2014. "Council Directors Bag Stands for a Song." *Zimbabwe Situation*, 24 February. Accessed on 24/2/14. http://www.zimbabwesituation.com/news/zimsit_council-directors-bag-stands-for-a-song.

Mushava, Everson. 2012. "Zanu PF Elites in Land Dog Fights." *Daily News*, 26–27 April. Accessed on 12 October 2014. http://wpr.net/report/zanu-pf-elites-in-land-dogfight.

Mutopo, Patience. 2011. "Women's Struggles to Access and Control Land and Livelihoods after Fast Track Land Reform in Mwenezi District, Zimbabwe." *Journal of Peasant Studies* 38(5): 1021–46.

Muzvidziwa, Victor N. 1998. "Cross Border Trade: A Strategy for Climbing out of Poverty in Masvingo, Zimbabwe." *Zambezia* XXIV: 29–58.

Presidential Land Review Committee (PLRC). 2003. *Report of the Presidential Land Review Committee under the Chairmanship of Dr Charles M.B. Utete.* Harare: Government of Zimbabwe.

Rukuni, Mandivamba. 1994. *Report of the Commission of Inquiry into Appropriate Agricultural Land Tenure Systems.* Harare: Government of Zimbabwe.

Schlyter, Ann. 1989. *Women Householders and Housing Strategies: The Case of Harare, Zimbabwe.* Oslo: National Swedish Institute for Building Research.

Scoones, Ian. 2014. "A1 Permits: Unleashing Contradictions in the Party State." *Zimbabweland blog*, 18 August. Accessed on 12 October 2014. https://zimbabweland.wordpress.com/2014/08/18/a1-permits-unleashing-contradictions-in-the-party-state/.

Sibanda, Nelson. 2013. "Mugabe, Chombo, Murerwa Fingered in Election Land Saga." *The Zimbabwean*, 9 October. Accessed 11/1/14. http://www.thezimbabwean.co/news/zimbabwe-news/68830/mugabe-chombo-murerwa-fingered-in.html.

Sithole-Fundire, Sylvia. 1994. "Housing Deprivation: A Study of Lodgers in One High Density Suburb of Marondera." Mimeo. Harare.

Sukume, Chrispen, Sam Moyo, and Prosper Matondi. 2003. "Farm Size, Viability and Land Use in The Fast Track Land Reform Programme." Mimeo. Harare: African Institute for Agrarian Studies.

Sunga, E. et al. 1990. "Farm Extension Baseline Survey Results." Harare: Zimbabwe Institute of Development Studies.

Weinrich, A.K. 1975. *African Farmers in Rhodesia*. Gweru: Mambo Press.

"Zanu-PF Embarks on Residential Stands Audit." (2012). *Bulawayo 24*, 11 March. Accessed 22/2/14. http://bulawayo24.com/index-id-news-sc-national-byo-13031-article-zanu-pf+%20embarks+on+residential+stands+audit.html.

"ZANU-PF Parcels out Harare." 2013. *NewsDay*, 9 September. Accessed on 12/1/14. https://www.newsday.co.zw/2013/09/09/zanu-pf-parcels-harare.

Zimbabwe National Statistics Agency (ZIMSTAT). 2012. *Zimbabwe Demographic and Health Survey 2010–11.* Calverton, Maryland: ZIMSTAT and ICF International Inc.

Chapter 9

Ecolonization and the Creation of Insecurity Regimes: The Meaning of Zimbabwe's Land Reform Programme in Regional Context

Pádraig Carmody

The future of Zimbabwe is absolutely vital to the future of capitalism in Africa. (Iliffe 1983: 43)

Introduction

According to a variety of commentators humanity now exists in, and reproduces itself through, a global informational economy. However, from continent-wide land grabbing to Zimbabwe's recent experience, land retains its centrality in African political economy. As the majority of the population of the continent derive their livelihoods from agriculture – in the Zimbabwean case 70 per cent (Pazvakavambwa 2011) – this is perhaps not surprising. Also as Iliffe noted in the quote above, the evolution of capitalism in Zimbabwe offers important lessons for the evolution of this mode of production on the continent as a whole.

The land question is a fundamentally biopolitical one, intertwining as it does power with survival. The classical agrarian question revolved around the extent to which capitalist social relations of production would penetrate agriculture. The round of large-scale land acquisitions taking place across the continent would appear to answer this question, however Zimbabwe's recent experience seems to offer a counterpoint. This chapter explores the extent to which Zimbabwe's experience can be considered unique, as it underwent a process of deindustrialization and reagrarianization, or is potentially also representative of broader political dynamics at play in the Southern African region.

African development is increasingly defined by a variety of meta-trends. Two of the most significant of these are 'land grabbing' and climate change. Much has been written about the recent massively increased interest in African land and the drivers of this (Cotula 2013). These drivers include recent food price increases, driven by changing diets, particularly more meat intensive diets in Asia, population growth, global urbanization (glurbanization) (Hodson and Marvin 2007), in addition to climate restructuring and substitution effects from food to biofuels (Smith 2010a). Increased land concentration would then seem to be a feature of current African development, although some caution should be exercised about the scale of reported land deals (McGrath 2013).

170 *State, Land and Democracy in Southern Africa*

On the other hand Zimbabwe's fast track, redistributive land reform is sometimes held up as a counterpoint to these trends, as it was generally redistributive 'downwards' to small farmers (Scoones et al. 2010). This chapter argues that despite the sometimes different logics and impetuses of the land tenure reforms in Zimbabwe from elsewhere in the continent, that they also share some common underlying (bio)political motivations – a politics of bodies, as well as 'bellies' (Bayart 1993). Also Zimbabwe's land reform arguably shares other similarities with elsewhere on the continent given the extent of land grabbing by domestic elites; often unremarked in the international media. This chapter argues that these trends across different African contexts are reflective of the ongoing tension between accumulation (partly for state elites) and strategies of rule combining legitimation with insecurity. Before exploring the political dynamics behind the Zimbabwean 'land grab', it is worthwhile examining the broader drivers of recent large-scale land acquisitions in Africa in order to reflect on their similarities and differences.

Land 'Grabbing' in Africa

There are a variety of drivers of climate change and land 'grabbing' operative at different scales in Africa. According to the Oxford English Dictionary grabbing is to take something quickly. In relation to recent large-scale land acquisitions and leases in Africa this term may be more or less appropriate depending on the particular situation (See Boamah 2014) and consequently it is important not to overgeneralize. Nonetheless there have been recent instances where large parcels of land have been taken quickly for transfer to foreign investors, as in Ethiopia, or for redistribution domestically to peasant farmers and state elites, as in the Zimbabwean case. Why have these different types of large-scale land reform taken place recently and what do they share in common?

Globalized capital accumulation results in both the demand for, and depletion of, source resources such as minerals and land, in addition to pressure on sink resources such as the oceans and atmosphere. Deepening globalization and the ecological contradiction (O'Connor 1994) which results from this lead to a search for new sources of supply of these sink and source resources. For example Zolli and Healy (2012) detail how Hurricane Katrina, which was perhaps associated with climate restructuring, knocked out oil supplies from the Gulf of Mexico for several months. This, in-turn, resulted in Congressionaly mandated targets for renewable energy production in the US – one of the primary drivers of the global 'land rush' (Li 2012).

Based on Sassen's (2013) calculations from the Land Matrix database, 40 per cent of the land acquired in recent years in large-scale land deals in Africa was for biofuels, 25 per cent for food and much of the remainder for forestry, carbon sequestration and other uses. Geographically Friis and Reenberg (2010) divide recent major investors in African farmland into: 1) oil rich Gulf States, 2) capital rich and populous Asian countries such as China and India, 3) Europe and the US and 4) private companies from around the world, although the division between the third and fourth category arguably overlaps.

In addition to resource depletion and scarcity resulting from economic growth there are a variety of other drivers of interest in large-scale land acquisitions in Africa, including global population growth and the change towards more meat and environmentally intensive diets in Asia in particular. Land and also 'green' grabbing, for carbon sequestration projects for example (Fairhead, Leach and Scoones 2012) are however fundamentally driven by the ecological contradiction between an almost constantly growing global economy and (relatively) fixed amounts of 'natural' resources. The first order 'global' drivers of the land rush result from the interaction between ecological scarcity and the opportunities this provides for capital accumulation – a form of insecurity, if not a manifestation of fully formed and broad scale 'disaster' capitalism (Klein 2007). However such dynamics may result in localized disasters for people who are dispossessed of their assets and livelihoods. Land tenure and reform not only entail access but also rely on 'powers of exclusion' from other potential claimants (Hall, Hirsch and Murray-Li 2011). While the global drivers of increased interest in African land have been well described (Pearce 2012; Cotula 2013), for our purposes it is also important to note that there are also other second and third order drivers operative at national and local scales.

Land and Biopolitics

As a basic input into the sustenance of human life, land is an implicit source of biopolitical power (Carmody 2013). Biopolitics refers to the power of life and death (Foucault et al. 2004). I am using the term somewhat more broadly here to refer to not only these powers, but the powers of population displacement and control through access and denial to the means of subsistence – land, in the case of much of Africa.

In some African countries political regime maintenance, such as Zimbabwe or Ethiopia, is tied to the exercise of biopower through granting and denial of access to land. This may represent coercion informed by consent which is essential to the construction of state hegemony (Marais 2010). In both of these cases consent on the part of some, such as land settlers in the Zimbabwean case, was mirrored by coercion for others, particularly 'white' farmers and some farmworkers. Together then this represented a form of violent hegemony, whereby disorder was instrumentalized (Chabal and Daloz 1999).

Another way of thinking of this is as a form of biopower. Granting of relatively larger parcels of land to regime loyalists, in Zimbabwe for example (Scoones et al. 2010), served to promote political accumulation and regime legitimacy in those networks. At the same time as land became state-owned this subjected them and other new settler farmers to potential discipline by the state. These political

172   *State, Land and Democracy in Southern Africa*

dynamics are also evident in large-scale land acquisitions across the rest of the continent, rather than them representing just the power of transnational land investors. How the 'global' drivers of land grabbing are refracted, expressed, or resisted through states depends on the balance of social forces and the possibilities such land acquisitions open up for political accumulation ('power and money') for state elites.

At national scales across much of Africa the attractions of increased tax revenue and exports, enhanced political control, perceived developmental impacts, ideologies of development, in addition to population growth often combine to make large-scale land acquisitions attractive to both foreign and domestic 'investors' and political elites; creating spatialized investment demand from them. National elites may also engage in land banking on a speculative basis in anticipation of increases in land prices or the potential discovery of minerals.[1]

Struggles over land in Africa centre over the creation and allocation of use, production and exchange values and the different forms of economic, political and biopower which derive from these. How these struggles play out is locally and contextually contingent, but the balance of power favours actors that derive structural power from mobility and capital, such as transnational capitals (TNCs), and/or states who often ultimately control access to territory. The power of this assemblage results from the integration of these different forms of power, and their legitimating discourses of climate mitigation, equity, development and conservation, although this may also generate localized resistances. How the Zimbabwean case relates to broader dynamics at play across much of Africa will be explored in more detail later in the paper.

Ecolonization and Land

Global discourses of climate change mitigation, development, food security and conservation can sometimes result in substantial land dispossession. Indeed these discourses, by and large, feed into a broader process of globalized colonization of ecological space.[2] Both climate restructuring[3] and land grabbing, rather than

---

1   For example in Kasenyi, Buliisa District in Uganda 'villagers here were beaten by hired thugs and detained by police this May after contesting the fraudulent sale of community land, including a plot where Tullow Oil's Kasmene-3 well is located, according to LC 1 Chairman, Eriakimi Kaseegu' (Musiime and Womakuyu 2012).

2   Ecological space is 'an equitable share of the planet's aggregate natural resources and environmental services that are available on a sustainable basis for human use' (Hayward 2007: 445).

3   The term climate restructuring is preferred to climate change or even climate disruption (Maass 2009) for a number of reasons. Climate as a term implies regularity, in contrast to "change." Climate restructuring captures the fact that increased unpredictability will be a feature of the new climate regime across much of Africa (Toulmin 2009).

simply being in contradiction are actually a part of a sub-process of globalization which can be thought of as ecological colonization (ecolonization).

Ecolonization is a primary feature of the current round of globalization, but has not previously been conceptualized as such, despite it largely driving the current global land rush. This ecolonization is paradoxically taking place in the context of nominally sovereign territories in the Global South, because state elites benefit from it. For example if people are dispossessed to make way for plantations to Reduce Emissions from Deforestation and Forest Degradation (REDD) it is sometimes governments that receive payments for those. Bumpus and Liverman (2008: 127) refer to the process of 'accumulation by decarbonisation'.

Under globalization tracing the scale and dimensions of food, biofuel feedstocks and carbon credit flows is difficult and it could be argued that interdependence has accelerated, rather than there being a new iteration of colonial type relations. However this terminology can be justified if the vast disparities across a variety of metrics of consumption between different people and world regions, whether measured by techniques such as the 'ecological footprint' or the fact that the average emissions from someone in Burundi is eight hundred times lower than that of someone in the United States, for example, are considered (World Bank 2014). Secondly there are yet clearer colonial dimensions or resonances to the current round of large-scale land acquisitions and also the recent land redistribution in Zimbabwe.

Colonialism was characterized by unequal social relations and exploitation, land dispossession, the extraction of resources for the benefit of metropolitan powers, and the denial of the rights of property and full citizenship to colonial subjects (Mamdani 1996). It was a system in which certain states claimed sovereignty over people and territory beyond their own boundaries and assumed the right of one set of people to impose their priorities and will upon others (Brett 1973 cited in Kanji 2008: 1). Current land grabs replicate these features in addition to sometimes establishing quasi-sovereignties[4] over land which has been purchased or leased. The oftentimes denial of rights by land grabbers and governments means that people who are dispossessed are subjects rather than citizens (Mamdani 1996).

Land, along with water, is the source for the reproduction of human life. As such embedded within its ownership and usage is biopolitical power. Regulating or denying access to land can have profoundly disciplining effects on the peasantry in Africa, as has been the case in Ethiopia for example (See Carmody 2013). Land dispossession also results in substantial climate service dispossession, as rainfall to

---

4   Sassen (2013: 25) states that land grabs are 'feeding the disassembling of national territory.' However as land in Africa is still typically and ultimately often owned by the state and state laws still apply this is not strictly speaking true. Rather there are 'graduated sovereignties' (Ong 2006) which may actually help with state-building through the projection of territorial control and greater tax revenues, for example. However this state-building is not necessarily associated with the development of rights, but divided citizenship.

grow crops is effectively denied for example. Consequently the political economy of climate vulnerability is refracted through land regimes and state formations, rather than being a 'natural' outcome of processes of climate restructuring.

The denial, or selective underminning of property and citizenship rights could be seen as a form of 'internal colonialism' (Hechter 1975) which results from the operation of the 'land grab' assemblage comprised of both 'national' and transnational actors and actants (including climate) (Latour 1987), which is also operative in Zimbabwe. There is a colonial precedent for this, in Uganda for example, where the British policy of indirect rule meant substantial amounts of land was given to the various indigenous kings, 'chiefs' and royals, such as the land grant to the king of Buganda. This 'turned the *Bakopi* (free peasants) and *Bataka* (clan leaders) into landless classes ... Although land given to the chiefs was supposed to be unoccupied rangelands, the chiefs abused the provisions of the agreement and laid claim to fertile lands in the densely populated areas' (Muhumuza 2007: 79). There are resonances of this in the recent Zimbabwean land redistribution.

Ecolonization is often associated with 'accumulation by dispossession' (Harvey 2003). In the literature to date this process has been associated with the operation of transnational corporations, however, it is also selectively practiced by other actors, such as state elites, depending on context. In the Zimbabwean case David Moore (2003) argues that the 'Fast Track Land Reform' (FTLR) was a form or primitive or primary accumulation by state elites, however Davies (2004) argues that primary accumulation had already taken place under colonialism.

Accumulation by dispossession is not only social, but extends to the natural environment which may be depleted of nutrients and biodiversity, which in turn feeds into social dispossession. The beneficiaries of ecolonization are, perhaps unsurprisingly, TNCs (or their owners) and state elites who are able to leverage their connections with these companies using Regalian theories[5] and practices of land to strengthen state power and expand accumulation for elites within its networks. As Hall (2011: 205) notes in relation to Southern Africa:

> media driven depictions of the rush for farmland for food and biofuels by the Chinese and Koreans with the backing of their governments and by Western corporations may be missing the mark, as equally profound but less visible transformations gather pace. As land is often leased, the 'grabber' is usually the state rather than foreign investors.

The geography of these processes is fundamental, as while land grabbing may result in climate mitigation and expanded incomes for some, for others it results in reduced incomes and climate service and land dispossession. The putative purposes of these projects, such as food security, then may be less important than their unstated motive logics of capital accumulation and/or state strengthening.

---

5   These theories hold that land should ultimately be owned by the state.

The ongoing ecolonization of Africa then has both internal and external dimensions to it. The theory of internal colonialism was developed in relation to South Africa and the 'Celtic fringe' in the United Kingdom (Wolpe 1975; Hechter 1975). It examined the way in which certain regions and people within the nation state were exploited and denied the full rights of citizenship in order to facilitate uneven development and capital accumulation (See Nally 2011). Land grabbing is a 'polymorphous crystalisation' involving aspect of state-building, elite accumulation and transnational ecological colonization (Mann 1990). Despite the very different outcome, in terms of land accumulation and holding patterns, these dynamics are evident across much of Africa and also in Zimbabwe.

Land may serve as a source of political power through a variety of channels. For example, the creation of poverty through land grabbing may serve not only capital accumulation, but political functions. 'It is easy to rule a poor man'[6] and land grabbing fits into a broader pattern of poverty perpetuation to ensure regime maintenance, as poor people are often preoccupied with survival rather than politics (Carmody 2007). On the other hand, in downward redistributive land reforms, as recently in Zimbabwe, land may serve as a source of legitimation for the ruling regime.

The current round of ecolonization shares similarities with, but is also different from formal colonialism. The ecolonial transnational assemblage extends even into Zimbabwe where small-holders who were granted land under the FTLR are now being dispossessed in some instances to make way for a sugar cane plantation, for example (Hall, 2011). I now turn to examine the specifics of the Zimbabwean case in more detail.

Zimbabwe's FTLR

Zimbabwe's political economy was characterized by a 'cascading collapse' from industry to agriculture (Carmody 2001). The dynamics of economic restructuring reconfigured power relations and set off large-scale spontaneous land invasions. According to Moyo (2011: 135) 'In the early stages of the FTLR (2000–2003), the leadership of the ruling party struggled to appease and co-opt the land occupation movement, and used force in the defence of the landless and against the political forces allied to the white agrarian monopoly and Western interests.' Quickly however this redistributive social movement was largely co-opted and steered by state elites for their own purposes – regime maintenance and economic accumulation.

According to Robin Palmer (1998: 1) 'The specific criticisms of Mugabe's land grab can briefly be summarized. Lack of funds, lack of planning, lack of capacity, lack of accountability and ... spectacular lack of diplomacy.' According to him the trajectory of land reform is influenced by previous colonial history.

---

6   Conversation with respondent (Kampala, September, 2013).

176   *State, Land and Democracy in Southern Africa*

For example, the fact that South Africa, Zimbabwe and Kenya had substantial land dispossession associated with 'white' settlement gave an impetus to later redistributive land reform in those countries.

There have been a number of studies which have shown how the land poor have benefitted from the land reform programme in Zimbabwe (Scoones et al. 2010; Hanlon, Manjengwa, and Smart 2013). However, the allocation of land was not always transparent. According to figures quoted in Sachikonye (2004) less than half of those who applied for land under the auspice of the 'fast track' reform received it. The distribution was politically influenced and as the state now owned the land, tenancy also became politically dependent. This was consistent with other techniques of control deployed by the ruling Zimbabwe African National Union – Patriotic Front (ZANU-PF) regime, such as the blocking of food aid to opposition areas in 2002, 2008 and 2013 – years in which Presidential or general elections were held.

The structure of power in rural areas in Zimbabwe was further evidenced in the 2013 election. 'In rural areas 99.97 per cent of voters were registered and 38 per cent of stations turned away voters, compared to 67.94 per cent registration and *82 per cent refusal* in urban areas' (Cendrowicz 2013, original emphasis). Reportedly ZANU-PF also spent 600 US million dollars of revenues from the Marange diamond fields to pay an Israeli company to rig the electoral roll (Amoore and Arbuthnott 2013). According to some non-government newspapers in Zimbabwe ZANU-PF has multi-billion dollar businesses through M&S Syndicate and Zidco Holdings (Hill 2005).

In Zimbabwe, such was the state of economic collapse that land serves both accumulation and legitimation functions, or the two simultaneously. According to some reports up to 40 per cent of land which was seized from white farmers was given to ZANU-PF loyalists (ZimOnline cited in Smith 2010b), although these figures are highly exaggerated. The majority of new farms benefitted landless or land poor peasants (Scoones et al. 2010). Hanlon, Manjengwa and Smart (2013) estimate that only 5 per cent of beneficiaries, taking 10 per cent of the land were political 'cronies.' However, the FTLR was then also a fast track land grab by politically connected elites and arguably peasants also. The sizeable farms and tracts of land that were allocated to political elites sometimes resulted in intra-ZANU-PF struggles over land. President Mugabe and his wife were said in the investigation cited above to own 14 farms of at least 16,000 hectares.

Matondi (2012: 6) notes in relation to the FTLR that 'it is even more confusing when some large commercial farms, which had been subdivided into smaller landholdings by the FTLR programme, are now re-emerging and promoting biofuels and agro-investments that apparently include foreigners.' This further suggests that the initial 'revolution from below' has been overtaken by a 'revolution from above' (Trimberger 1978). The fact that land which was redistributed in Zimbabwe was granted on the basis of either an 'offer letter' or on a leasehold basis made property tenure insecure and people dependent on state tolerance or 'largesse.' Land then serves as an important component of both the extraversion and introversion portfolios of ZANU-PF (Peiffer and Englebert 2012): serving both to promote politicized accumulation for state elites, sources of foreign exchange and diplomatic support, from China in particular, and legitimacy/insecurity amongst the broader population. There have been several instances where land which was redistributed has now been reappropriated by domestic elites or given to foreign investors. In one case a resettlement farmer was told to stop farming so that a Chinese-owned brick making factory could access a nearby road (Matondi 2012). The fact that the judiciary has been politicized in Zimbabwe has contributed to these processes.

Zimbabwe's Experience in Regional Context

There is a dialectic of land concentration and dispersion at play in Southern Africa. Processes of deindustrialization, in relative if not absolute terms, across the continent (United Nations Conference on Trade and Development 2012) have given land greater, not less, political salience despite rhetoric around Africa's information revolution (see for example Smith, Spence, and Rashid 2011) or the discourse of 'Africa Rising' (Mahajan 2008). In the context of rising values, consequent to higher food prices and demand for biofuels, land has assumed greater importance for maintenance of political power and opportunities for accumulation for state elites, the two of which are inter-twinned. Thus, while exceptional in some respects, Zimbabwe's recent experience is reflective of a broader politicization of land taking place across the continent.

The land insecurity regime which has been created in Zimbabwe is fundamental to the maintenance of the ZANU-PF regime in the country. The ZANU-PF government has sought to create an insecurity regime across the different sectors of the economy through land invasions, Operation *Murambatsvina* in 2005 (directed against the informal sector), Operation No Return (directed against informal miners), and the Indigenization and Economic Empowerment Act which affected manufacturing. The creation of insecurity regimes is also in evidence in other countries in sub-Saharan Africa, in Ethiopia for example.

According to a farmer displaced by the massive investment by the Indian conglomerate Karuturi in Ethiopia, 'when they first came they told us an investor was coming and we would develop the land alongside one another. They didn't say the land would be taken away from us entirely. I don't understand why the government took the land' (Gemechu cited in Rugman 2012). His spouse noted 'since the land was taken away from us we are impoverished. Nothing has gone right for us since these investors came.' However, the dispossession has a profound disciplinary effect in Ethiopia as large-scale land acquisitions serve as 'a constant reminder of the danger hanging over small farmers and pastoralists and their way of life' (Rahmato 2011: 5), thus creating a new land (in)security regime.

In Zimbabwe 'a few land-reform farmers have 99-year leases, but most only have a permit or letter (usually called an 'offer letter') allocating land to them, and many have nothing and officially are still 'squatting' on their land' (Hanlon, Manjengwa, and Smart 2013: 200). This insecurity makes them dependent on the state which has adopted a neo-feudal form of rule (Carmody 2007).

Feudalism was a social system which revolved around usufruct rights to land being exchanged for service or labour. According to David Moore (2001: 44) Zimbabwe is 'approaching a feudal mode of political rule – in which problems of leadership succession have society-wide consequences.' In the Zimbabwean case usufruct rights to land are held in exchange for political quiescence. The vesting of ownership of land in the state was done under the pretext that freehold tenure would be insecure for the poor as circumstances might force them to sell it thereby reversing the land reform process (Matondi 2012).

Conclusion

Zimbabwe's fast track land reform came about as a result of different motivations and a short-term confluence of interests amongst different state and non-state actors. This has also been the case for other 'upward' recent land reforms elsewhere in Africa, although the 'land grab' assemblages have had different social configurations elsewhere.

According to Sam Moyo (2013: 49) in Africa 'the agrarian accumulation model continues to be based on an outward-looking agricultural strategy, except in the case of Zimbabwe, which is veering towards internal markets, food sovereignty and autonomous development.' The argument of this chapter is different. It is that the increasing politicization of land in Zimbabwe is reflective of broader trends across the continent. The Zimbabwean state, while always having to negotiate and create various channels of regime maintenance, orients itself more externally or internally depending on the particular conjuncture (Carmody and Taylor 2003).

There are many new agrarian questions in Africa. These include ones around the sustainability of agriculture on the continent and the extent of commoditization of land. This chapter has argued however that the primary new agrarian question in Africa revolves around the politics of land. For Kautsky (1988) the agrarian question centred on the political orientation of the peasantry based on the social relations of production in agriculture. In Africa the central new agrarian question is the role which land plays as a resource in political struggles for regime maintenance and change. Zimbabwe has important lessons to teach us in this regard, as well as providing warnings around commoditization and concentration of land ownership in the context of the deepening of capitalism on the continent.

References

Amoore, Miles and George Arbuthnott. 2013. "Diamonds Ensure Mugabe is Forever." *Sunday Times*, 4 August: 16.

Bayart, Jean-François. 1993. *The State in Africa: The Politics of the Belly*. London: Longman.

Boamah, Festus. 2014. "Imageries of the Contested Concepts 'Land Grabbing' and 'Land Transactions': Implications for Biofuels Investments in Ghana." *Geoforum* 54: 324–34.

Brett, Edward A. 1973. *Colonialism and Underdevelopment in East Africa: The Politics of Economic Change 1919–1939*. London: Heinemann Educational Books.

Bumpus, Adam and Diana Liverman. 2008. "Accumulation by Decarbonization and the Governance of Carbon Offsets." *Economic Geography* 84(2): 127–55.

Carmody, Pádraig. 2001. *Tearing the Social Fabric: Neoliberalism, Deindustrialization, and the Crisis of Governance in Zimbabwe*. Portsmouth, NH: Heinemann.

——. 2007. *Neoliberalism, Civil Society and Security in Africa*. Basingstoke: Palgrave Macmillan.

——. 2013. *The Rise of the BRICS in Africa : the Geopolitics of South-South Relations*. London: Zed Books.

Carmody, Pádraig and Scott Taylor. 2003 "Industry and the Urban Sector in Zimbabwe's Political Economy." *African Studies Quarterly* 7(2 and 3). http://web.africa.ufl.edu/asq/v7/vi2a3.htm.

Cendrowicz, Leo. 2013. "Zimbabwe election results: Opposition leaders claim vote tainted by 'monumental rigging' as Robert Mugabe's Zanu-PF claims victory." *The Independent*. Accessed 16 March 2015. http://www.independent.co.uk/news/world/africa/zimbabwe-election-results-opposition-leaders-claim-vote-tainted-by-monumental-rigging-as-robert-mugabes-zanupf-claims-victory-8741646.html.

Chabal, Patrick and Jean Pascal Daloz. 1999. *Africa Works: Disorder as Political Instrument*. Oxford: International African Institute in association with James Currey.

Cotula, Lorenzo. 2013. *The Great African Land Grab?: Agricultural Investments and the Global Food System*. London: Zed Books in association with International African Institute, Royal African Society, World Peace Foundation.

Davies, Robert. 2004. "Memories of Underdevelopment: A Personal Interpretation of Zimbabwe's Economic Decline," in *Zimbabwe: Injustice and Political Reconciliation*, edited by Brian Raftopoulos and Tyrone Savage, 19–42. Cape Town: Institute for Justice and Reconciliation.

Fairhead, James, Melissa Leach and Ian Scoones. 2012. "Green Grabbing: A New Appropriation of Nature." *Journal of Peasant Studies* 39(2): 237–61.

Foucault, Michel, François Ewald, Alessandro Fontana, and Michel Senellart. 2004. *Naissance de la Biopolitique: Cours au Collège de France (1978–1979)*. Paris: SeuilGallimard.

Friis, Cecilie and Anette Reenberg. 2010. *Land Grab in Africa: Emerging Land System Drivers in a Teleconnected World*. Copenhagen: GLP.

Hall, Derek, Philip Hirsch and Tania Murray-Li. 2011. *Powers of Exclusion: Land Dilemmas in Southeast Asia*. Honolulu: University of Hawaii Press.

Hall, Ruth. 2011. "Land Grabbing in Southern Africa: The Many Faces of the Investor Rush." *Review of African Political Economy* 38(128): 193–214.

Hanlon, Joseph, Jeanette Manjengwa, and Teresa Smart. 2013. *Zimbabwe Takes Back its Land*. 1st ed. Sterling, VA.: Kumarian Press.

Harvey, David. 2003. *The New Imperialism*. Oxford and New York: Oxford University Press.

Hayward, Tim. 2007. "Human Rights Versus Emissions Rights: Climate Justice and the Equitable Distribution of Ecological Space." *Ethics and International Affairs* 21(4): 431–50.

Hechter, Michael. 1975. *Internal Colonialism: The Celtic Fringe in British National Development*. Berkeley, CA: University of California Press.

Hill, Geoff. 2005. *What Happens After Mugabe?* Cape Town: Zebra Press.

Hodson, Mike and Simon Marvin. 2007. "Understanding the Role of the National Exemplar in Constructing 'Strategic Glurbanization.'" *International Journal of Urban and Regional Research* 31(2): 303–25.

Iliffe, John. 1983. *The Emergence of African Capitalism: the Anstey Memorial Lectures in the University of Kent at Canterbury 10–13 May 1982*. London: Macmillan.

Kanji, Kamil. 2008. "The Ecological and Political Impact of Colonialism in the Third World During the Nineteenth and Twentieth Centuries." Accessed 16 March 2015. http://www.articlesbase.com/politics-articles/the-ecological-and-political-impact-of-colonialism-in-the-third-world-during-the-nineteenth-and-twentieth-centuries-306767.html.

Kautsky, Karl. 1988. *The Agrarian Question*. London: Zwan.

Latour, Bruno. 1987. *Science in Action*. Cambridge, MA: Harvard University Press.

Klein, Naomi. 2008. *The Shock Doctrine: The Rise of Disaster Capitalism*. London. Picador.

Li, Tania. 2012. "What is Land? Anthropological Perspectives on the Global Land Rush." Paper presented at the International Conference on Global Land Grabbing II, 17–19 October, 2012 Organized by the Land Deals Politics Initiative (LDPI) and hosted by the Department of Development Sociology at Cornell University, Ithaca, NY. Accessed 16 March 2015. http://www.cornell-landproject.org/download/landgrab2012papers/li.pdf.

Maass, Peter. 2009. *Crude World: The Violent Twilight of Oil*. London: Allen Lane.

Mahajan, Vijay. 2008. *Africa Rising: How 900 million African Consumers Offer More Than You Think*. New Jersey: Wharton School Publishing.

Mamdani, Mahmood. 1996. *Citizen and Subject: Contemporary Africa and the Legacy of Late Colonialism*. London: James Currey.

Mann, Michael. 1990. *The Sources of Social Power*. Cambridge and New York: Cambridge University Press.

Marais, Hein. 2010. *South Afri.ca Pushed to the Limit: The Political Economy of Change*. Claremont, Cape Town: UCT Press.

Matondi, Prosper B. 2012. *Zimbabwe's Fast Track Land Reform*. London: Zed Books.

McGrath, Matt. 2013. "Database Says Level of Global 'Land Grabs' Exaggerated." *BBC News*. Accessed 16 March 2015. http://www.bbc.com/news/science-environment-22839149.

Moore, David. 2001. "Neoliberal Globalisation and the Triple Crisis of 'Modernisation' in Africa: Zimbabwe, the Democratic Republic of the Congo and South Africa." *Third World Quarterly* 22(6): 909–29.

——. 2003. "Zimbabwe: Twists in the Tale of Primitive Accumulation," in *Globalizing Africa*, edited by Malinda Smith, 246–70. Trenton, NJ: Africa World.

Moyo, Sam. 2011. "Agrarian Reform and Prospects for Recovery," in *Zimbabwe: Picking up the Pieces*, edited by Hany Besada, 129–56. Basingstoke and New York: Palgrave MacMillan.

——. 2013. "Agrarian Transformation in Africa and its Decolonisation," in *Agricultural Development and Food Security: The Impact of Chinese, Indian and Brazilian Investments*, edited by Fantu Cheru and Renu Modi, 38–58. London: Zed Books.

Muhumuza, William. 2007. *Credit and Reduction of Poverty in Uganda: Structural Adjustment Reforms in Context*. Kampala: Fountain Publishers.

Musiime, Chris and Frederick Womakuyu. 2012. "The Great Land Rush." *Oil in Uganda* August, Issue 2. Accessed 16 March 2015. http://www.oilinuganda.org/wp-content/plugins/downloads-manager/upload/OIL%20IN%20UGANDA%20ISSUE%202%20(AUGUST%202012).pdf.

Nally, David P. 2011. *Human Encumbrances: Political Violence and the Great Irish Famine*. Notre Dame, Ind: University of Notre Dame Press.

O'Connor, Martin. 1994. *Is Capitalism Sustainable? Political Economy and the Politics of Ecology*. New York and London: Guilford Press.

Ong, Aihwa. 2006 *Neoliberalism as Exception: Mutations in Citizenship and Sovereignty*. Durham: Duke University Press.

Palmer, Robin. 1998. "Mugabe's 'Land Grab' in Regional Perspective." Accessed 16 March 2015. http://www.mokoro.co.uk/files/13/file/lria/mugabes_land_grab_in_regional_perspective.pdf.

Pazvakavambwa, Simon. 2011. "Addressing Food Security: A View from Multilateral Institutions," in *Zimbabwe: Picking up the Pieces*, 157–80, edited by Harry Beseda. Basingstoke and New York: Palgrave MacMillan.

Pearce, Fred. 2012. *The Land Grabbers: The New Fight Over Who Owns the Earth*. Boston: Beacon.

Peiffer, Caryn and Pierre Englebert. 2012. "Extraversion, Vulnerability to Donors, and Political Liberalization in Africa." *African Affairs* 111(444): 355–78.

Rahmato, Dessalegn. 2011. "Land to Investors: Large-scale Land Transfers in Ethiopia." Addis Ababa: Forum for Social Studies. http://www.landgovernance.org/system/files/Ethiopia_Rahmato_FSS_0.pdf.

Rugman, Jonathan. 2012. "Africa Succumbs to Colonial-style Land Grab." *Channel 4 News*. 7 January. http://www.channel4.com/news/africa-succumbs-to-colonial-style-land-grab.

Sachikonye, Lloyd. 2004. "The Promised Land: From Expropriation to Reconciliation and Jambanja," in *Zimbabwe: Injustice and Political Reconciliation*, edited by Brian Raftopoulos and Tyrone Savage, 1–18. Cape Town: Institute for Justice and Reconciliation.

Sassen, Saskia. 2013. "Land Grabs Today: Feeding the Disassembling of National Territory." *Globalizations* 10(1): 25–46.

Scoones, Ian, Nelson Marongwe, Blasio Mavedzenge, Jacob Mahenehene, Felix Murimbarimba, and Chrispen Sukume. 2010. *Zimbabwe's Land Reform: Myths & Realities*. Woodbridge: James Currey; Harare: Weaver Press; Johannesburg: Jacana Media.

Smith, David. 2010a. "Mugabe and Allies Own 40% of Land Seized from White Farmers – Inquiry." *The Guardian*. Accessed 16 March 2015. http://www.theguardian.com/world/2010/nov/30/zimbabwe-mugabe-white-farmers.

Smith, James. 2010b. *Biofuels and the Globalization of Risk: The Biggest Change in North-South Relationships Since Colonialism?* London: Zed Books.

Smith, Matthew, Randy Spence, and Ahmed Rashid. 2011. "Mobile Phones and Expanding Human Capabilities." *Information Technologies & International Development and Change* 7(3): 77–88.

Toulmin, Camilla. 2009. *Climate Change in Africa*. London and New York: Zed Books in association with International African Institute, Royal African Society. Distributed in the USA exclusively by Palgrave Macmillan.

Trimberger, Ellen Kay. 1978. *Revolution from Above: Military Bureaucrats and Development in Japan, Turkey, Egypt, and Peru*. New Brunswick, NJ: Transaction Books.

United Nations Conference on Trade and Development. 2012. *Economic Development in Africa Report 2012: Structural Transformation and Sustainable Development in Africa*. Geneva: UNCTAD.

Wolpe, Harold. 1975. "The Theory of Internal Colonialism: The South African Case," in *Beyond the Sociology of Development: Economy and Society in Latin America and Africa*, edited by Ivar Oxhaal, Tony Barnett, and David Booth, 229–52. London: Routledge.

World Bank. 2014. "World Bank Open Data." http://data.worldbank.org.

Zolli, Andrew and Ann Marie Healy. 2013. *Resilience: Why Things Bounce Back*. New York: Simon and Schuster.

Index of Names

Acemoglu, Daron 71n24
Adam, Christopher 31
Alexander, Jocelyn 90, 92
Allina, Éric 84, 88
Amin, Idi 43

Banda, Joyce 11, 25, 28, 32, 35
Barnes, Teresa 152, 154
Battera, Federico 13, 14
Bere, Francis 165
Bernstein, Henry 2–4, 7
Birner, Regina 6
Boesen, Jannik 43
Boone, Catherine 2, 7
Borras, Saturnino M. Jr. 1, 2, 71n25
Botha, Roelof Frederik 109, 112
Bratton, Michael 115
Brewster, Kingman 116, 121
Brown, Mervyn 118
Brown, Taylor 70
Bumpus, Adam 173
Byres, Terence J. 2, 3, 5

Carmody, Pádraig 10, 12
Carrilho, João 94
Carrington, Peter 117–22
Carter, Jimmy 116, 117, 120, 121
Chachage, Chachage 45
Chapoto, Antony 70
Chaumba, Joseph 127n1
Cheater, Angela 152
Cheeseman, Nic 67n15
Chikulo, Bornwell 71
Chikwanda, Alexander 74
Chiluba, Frederick 65n10, 67
Chinsinga, Blessings 11, 28
Chipungu, Samuel N. 64n8
Chirwa, Ephraim 28
Chiwenga, Constantine 165
Chiwenga, Jocelyn 165

Chiyangwa, Philip 164
Chombo, Ignatious 164
Chombo, Marian 164
Chung, Fay 115
Consul, António 93n13
Cooksey, Brian 50
Coulson, Andrew 42
Cousins, Ben 8
Cramer, Christopher 97
Crosland, Anthony 109

das Neves Têmbe, Joel 85–7
Davidow, Jeffrey 116
Davies, Robert 174
Dercon, Stefan 31
Direito, Bárbara Pinto Teixeira 84
Dumont, René 42
Du Toit, Andries 40

Erdmann, Gero 67n15

Fourie, Johan 93n12, 93n14
Friis, Cecilie 170

Gaidzanwa, Rudo B. 9, 10, 150,
    155, 159
Gama, L.A. João 94n18
Gould, Jeremy 14

Hall, Ruth 6, 174
Hanlon, Joseph 95–7, 176
Hazeel, Peter 15
Healy, Ann Marie 170
Hinfelaar, Marja 67n15

Iliffe, John 169

Jayne, Thomas S. 70–72

Kaarhus, Randi 26

Kabamba, Pamela 75
Kaseegu, Eriakimi 172n1
Kaunda, Kenneth 63, 64, 66, 68, 75, 106, 118
Kautsky, Karl 6, 178
Kilama, Blandina 49
Kissinger, Henry 105–14, 118

Lake, Anthony 120
Lerche, Jens 2, 3, 7
Lipton, Michael 6
Liverman, Diana 173
Lokina, Razack B. 12
Lund, Christian 2, 7
Lyne, Roderic 117, 118

Machel, Samora 106, 115, 119
Maghimbi, Sam 12
Mahenehene, Jacob 127n1
Makura-Paradza, Gaynor 156, 157, 161, 163
Manjengwa, Jeanette 176
Manji, Ambreena 3
Marongwe, Nelson 127n1, 150
Marx, Karl 2
Mason, Nicole M. 67
Masunda, Langton 166
Matondi, Propser 150, 159, 176
Mavedzenge, Blasio 127n1
Minae, Susan 6
Mofya-Mukuka, Rhoda 74n35
Mohadi, Kembo 165
Moore, David 174, 179
Moose, Richard 121
Mosca, João 11
Moyo, Clement 166
Moyo, Sam 5, 150, 175, 179
Mugabe, Robert 106, 115–17, 119, 122, 165, 175, 176
Mukori, Wilbert 165
Munanavire, Bridget 165
Munishi, Gaspar 43
Munyuki-Hungwe, Mabel 150, 159, 160
Murimbarimba, Felix 127n1
Mushava, Everson 166
Mussimwa, Chief 95
Mutopo, Patience 150, 159, 160
Muzorewa, Abel 117, 118, 122

Muzvidziwa, Victor 150
Myers, Gregory W. 92
Mwanawasa, Levy 73
Mwinyi Ali Hassan 44

Nkomo, John 166
Nkomo, Joshua 106, 108, 110, 116, 117, 119, 120, 122
Nkonde, Chewe 72n28
Nolte, Kerstin 70
Nyerere, Julius 41–3, 106–11, 118, 119
Nyirenda, Ramji 26

O'Laughlin, Bridget 8, 90, 98
Onslow, Sue 117
Otsuka, Keijiro 5
Oya, Carlos 4, 97
Owen, David 115

Pallotti, Arrigo 13, 109n1, 113n2
Palmer, Robert 175
Patnaik, Utsa 5
Peters, Pauline E. 15
Place, Frank 5
Plaut, Martin 116
Posner, Daniel N. 66, 67n15

Rakner, Lise 66
Ramphal, Shridath 116, 120–23
Reed, Tristan 71n24
Reenberg, Anette 170
Resnik, Danielle 6
Richard, Ivor 115
Ricker-Gilbert, Jacob 67
Robinson, James A. 71n24
Rogers, William 111–13
Rungo, Cremildo 95n19

Sachikonye, Lloyd 176
Salazar, António de Oliveira 84
Sassen, Saskia 169, 173n4
Sata, Michael 73, 75
Scarnecchia, Timothy 8
Schaufele, William 113
Schlyter, Ann 155, 160, 161
Scoones, Ian 8, 9, 71n24, 166
Scott, Guy 66
Scott, James, 41

Index of Names

Sembeséa, Chief 95
Sender, John 97
Senga, Mathew A. 12
Serra, Carlos Manuel 94
Shivji, Issa 43, 45
Short, Clare 157
Simutanyi, Neo 65n10
Sithole-Fundire, Sylvia 155
Sitko, Nicholas J. 71
Skastein, Rune 49
Smart, Teresa 96, 97, 176
Smith, David 112
Smith, Ian 106–8, 110, 112, 113, 115, 118, 122
Sukume, Chrispen 127n1, 150
Sunga, E. 155

Thatcher, Margaret 119, 122

Tornimbeni, Corrado 12, 88n3, 94n16, 98n20
Tygesen, Peter 11

Vance, Cyrus 120, 121
Vorster, Balthazar 109–13

Weinrich, A. 152, 159
Wicker, Tom 106
Wily, Liz Alden 4, 11, 46
Win, Everjoyce 152, 154
Wolmer, Will 127n1
Woodhouse, Philip 4, 35
Wuyts, Mark 49, 90, 91, 98

Zolli, Andrew 170